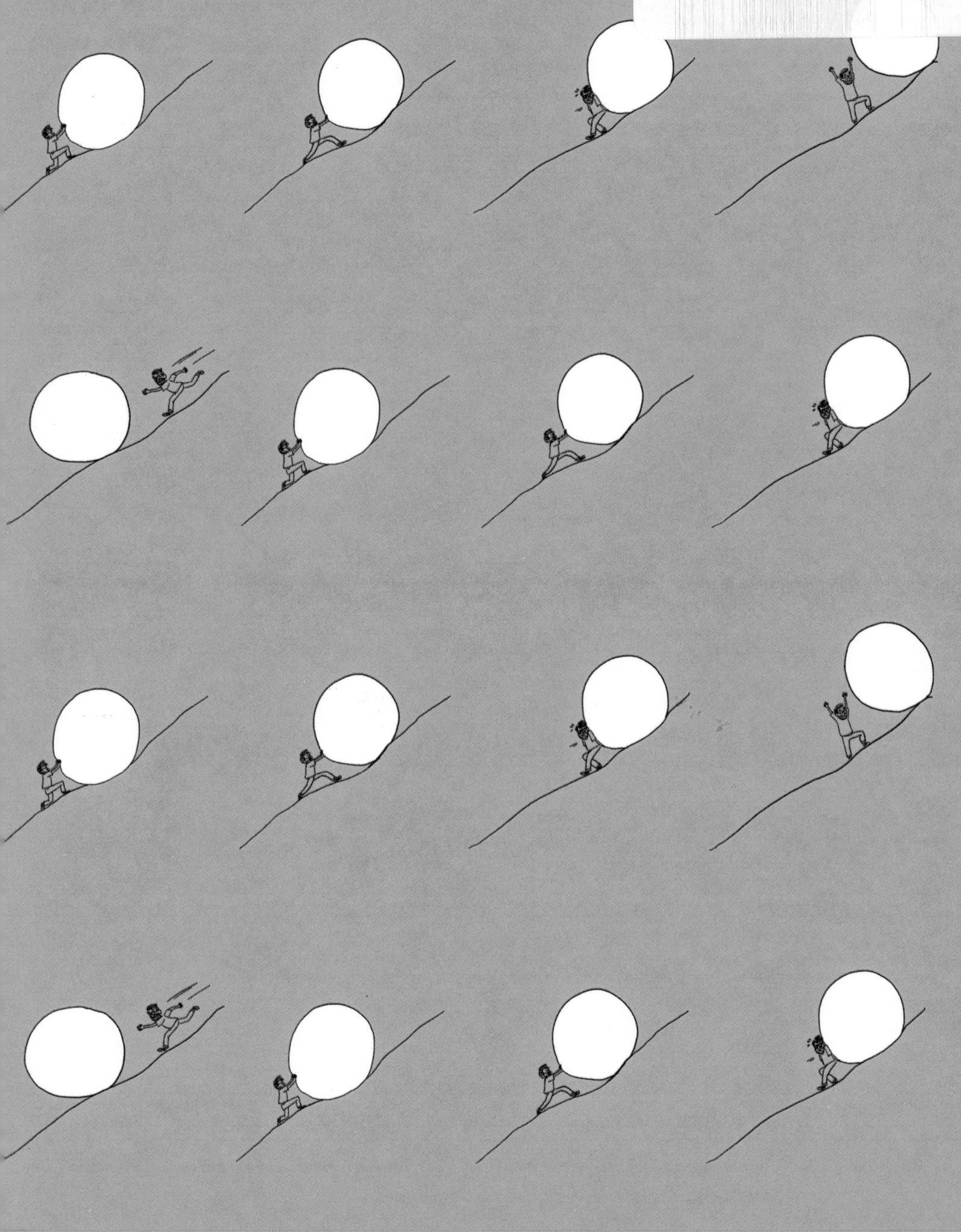

EVERYTHING IS AN EMERGENCY

EVERYTHING IS an EMERGENCY

An OCD Story in Words and Pictures

Jason Adam Katzenstein

HARPER ● PERENNIAL

NEW YORK ● LONDON ● TORONTO ● SYDNEY ● NEW DELHI ● AUCKLAND

HARPER ● PERENNIAL

HarperCollins books may be purchased for educational, business, or sales promotional use. For information, please email the Special Markets Department at SPsales@harpercollins.com.

FIRST EDITION

Designed by Jen Overstreet

Cartoon on page 128 originally appeared in The New Yorker.

Library of Congress Cataloging-in-Publication Data has been applied for.

ISBN 978-0-06-295007-9

20 21 22 23 24   LSC   10 9 8 7 6 5 4 3 2 1

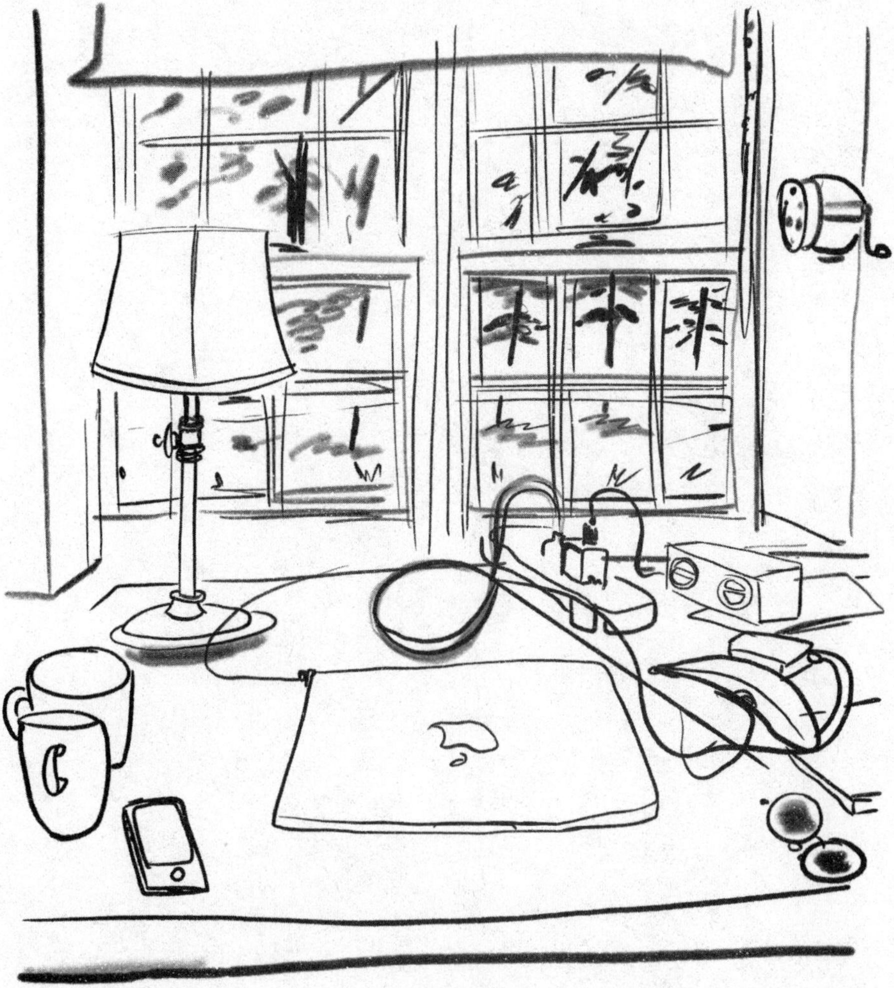

This comic was written, drawn, rewritten
and redrawn, shared, agonized over, and given life
at the MacDowell Colony. My love and gratitude
to this wonderful place and everyone in it.

In surrealism, as in dreams and cartoons,
things turn into other things without any preamble.
—David Salle

What, me worry?
—Alfred E. Neuman

EVERYTHING IS AN EMERGENCY

The first thing I'm ever afraid of is this statue in my grandparents' house.

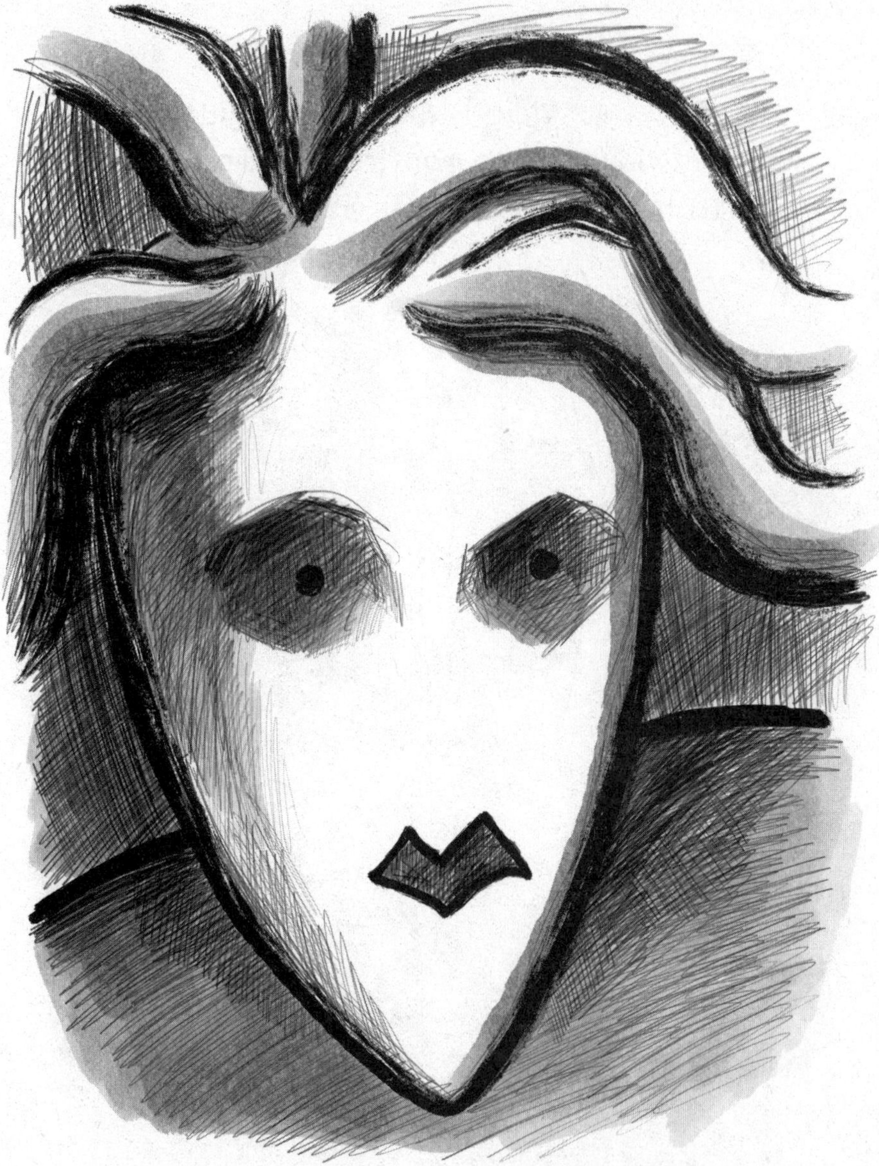

I've always been creative with my fears.

Whenever we visit, I take a quick glance
into the living room to confirm that the statue
that terrifies me is in its proper place.

She always is.

Until, one day, my parents figure out
I've been hiding from her.

The next time we go to my grandparents':

I know she's still under there, but for now she's neutralized.

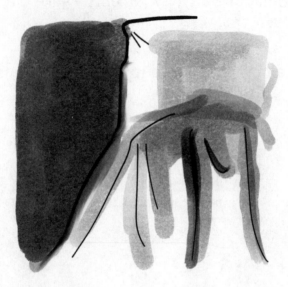

And for now that's enough.

Another early fear is Madeleine L'Engle's *A Wrinkle in Time.*

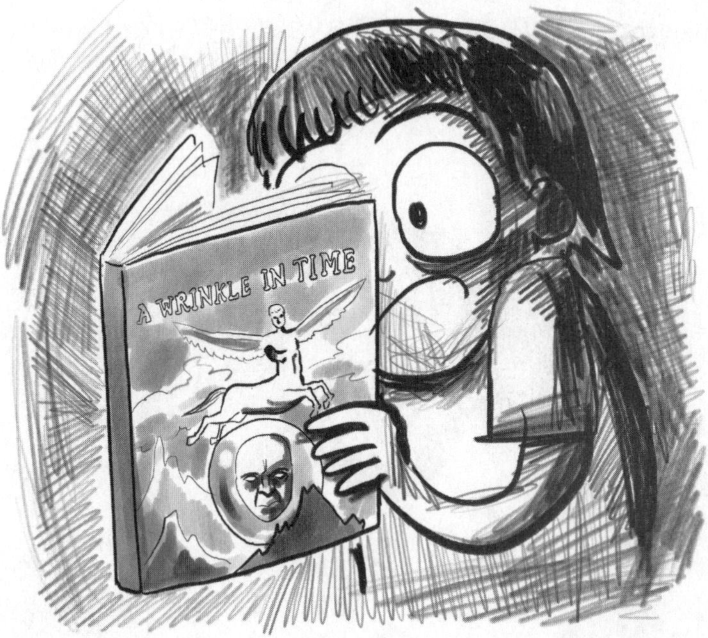
A WRINKLE IN TIME

My nightmares are original stories my subconscious writes about the Man with Red Eyes, eerie fan fiction.

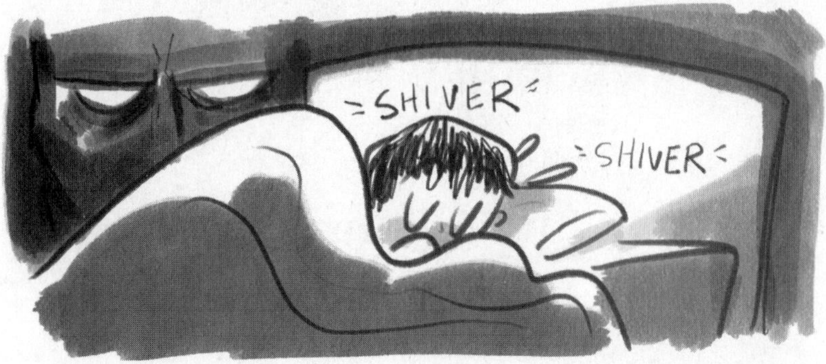
SHIVER
SHIVER

My dad teaches me that if you have a nightmare, you wake up and turn your pillow over, and when you go back to sleep you'll have a different dream.

This comforts me.

As an extra precaution, when I go back to sleep
I hide myself completely under the comforter.
That way nothing and nobody will find me.

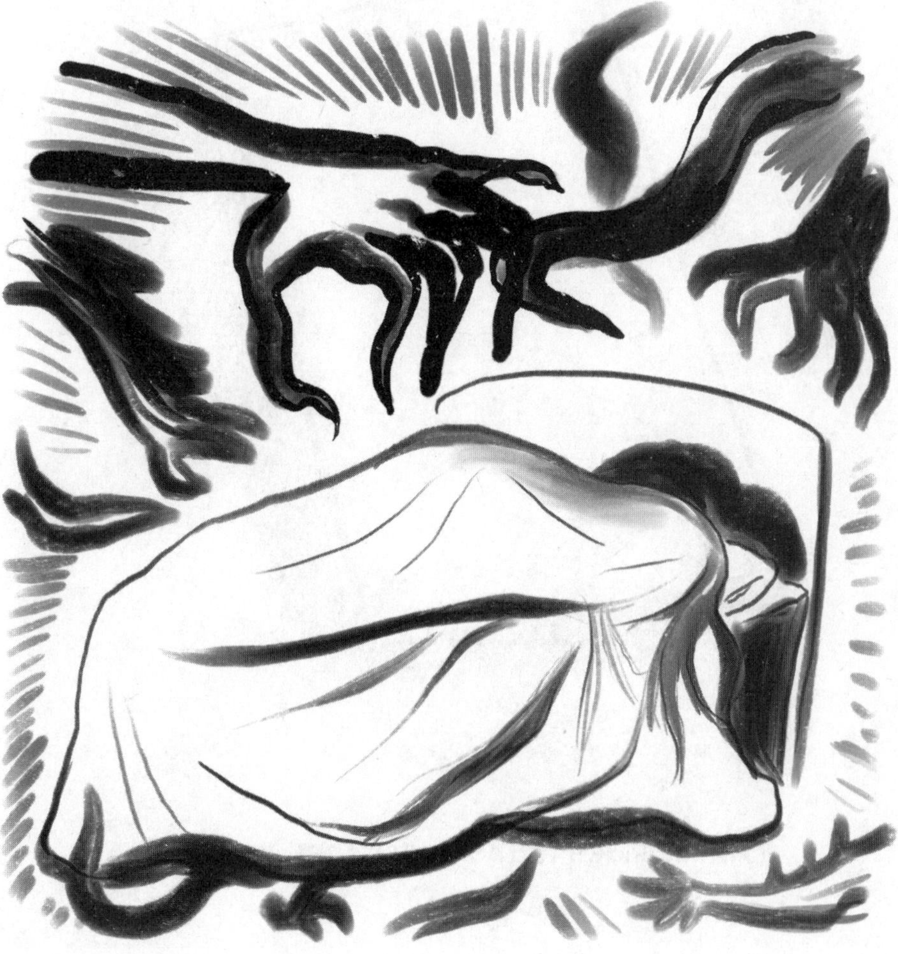

In the morning my dad tapes a piece of brown
paper over the cover of *A Wrinkle in Time.*

Then he hides it and doesn't tell me where.

I'm safe again for now.

When my parents go out, I stay awake in bed
imagining every terrible way they could die.

I can't fall asleep until I hear the sound
of the garage door opening.

I tell my mom that when I close my
eyes I see pictures in my head.

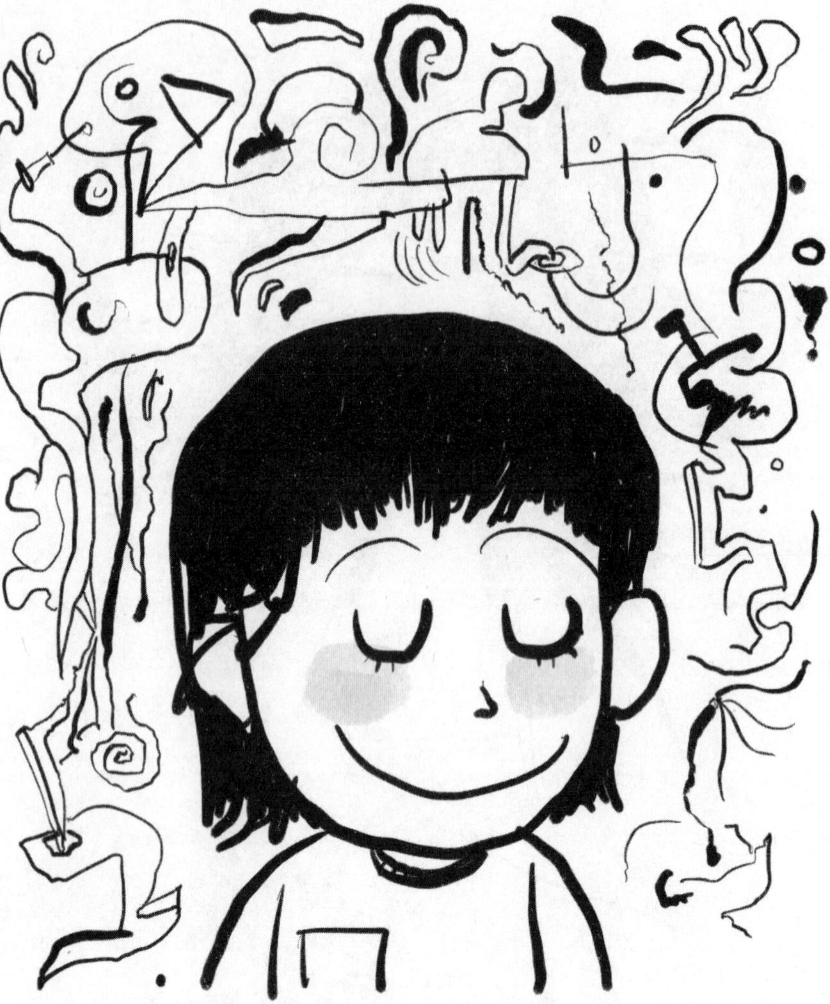

When I'm in control of these pictures,
it's the thing I like to do best.

I've been seeing a child development specialist named Mary. I don't know it at the time, but my mom has hired her to prepare me for my parents' divorce. Mary is, in fact, the one to break the news to me.

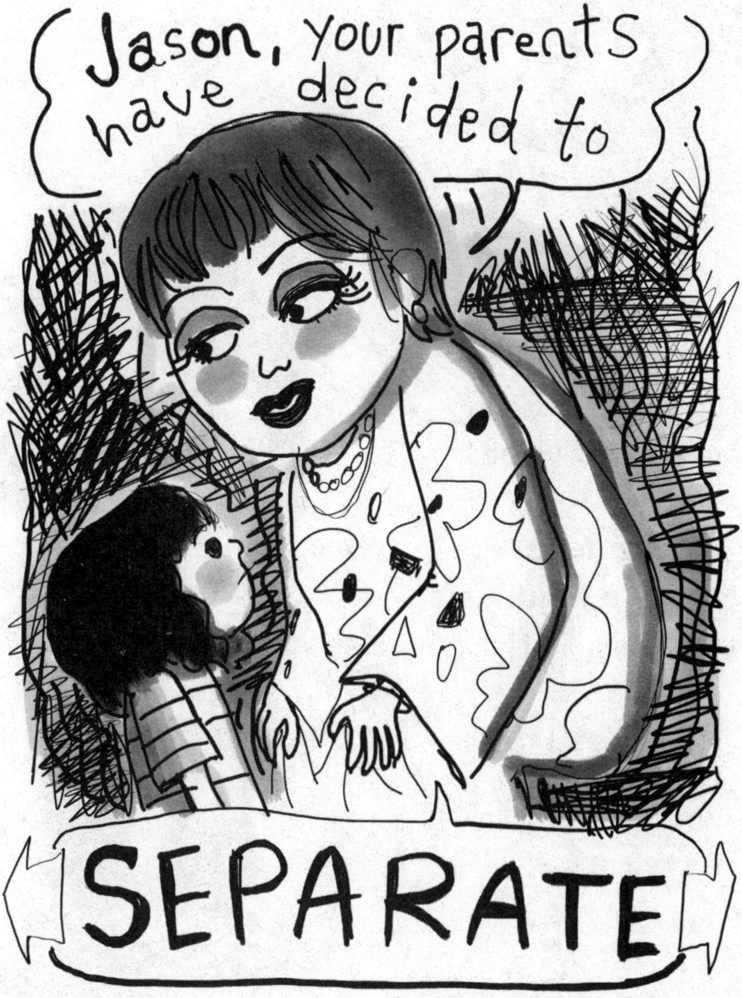
Jason, your parents have decided to
SEPARATE

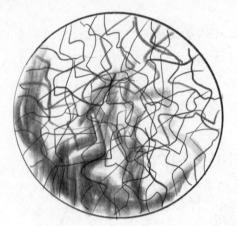

Cracks form in my world,
little gaps between what
should be and what is.

The cracks make me
furious. Everything
makes me furious.

If the terms of my
reality are negotiable,
well, I will be rigid.

Things need to BE
a certain way.

The cereal in my bowl doesn't match the way it looks on the box. . . .

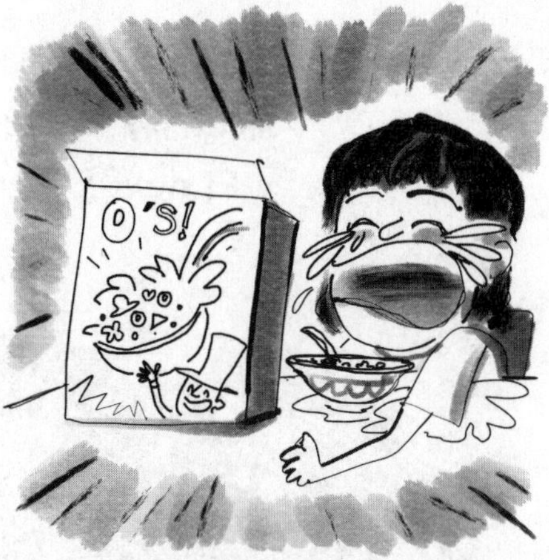
O'S!

I watch *The Parent Trap*, and I learn that if I'm mean enough to my dad's dates, they'll go away and he'll realize he belongs with my mom.

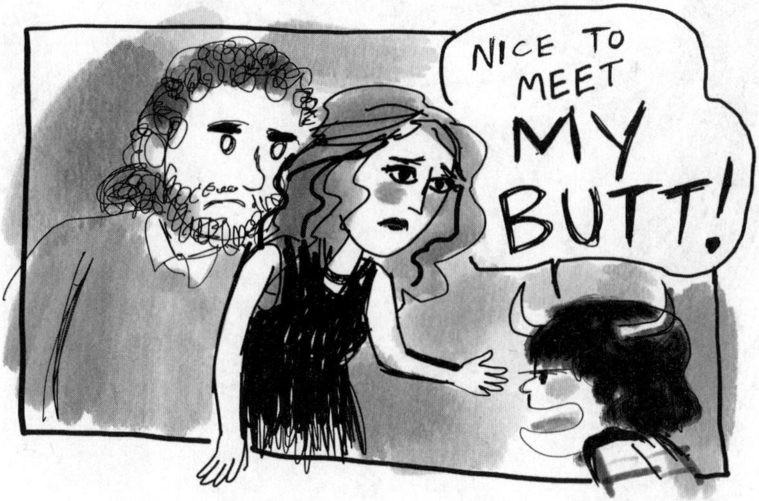
NICE TO MEET MY BUTT!

It never turns out like it did in the movie.

I don't know what happens
when my world splits open, and
I never want to find out.

When I close my eyes, I see the world I want.

I imagine a machine that can turn the things in my head into reality.

PERFECT CEREAL-TO-MILK RATIO!

I draw things the way they SHOULD be.

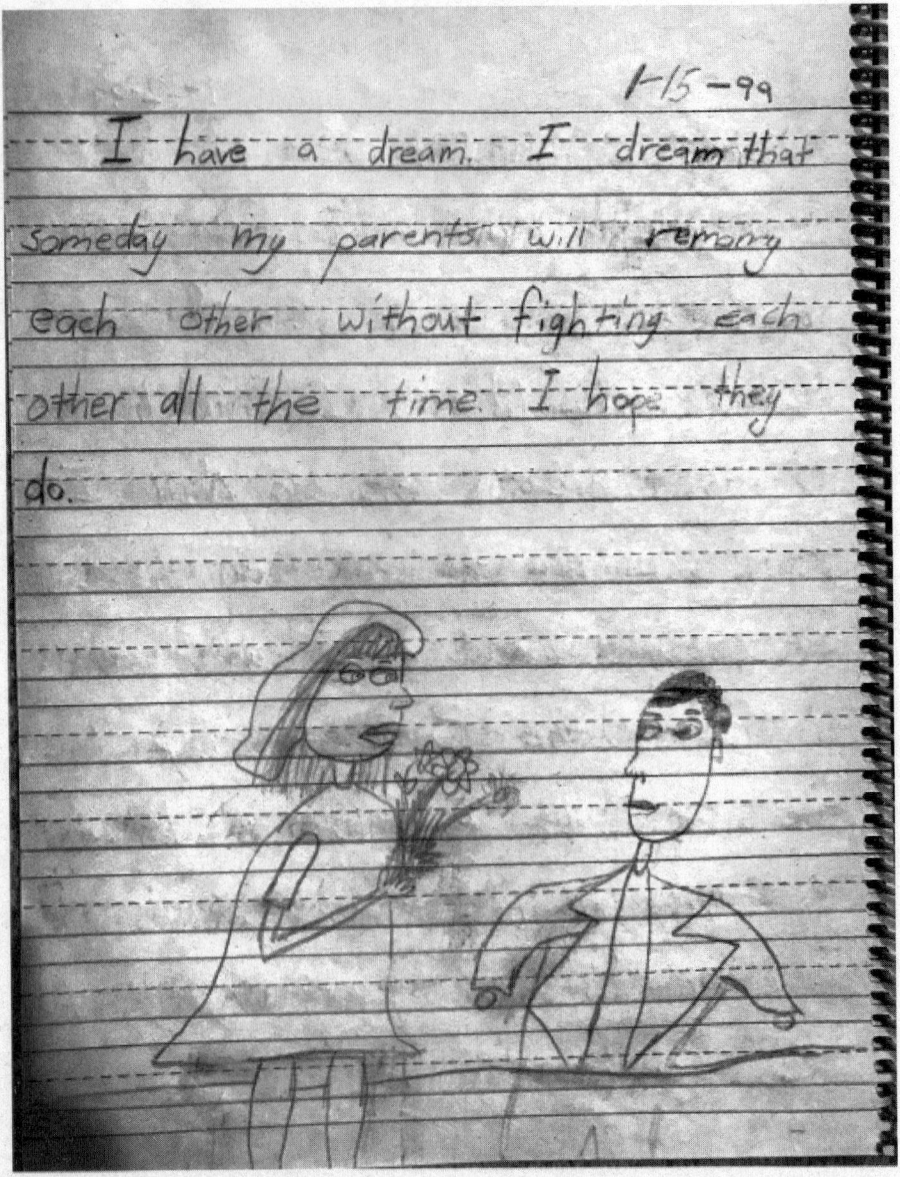
1-15-99
I have a dream. I dream that
someday my parents will remarry
each other without fighting each
other all the time. I hope they
do.

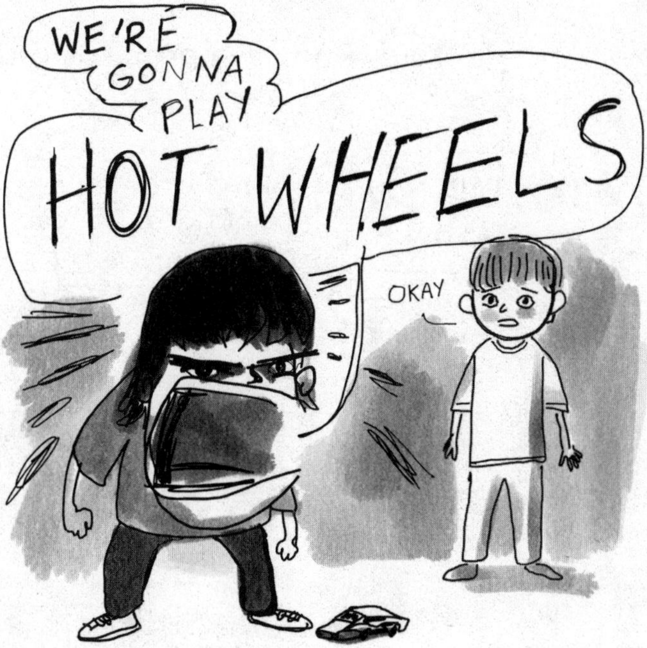
WE'RE GONNA PLAY
HOT WHEELS
OKAY

I am aggressive on playdates.

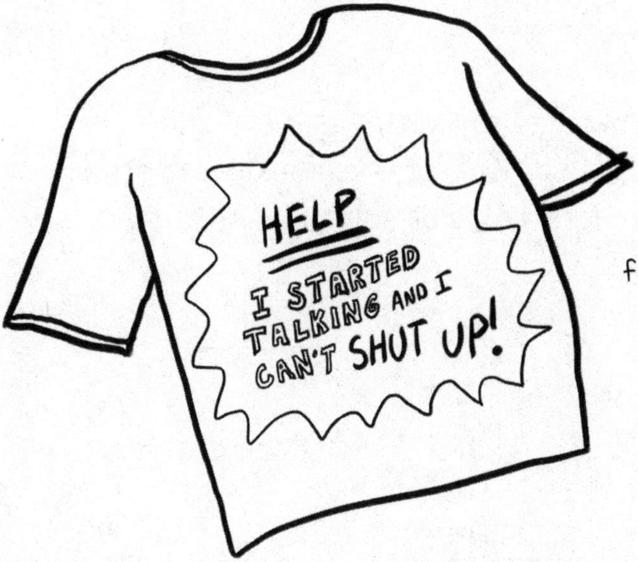
HELP
I STARTED TALKING AND I CAN'T SHUT UP!

I'll never forget this T-shirt my friend's mom gave to me as a "gift."

I meet with Mary in a group of other boys.

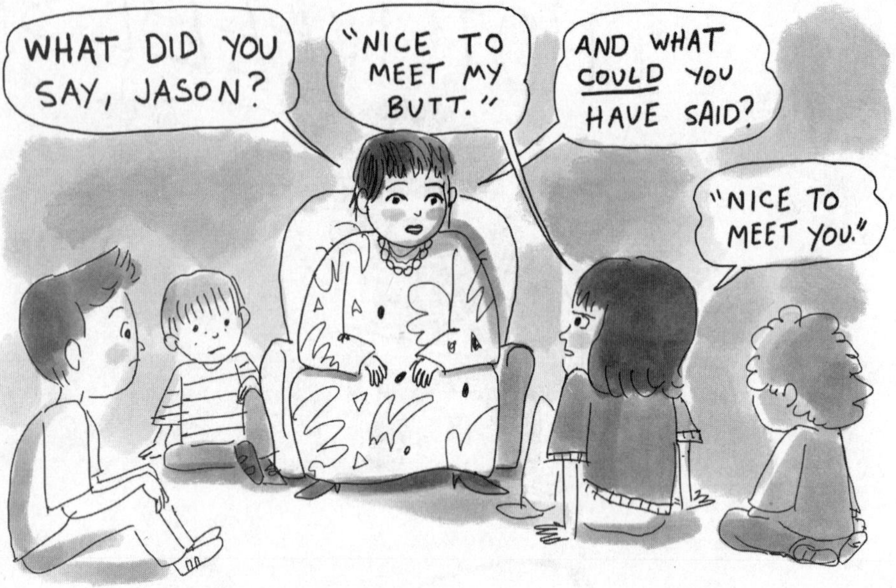
WHAT DID YOU SAY, JASON?
"NICE TO MEET MY BUTT."
AND WHAT COULD YOU HAVE SAID?
"NICE TO MEET YOU."

Our common denominator is all of our parents can — and do — spend money sending us to a children's group therapist.

Mary asks each of us to write a story. We're supposed to think of some deficient quality in ourselves, and then give that quality to a fictional character.

Once upon a time there was a duck named Quacky. He was sooooooooo bossy.

I write my magnum opus, "The Very Bossy Duck."

I get lost in this story. I send Quacky on adventures. I draw him in MS paint. I forget that I'm supposed to be working on myself and focus on my character design.

Portrait of the Artist as a Very Bossy Duck

In the bed I share with my little brother in my dad's new apartment, I toss and turn. And in the mornings:

I can't sleep. I don't like the bed. I don't want to be in this apartment. The world as it presently exists keeps making me furious.

Now when I'm feeling this way I work on Quacky.

Finally, I control the machine that turns my thoughts into reality.

I get into screaming matches with my stepfather.

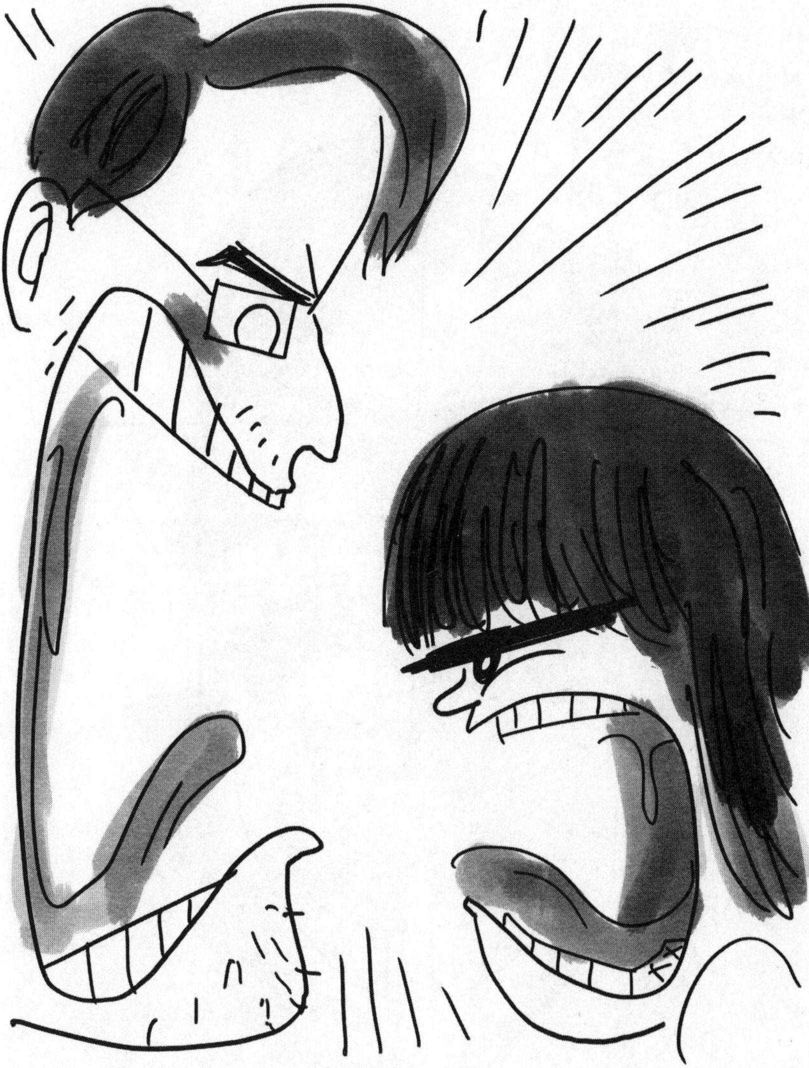

He wins because he's louder.

I study his face like I'm drawing him.

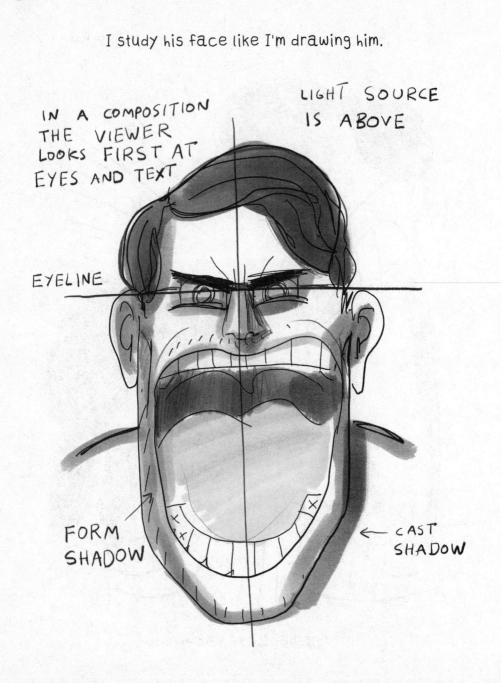

IN A COMPOSITION
THE VIEWER
LOOKS FIRST AT
EYES AND TEXT

LIGHT SOURCE
IS ABOVE

EYELINE

FORM
SHADOW

← CAST
SHADOW

After these fights I cry loudly in my room. I want to be left alone. I also want him to hear me and come in and apologize.

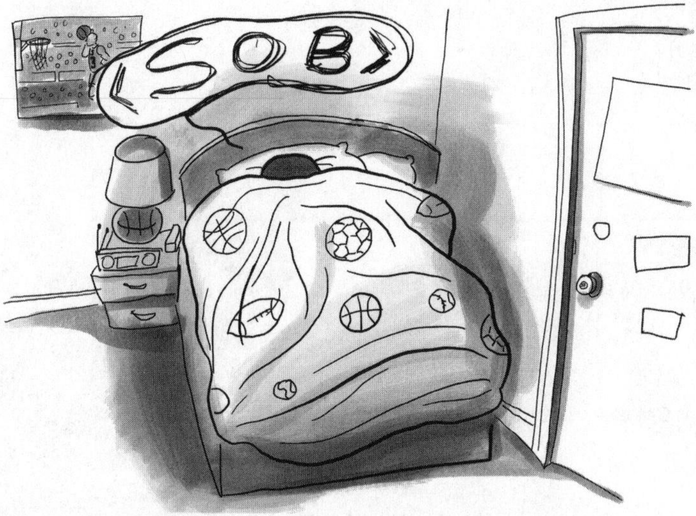
<SOB>

I try to remember the way I'm feeling, and commit to never making someone else feel this way.

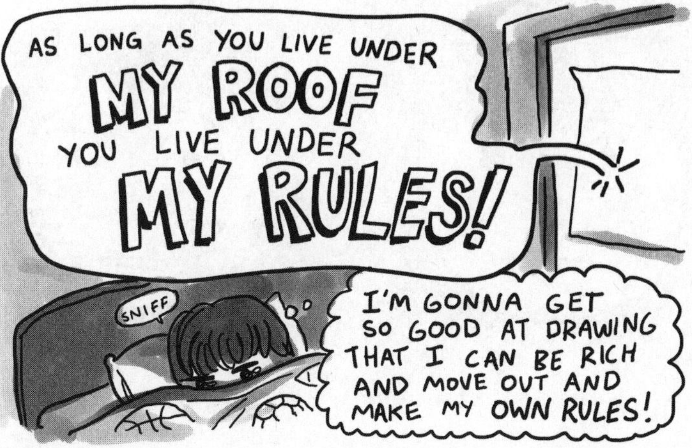
AS LONG AS YOU LIVE UNDER MY ROOF YOU LIVE UNDER MY RULES!
SNIFF
I'M GONNA GET SO GOOD AT DRAWING THAT I CAN BE RICH AND MOVE OUT AND MAKE MY OWN RULES!

I have this recurring nightmare.

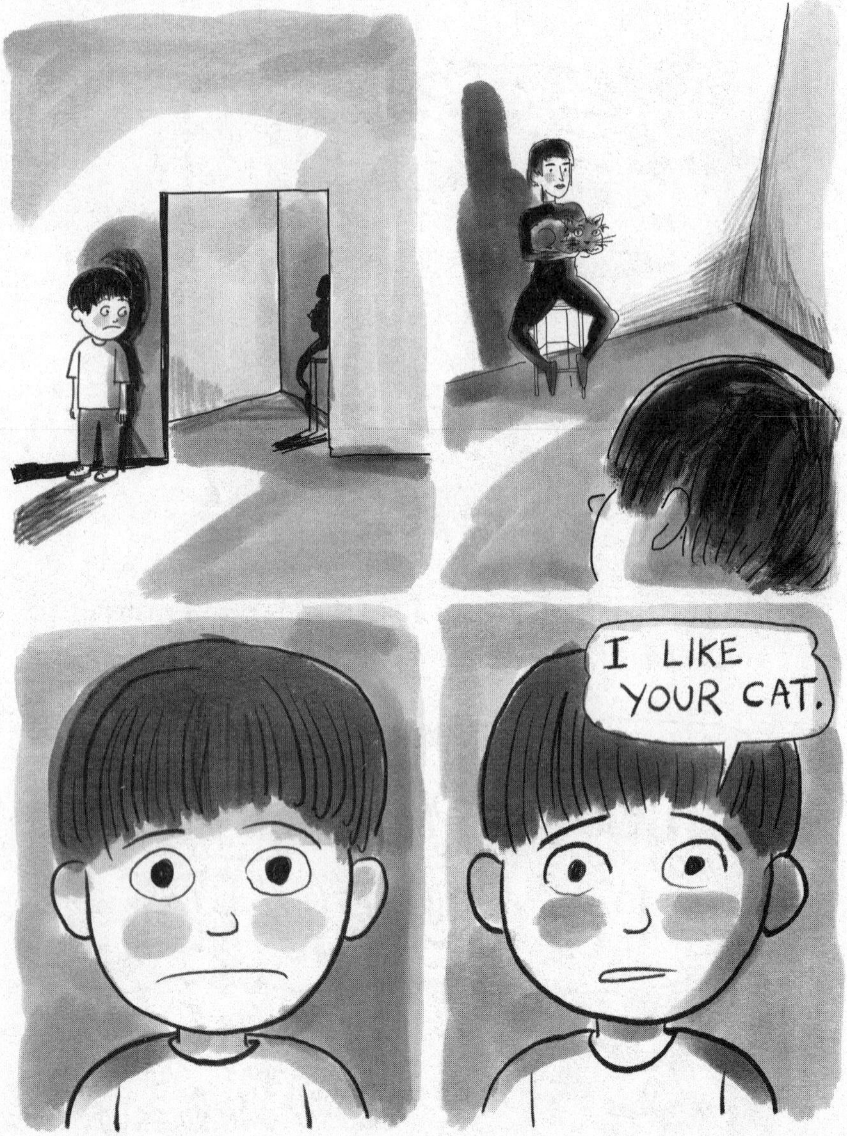
I LIKE YOUR CAT.

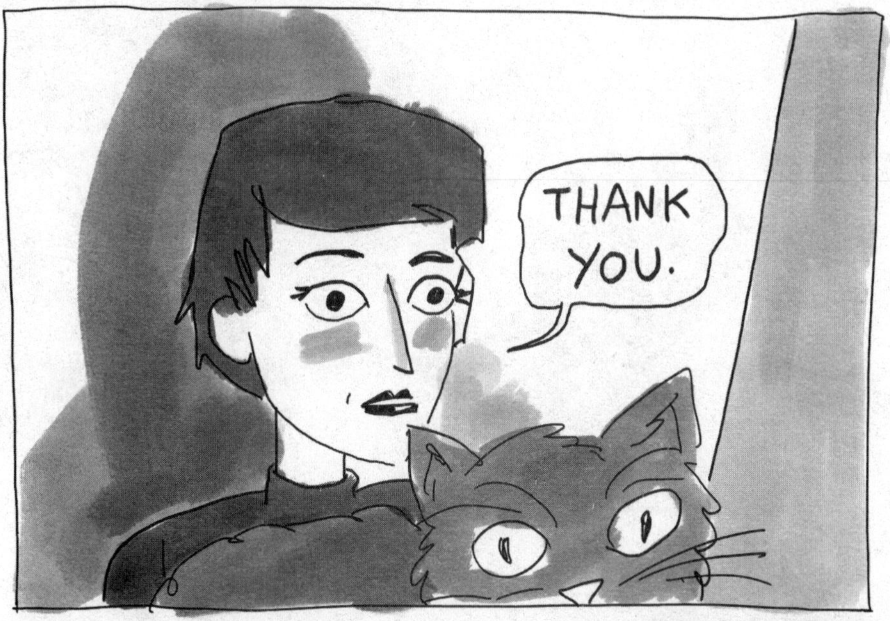
THANK YOU.

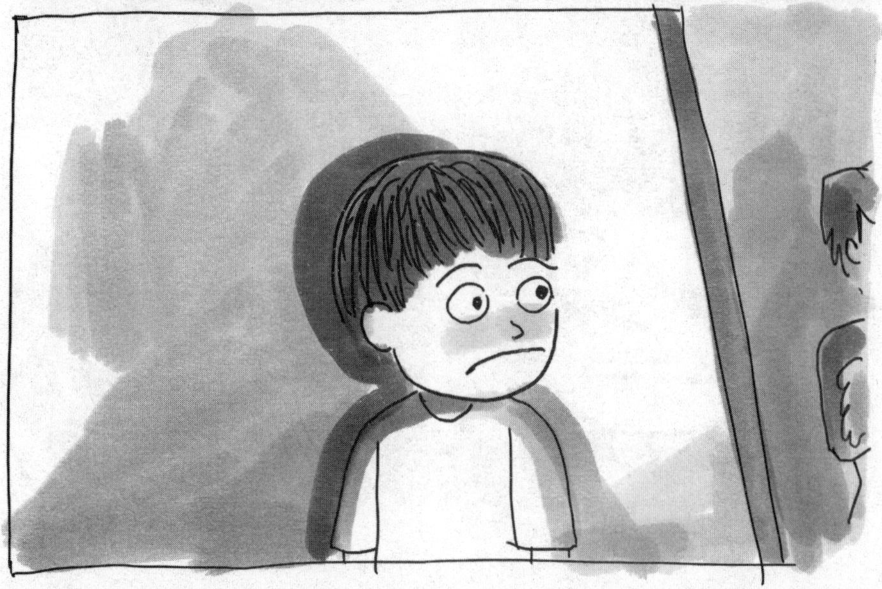

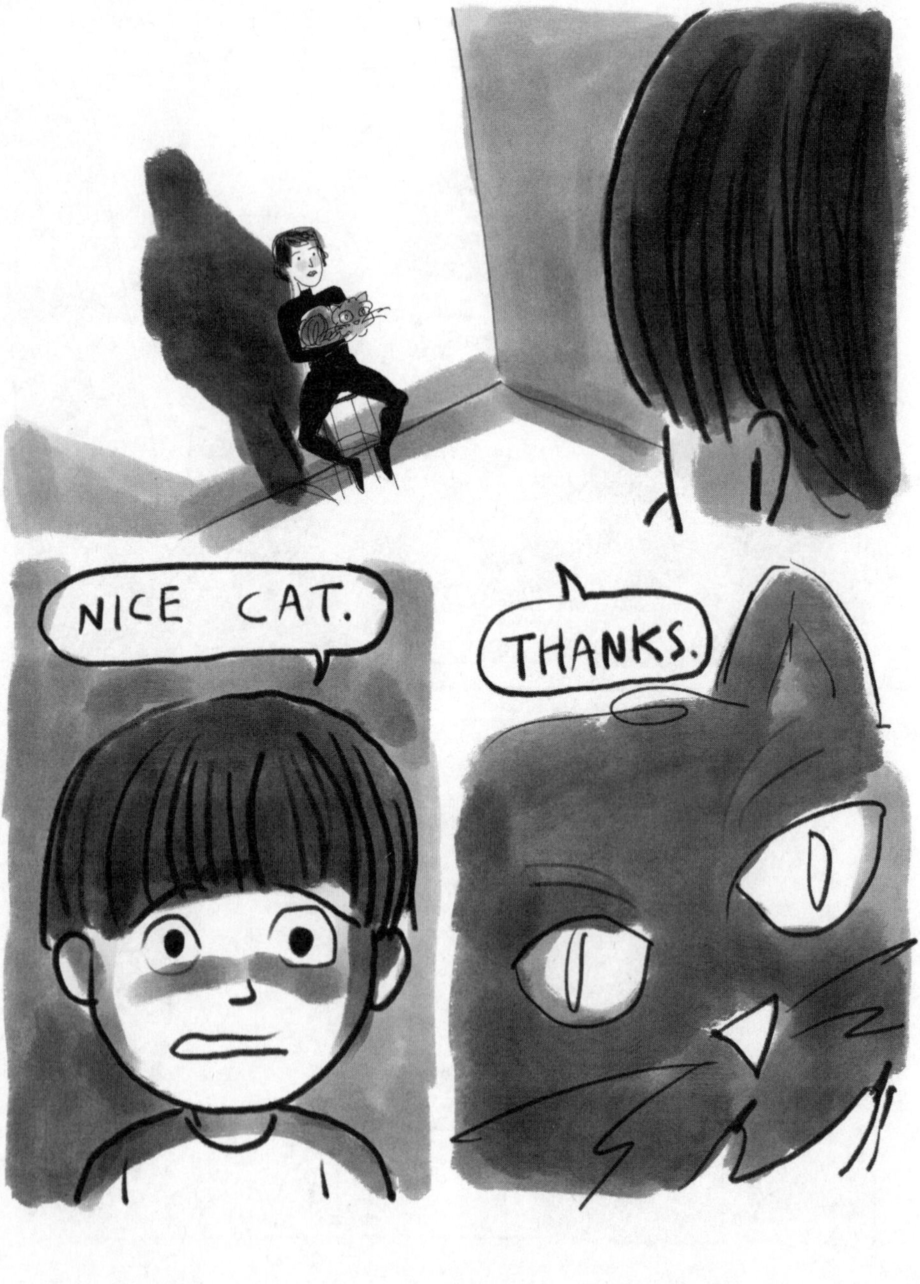
NICE CAT.
THANKS.

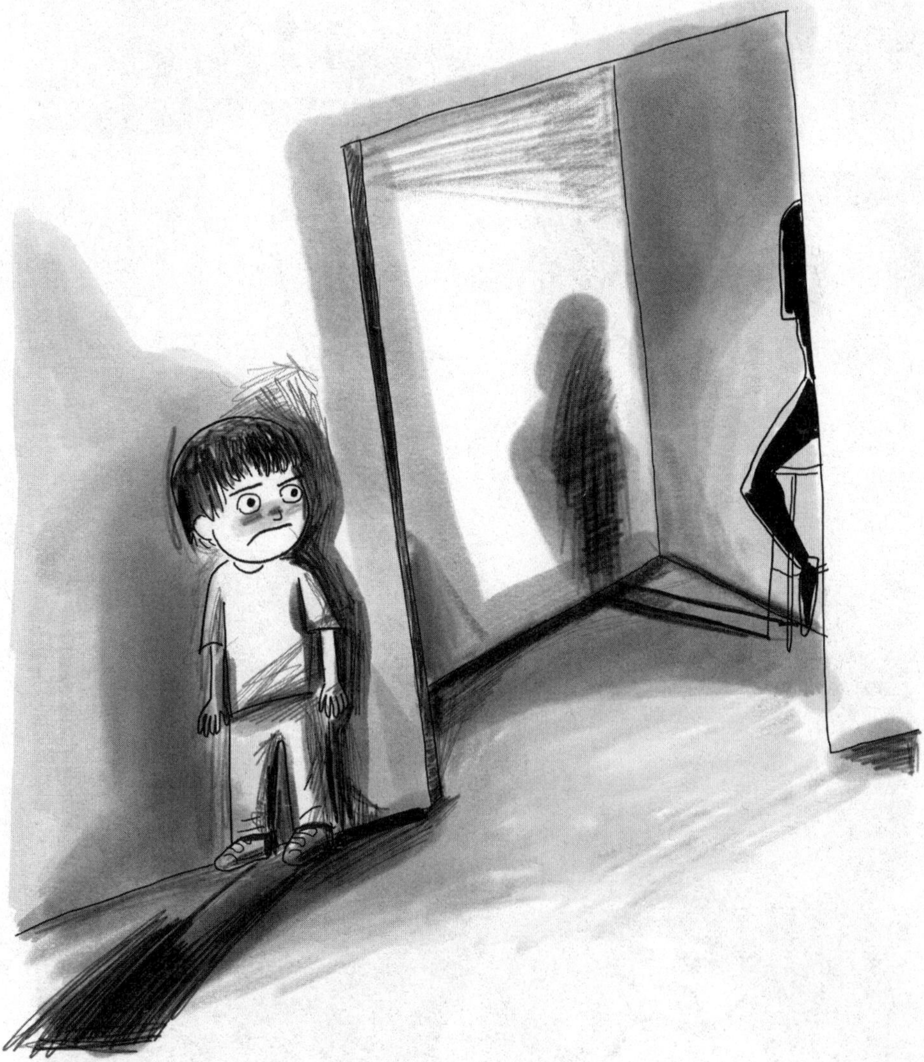

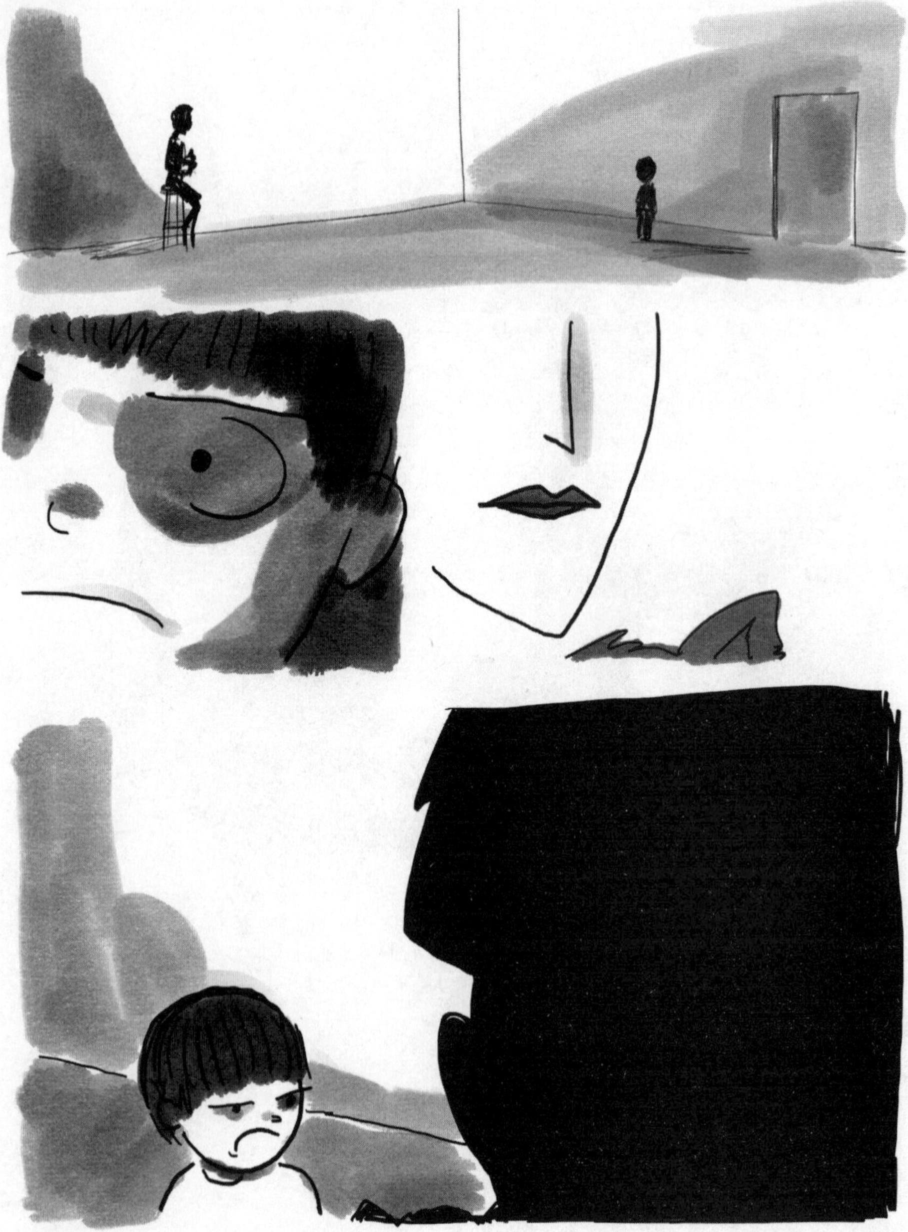

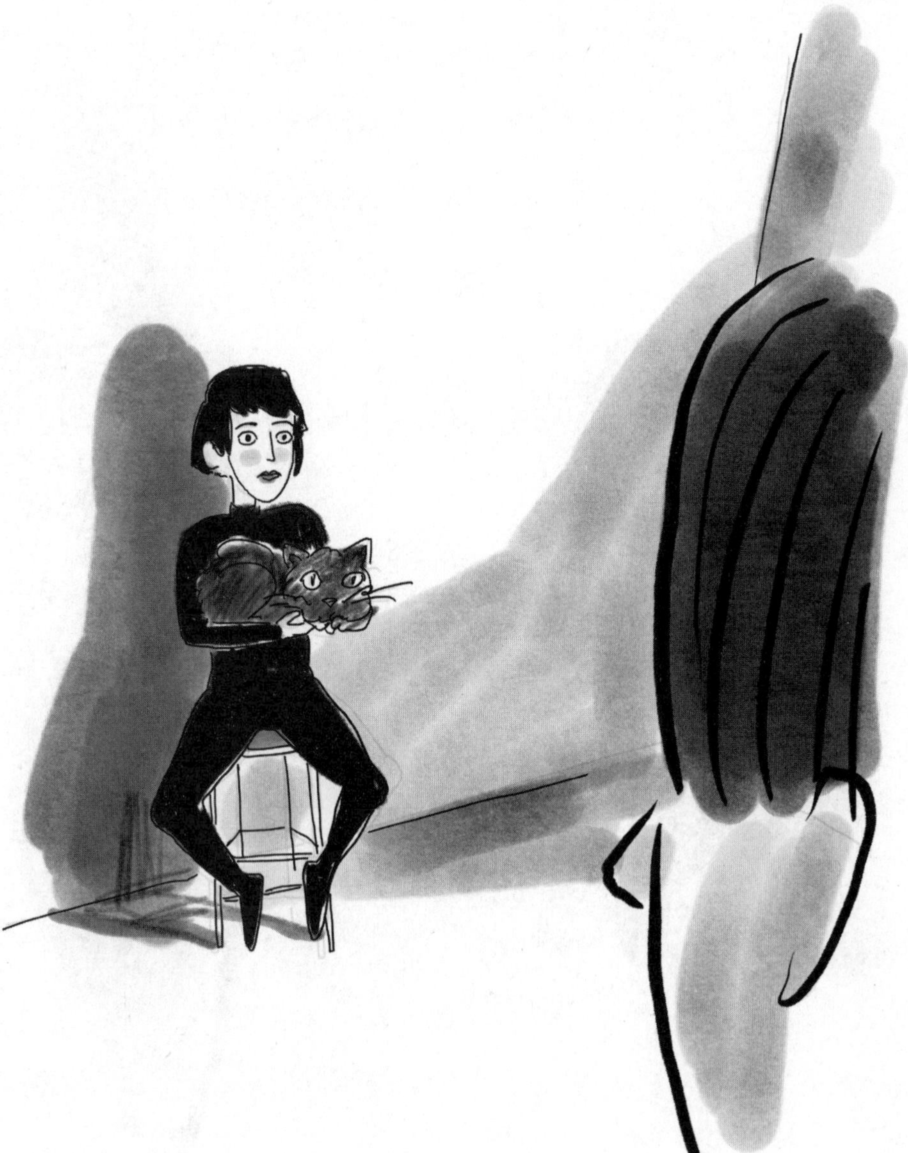

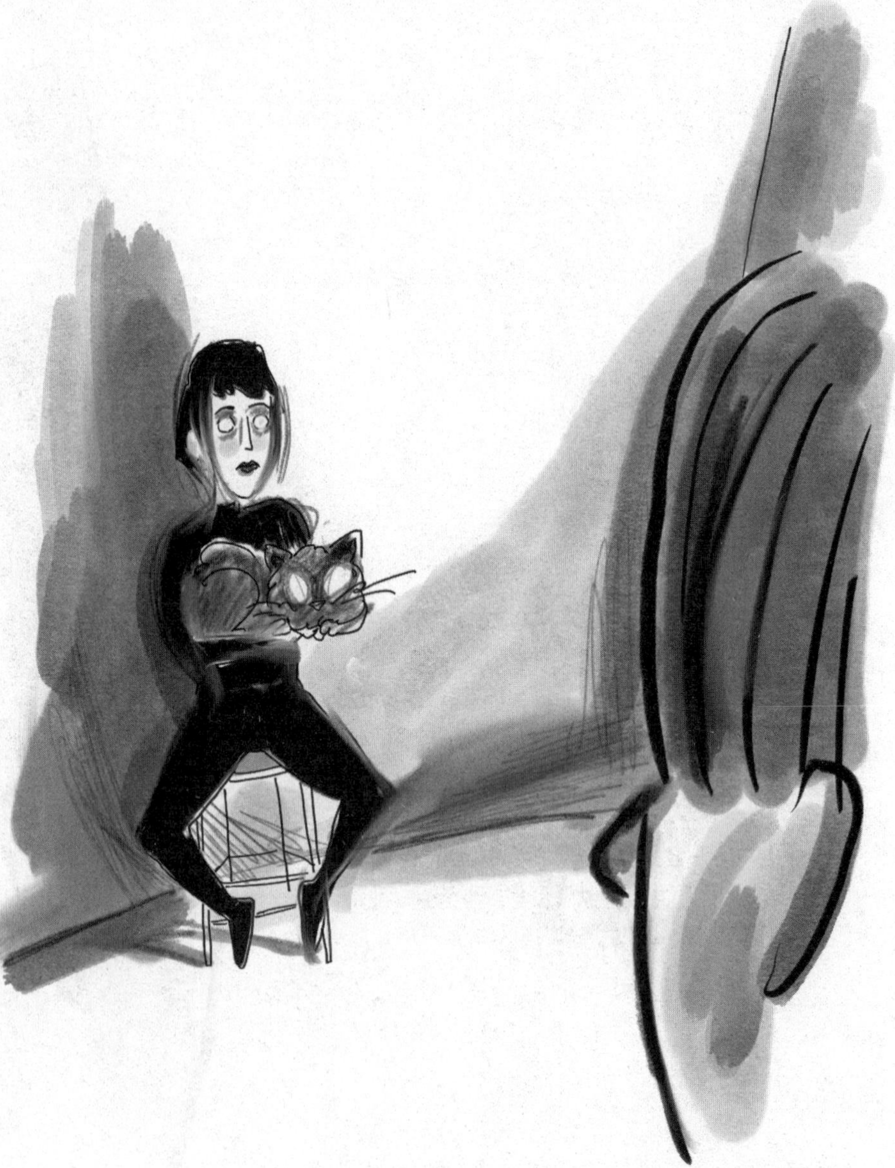

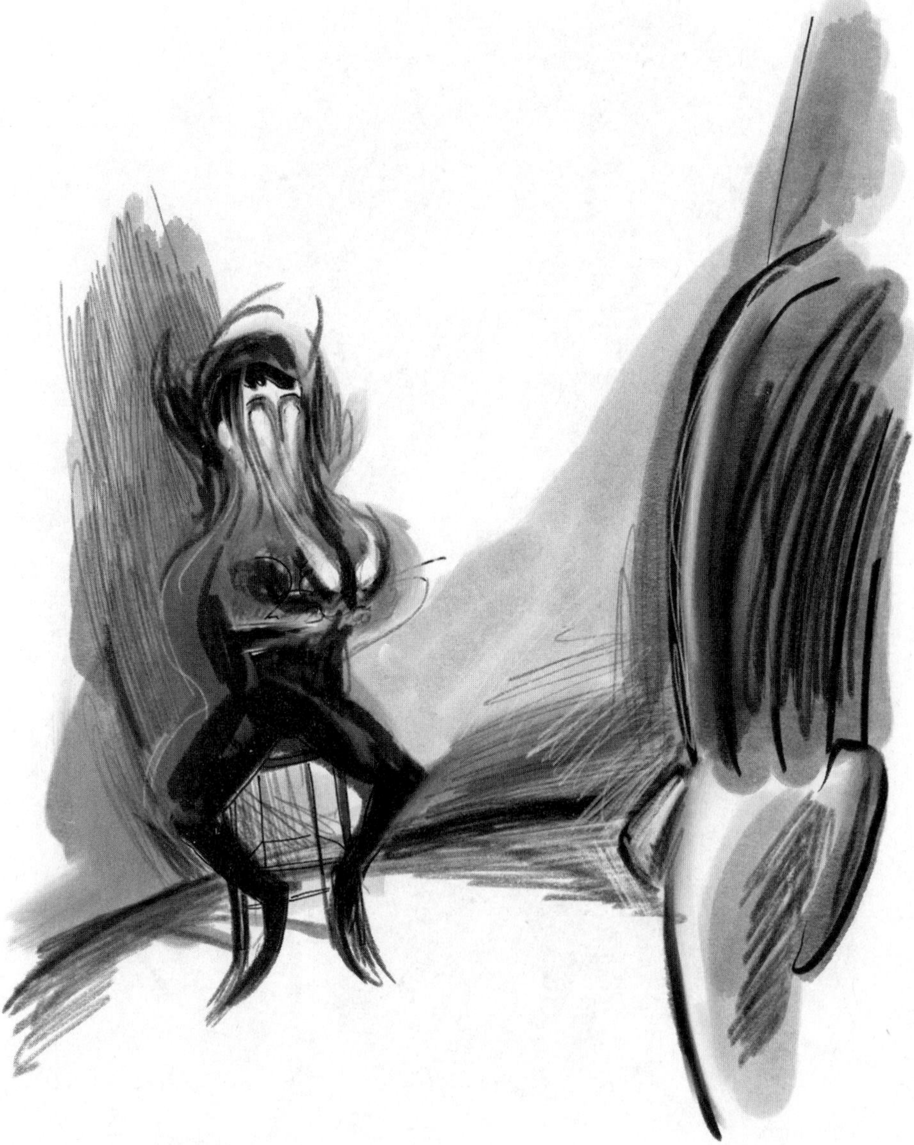

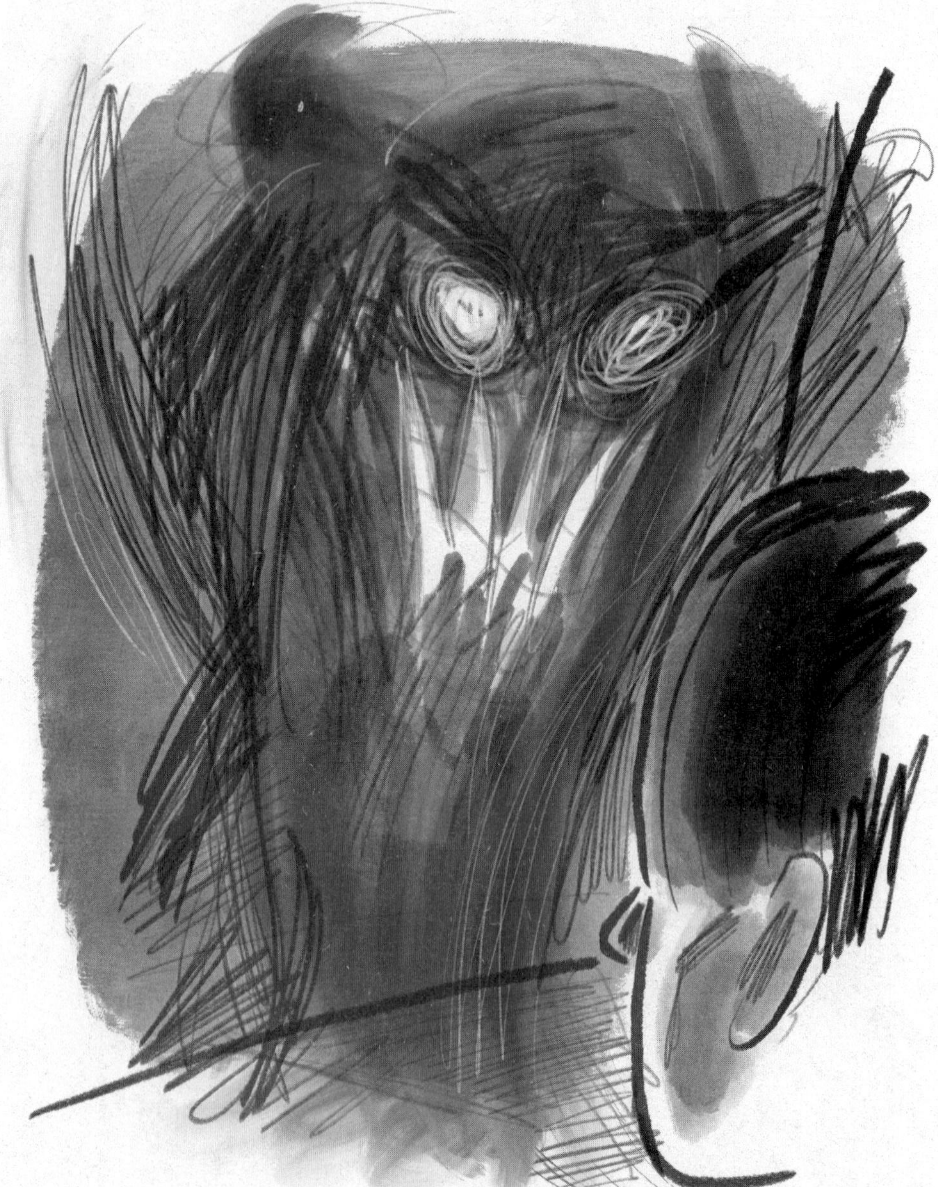

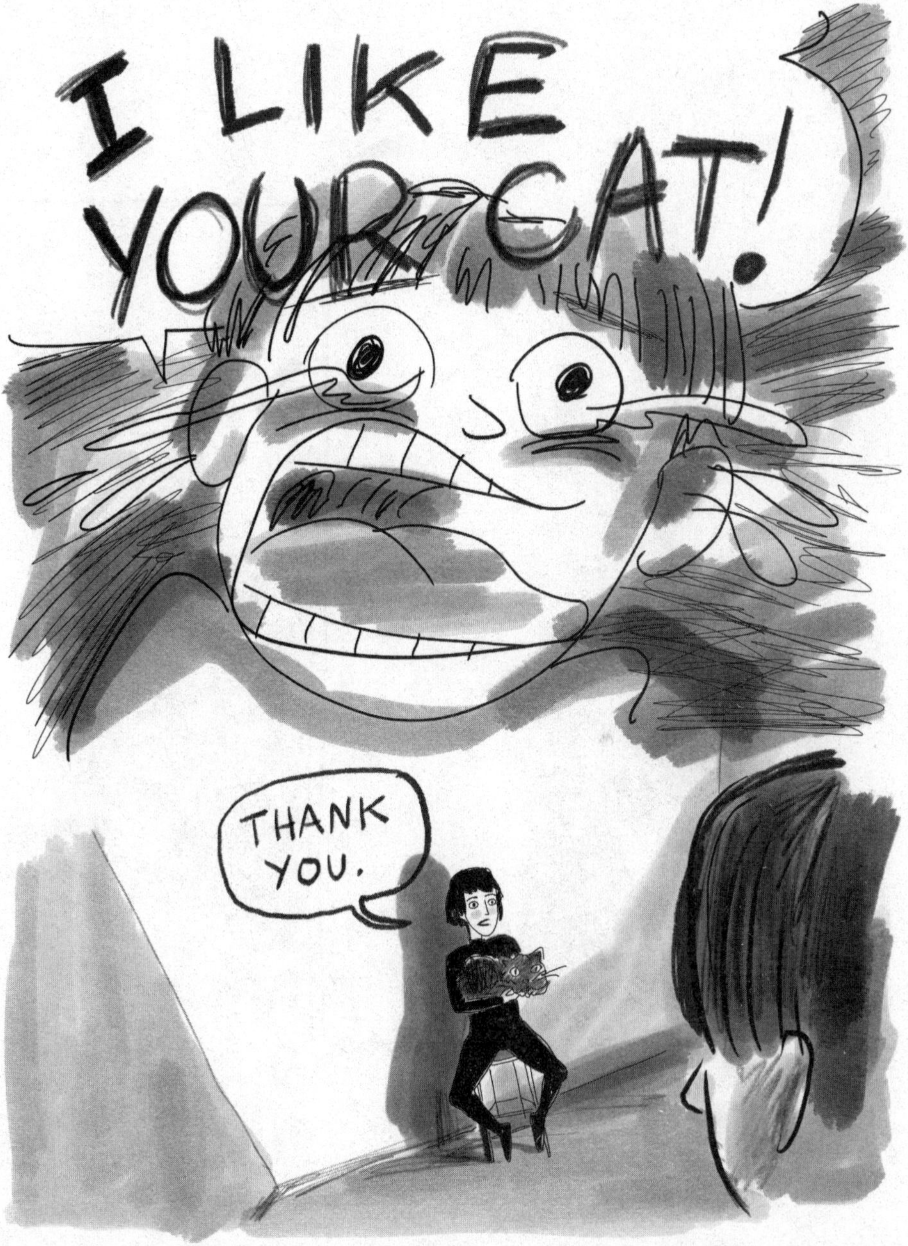
I LIKE YOUR CAT!
THANK YOU.

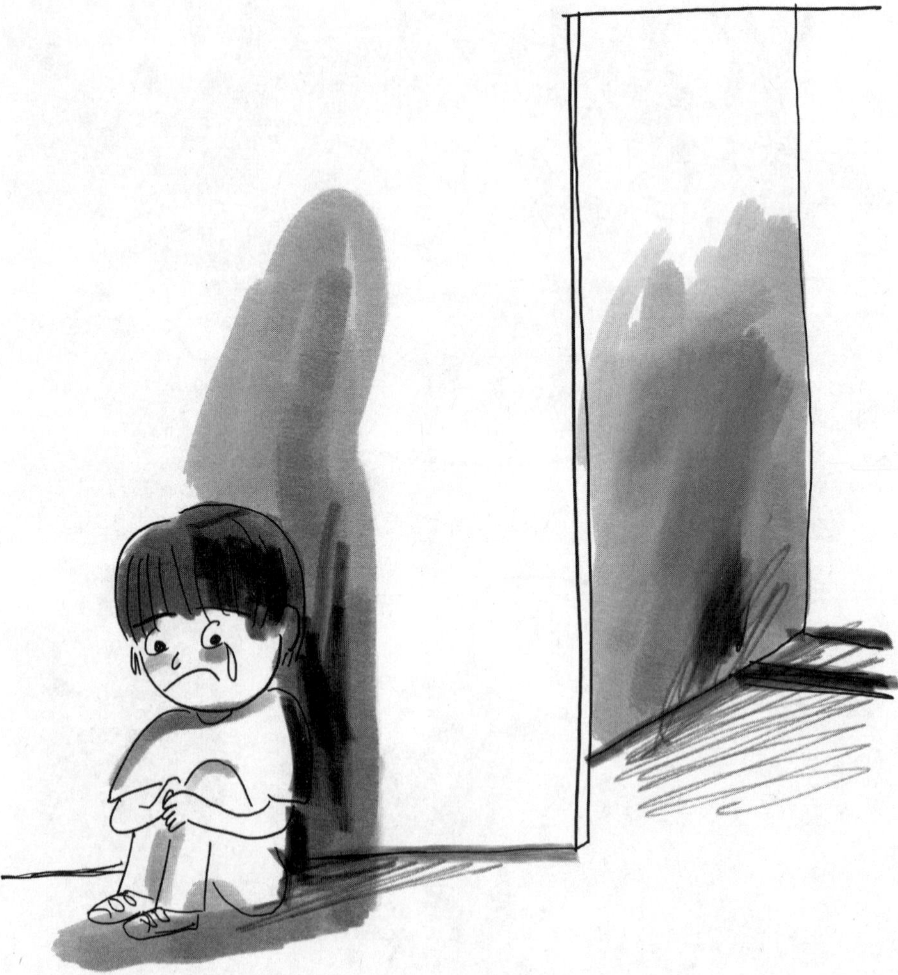

In my waking life, I look for anything I can control. I fixate on my body, which looks nothing like the bodies in the comics I read.

I put myself on a no-carb diet. I do one hundred sit-ups a day, and I run on the treadmill for hours until I'm drenched in sweat. I start reading workout magazines.

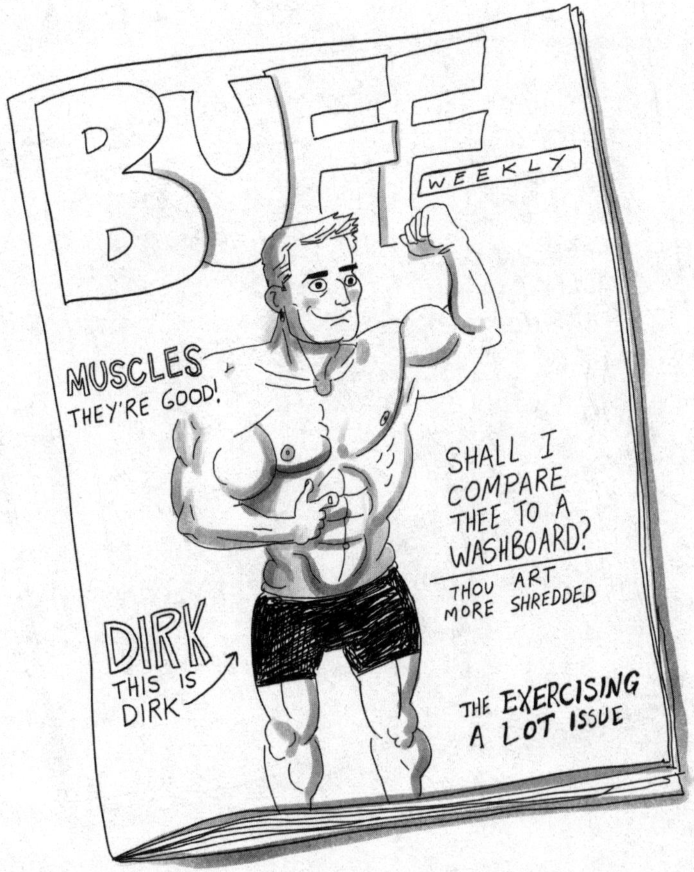
BUFF
WEEKLY
MUSCLES
THEY'RE GOOD!
SHALL I COMPARE THEE TO A WASHBOARD?
THOU ART MORE SHREDDED
DIRK
THIS IS DIRK
THE EXERCISING A LOT ISSUE

I disappoint myself.

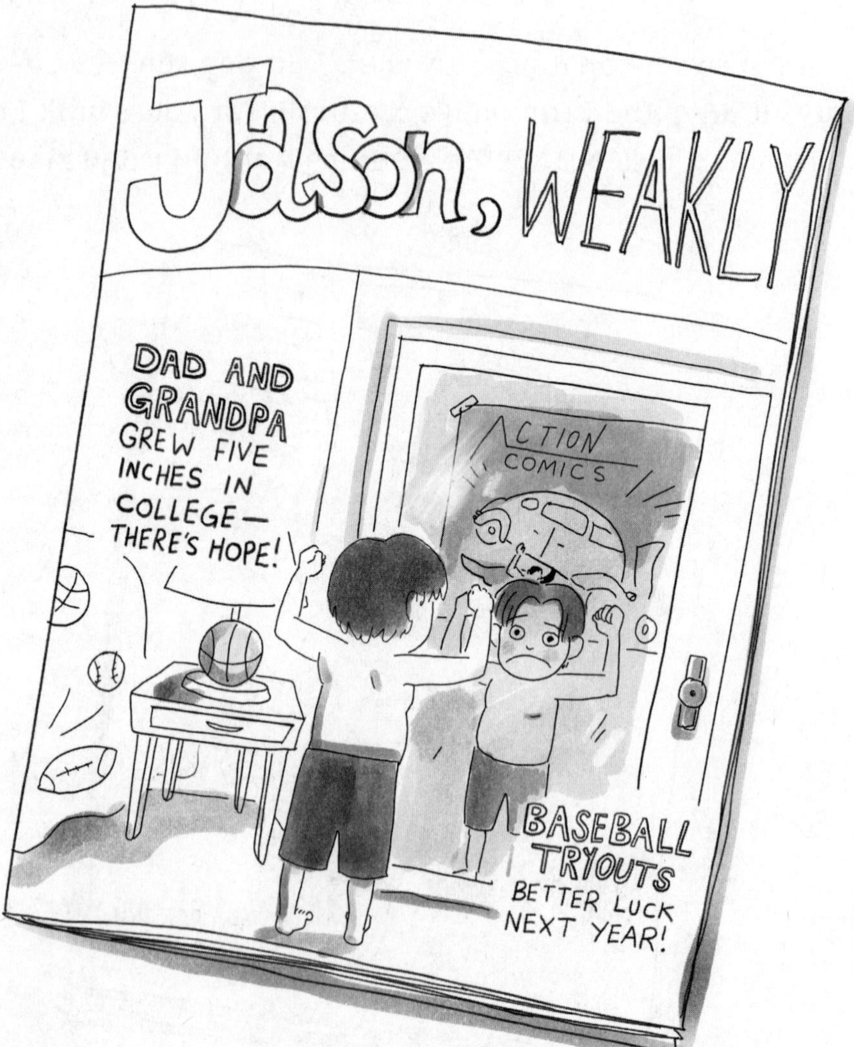
Jason, WEAKLY
DAD AND GRANDPA GREW FIVE INCHES IN COLLEGE— THERE'S HOPE!
ACTION COMICS
BASEBALL TRYOUTS BETTER LUCK NEXT YEAR!

My dad finds the magazines.

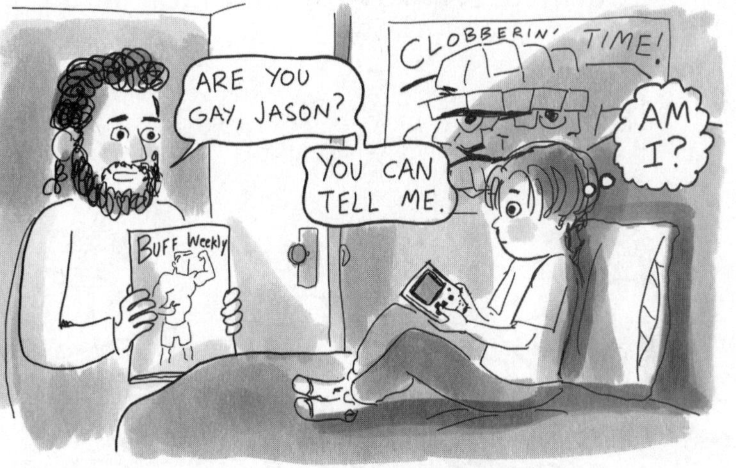
CLOBBERIN' TIME!
ARE YOU GAY, JASON?
YOU CAN TELL ME.
AM I?
BUFF Weekly

I'm thirteen, and I've never kissed anyone, so I don't have much to go on.

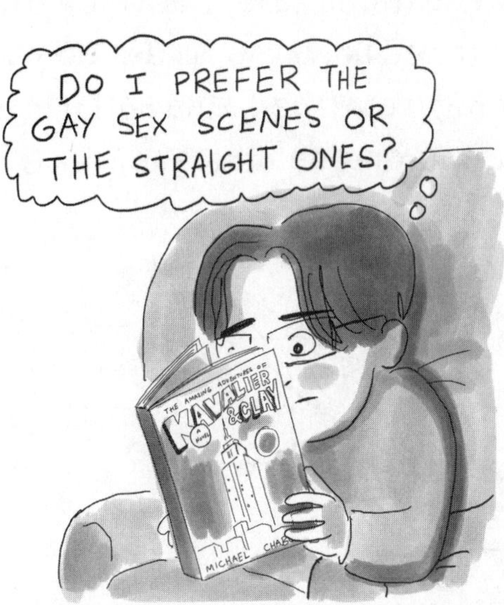
DO I PREFER THE GAY SEX SCENES OR THE STRAIGHT ONES?
THE AMAZING ADVENTURES OF KAVALIER & CLAY
MICHAEL CHAB

It terrifies me that there are questions about my identity that only I can answer.

I go away to summer camp and hate it. I abstain from camp activities; I'm what you'd call an "indoor kid."

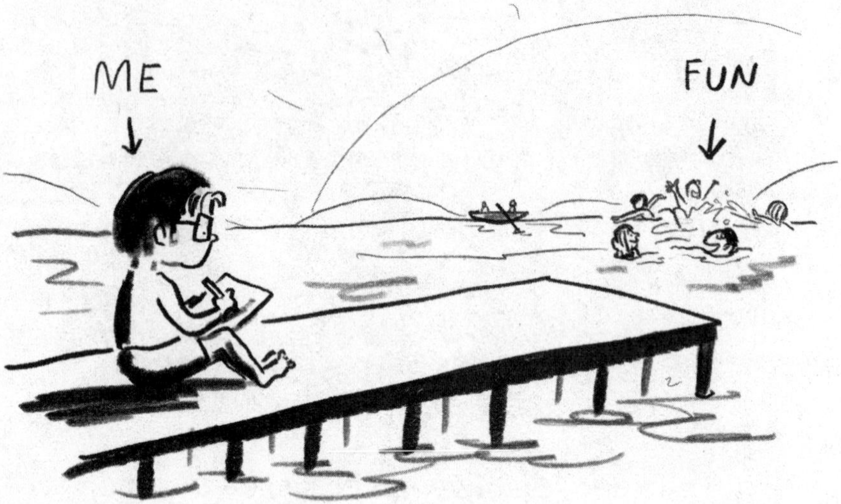
ME
FUN

With too much unsupervised alone time, I develop an idea of a perfectly balanced universe, where doing good things is proportionally rewarded, and bad things are punished. I develop a one-on-one dialogue with God.

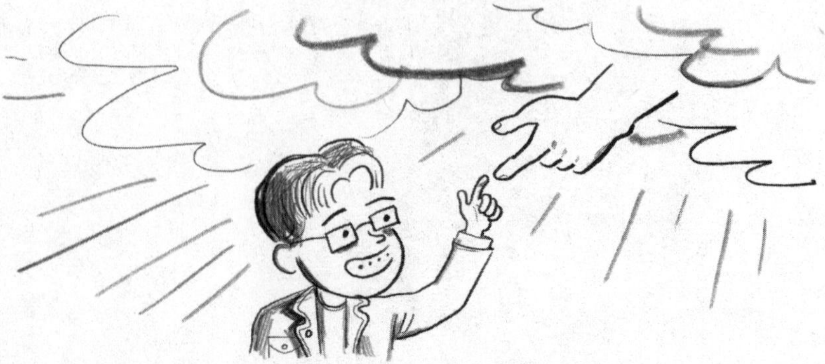

When I get home, I'm fixated on picking up every piece of trash I see on the ground.

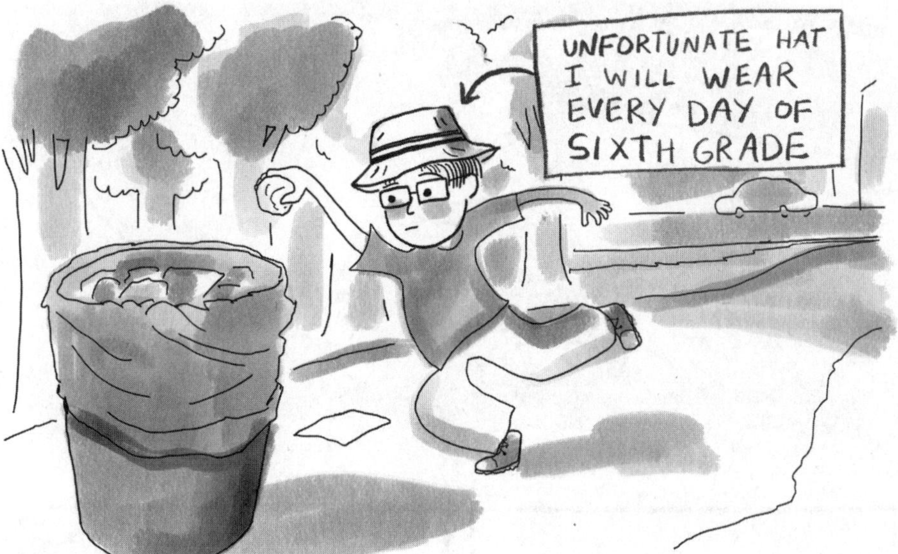
UNFORTUNATE HAT I WILL WEAR EVERY DAY OF SIXTH GRADE

What a little weirdo I am.

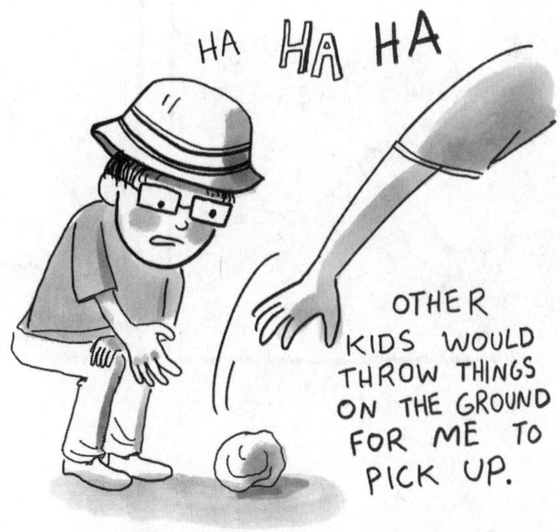
HA HA HA
OTHER KIDS WOULD THROW THINGS ON THE GROUND FOR ME TO PICK UP.

I visit New York with my mom.

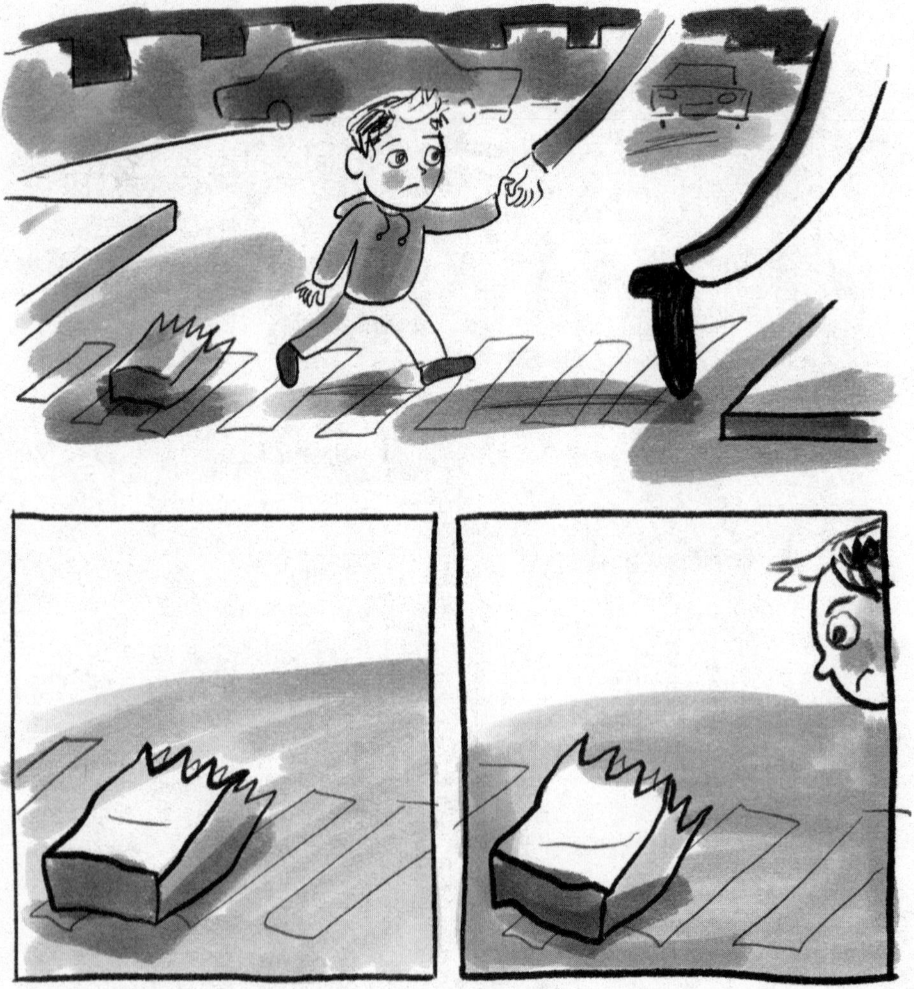

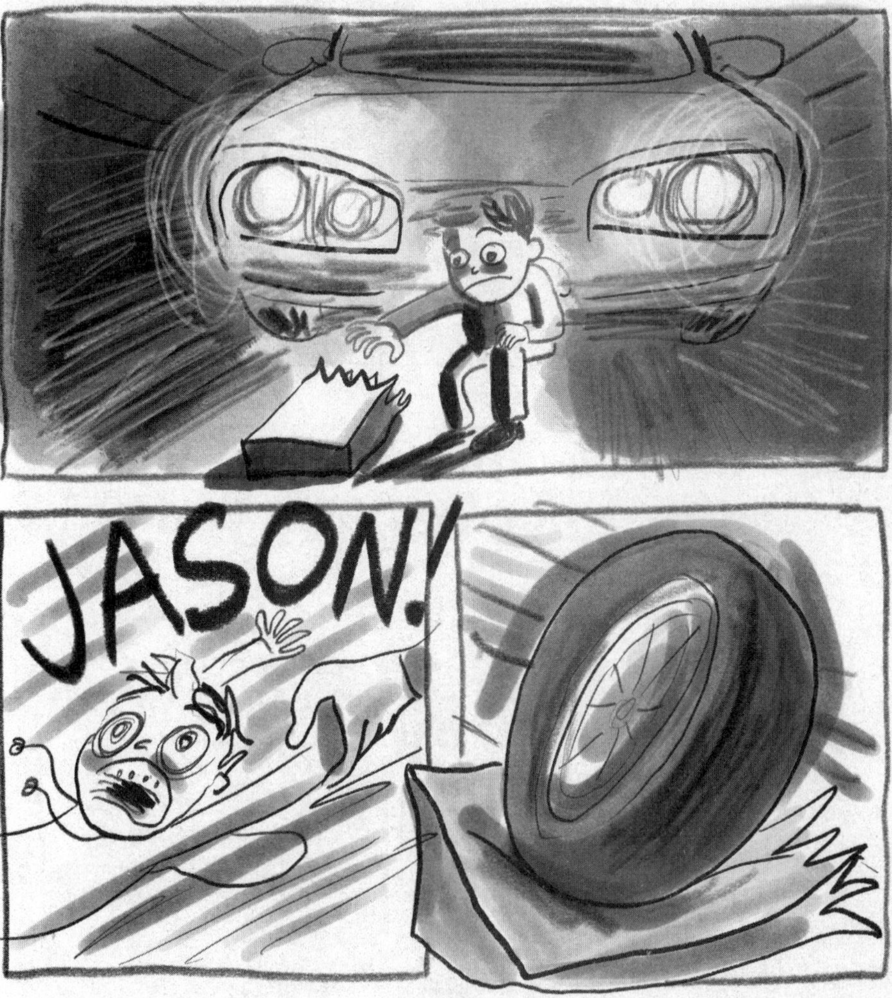
JASON!

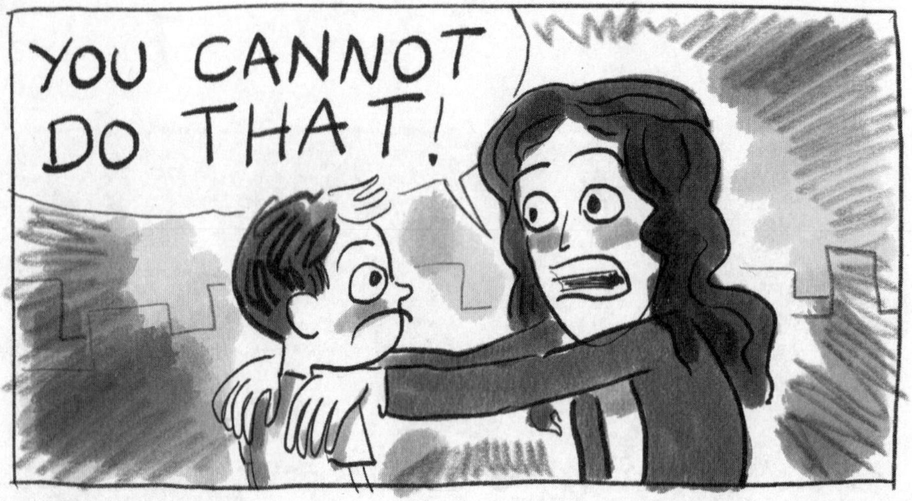
YOU CANNOT DO THAT!

I don't know why I'm doing that, and I don't know how to stop.

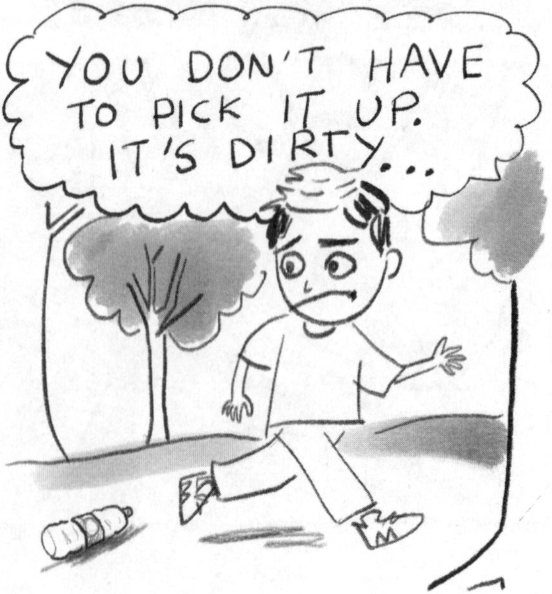
YOU DON'T HAVE TO PICK IT UP. IT'S DIRTY...

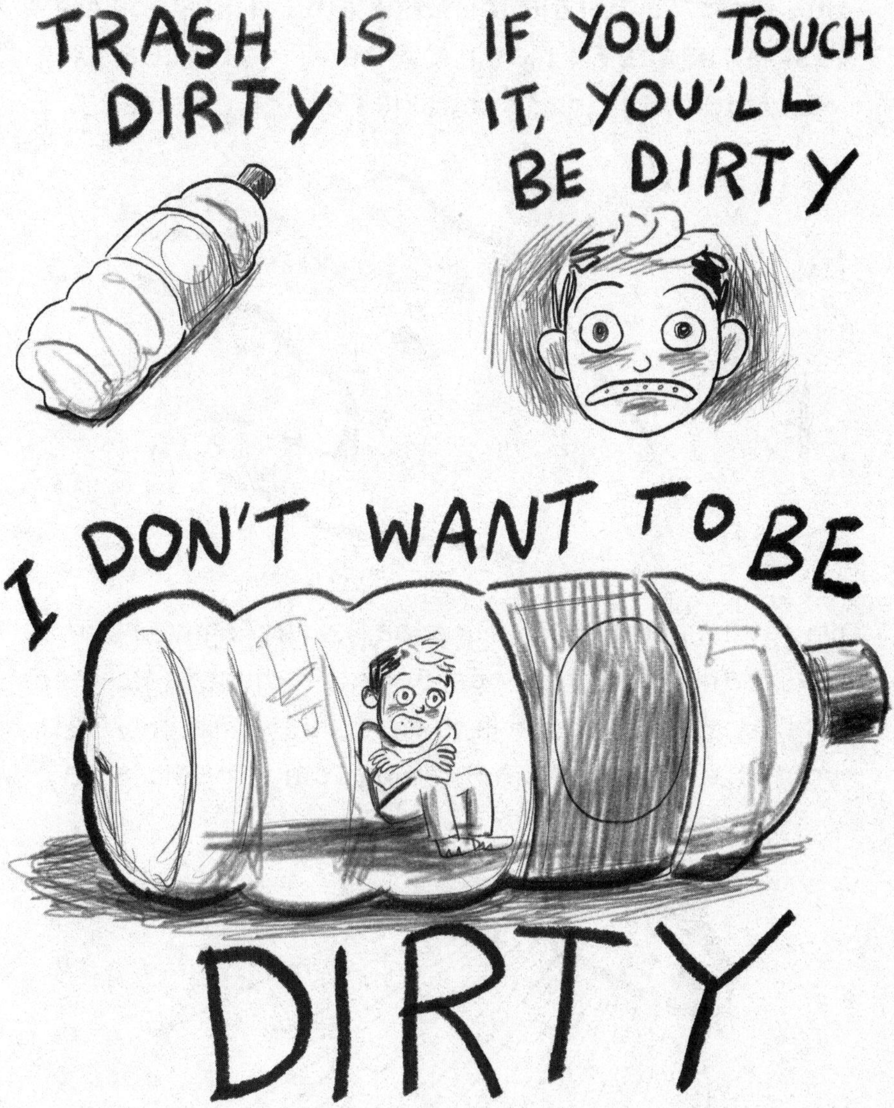
TRASH IS DIRTY
IF YOU TOUCH IT, YOU'LL BE DIRTY
I DON'T WANT TO BE
DIRTY

Suddenly, I'm afraid to shake hands with people. I wash my hands all the time. Often I'll finish washing and start again. My knuckles crack and bleed.

"Dirty" turns into "contaminated," a feeling that's more abstract and more insidious. Something just feels wrong, and that something clings to me all day. The only safe spot is the shower. I start taking four showers a day.

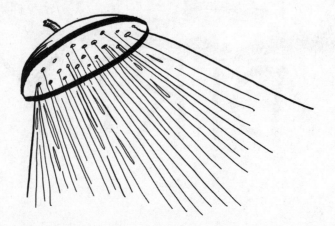

Every time I go to the bathroom I am contaminated and need to shower. This means I hold my piss all day at school.

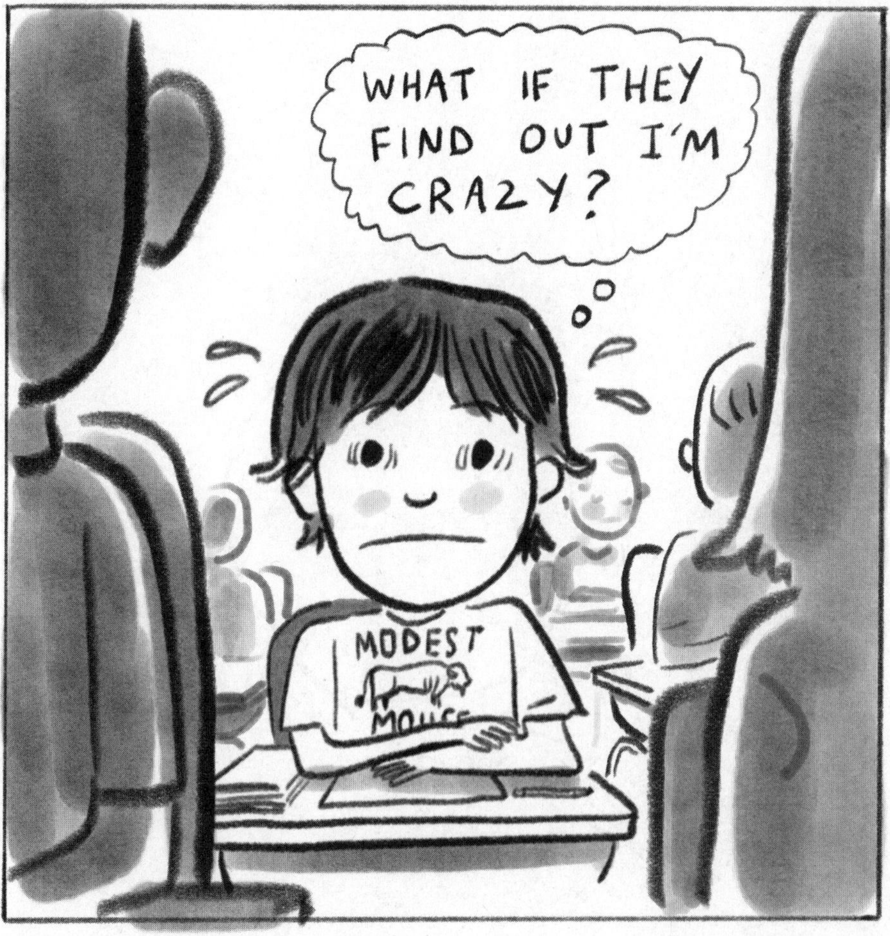
WHAT IF THEY FIND OUT I'M CRAZY?
MODEST

I'm uncomfortable, and I'm ashamed.

I'm a teenager.

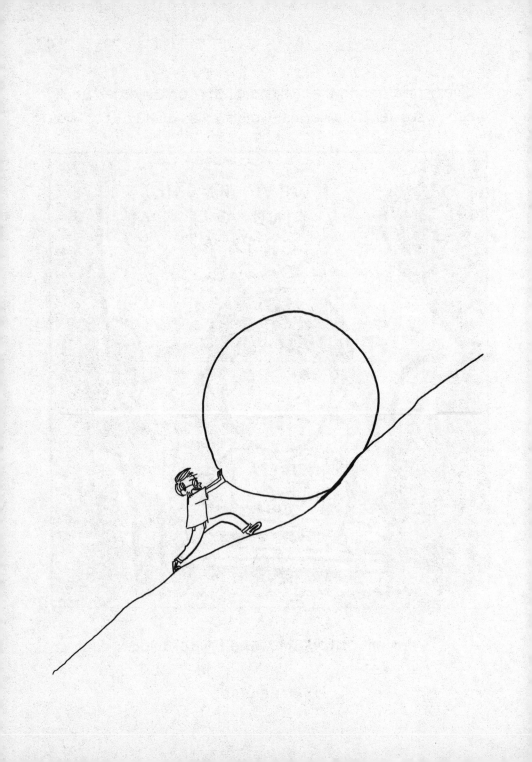

It is with profound embarrassment
that I introduce you to . . .

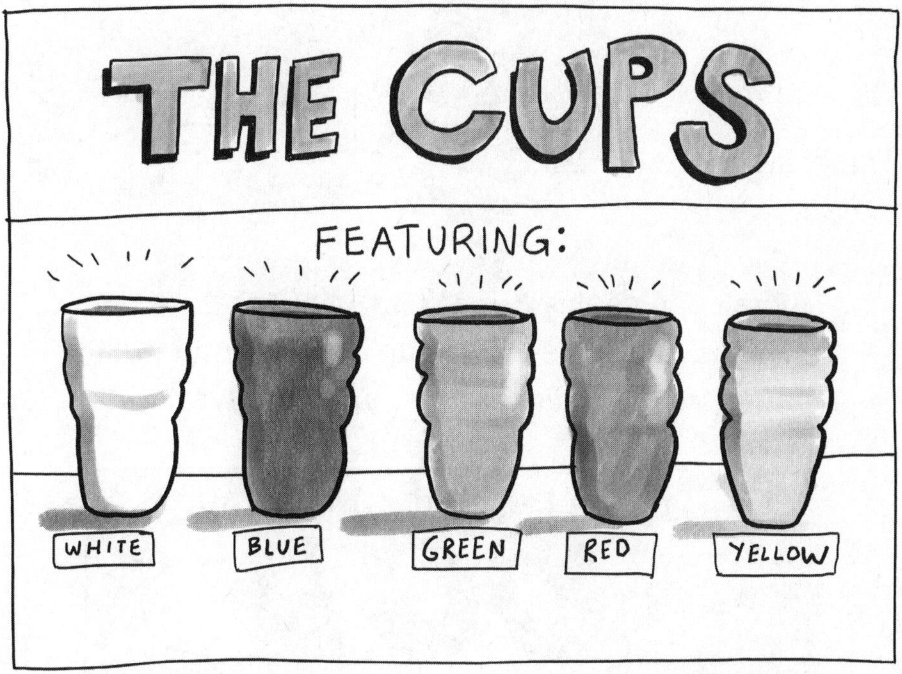
THE CUPS
FEATURING:
WHITE
BLUE
GREEN
RED
YELLOW

My family has a set of cups in these colors. It's my job to set the table. For some reason, I've decided that the color of the cup is a harbinger of your next twenty-four hours.

White is neutral, blue is sadness, green is sickness, red is passion, and yellow is extraordinary.

I feel too powerful.

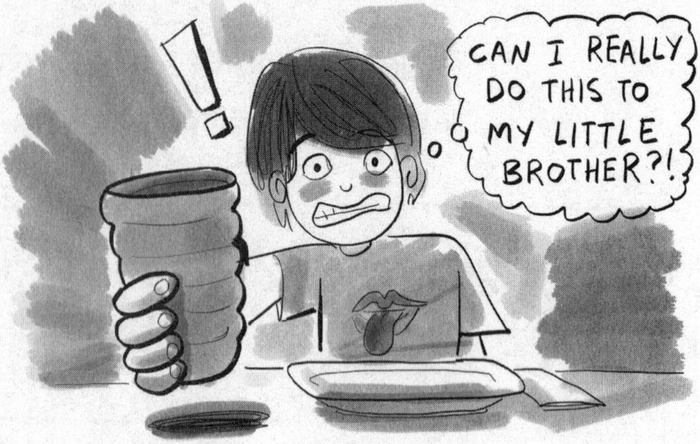
CAN I REALLY DO THIS TO MY LITTLE BROTHER?!

Also, insane.

I've been seeing a new therapist for a year. He knows about the picking up of trash and talking to God, and now the cups. He says:

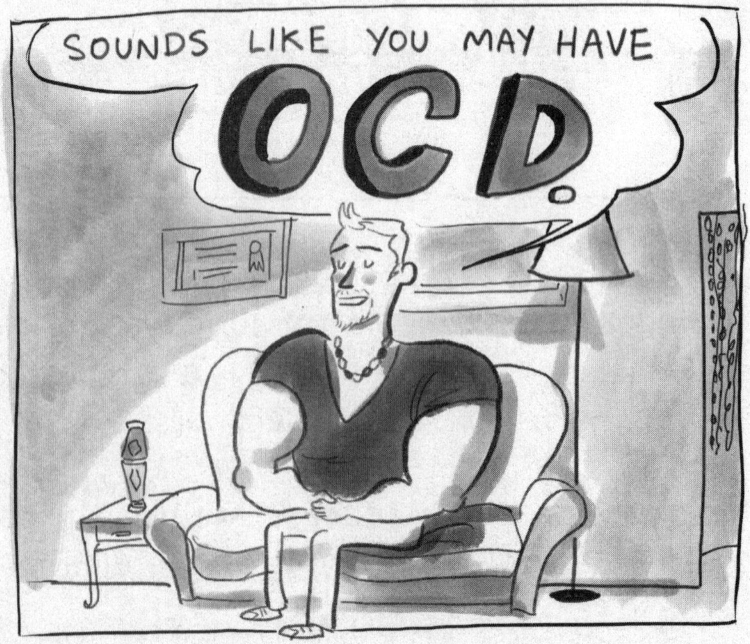
SOUNDS LIKE YOU MAY HAVE OCD.

What I know about OCD begins and ends with what I've read in *Xenocide*, one of the Ender's Game series books.

In *Xenocide*, the inhabitants of the planet Path have been infected by their government with intrusive thoughts. These thoughts sound to them like the voices of gods, and the only way to shut out these voices is to count the grains in floor patterns.

I find a book on the subject that has fewer alien planets. The firsthand testimonials scare the shit out of me.

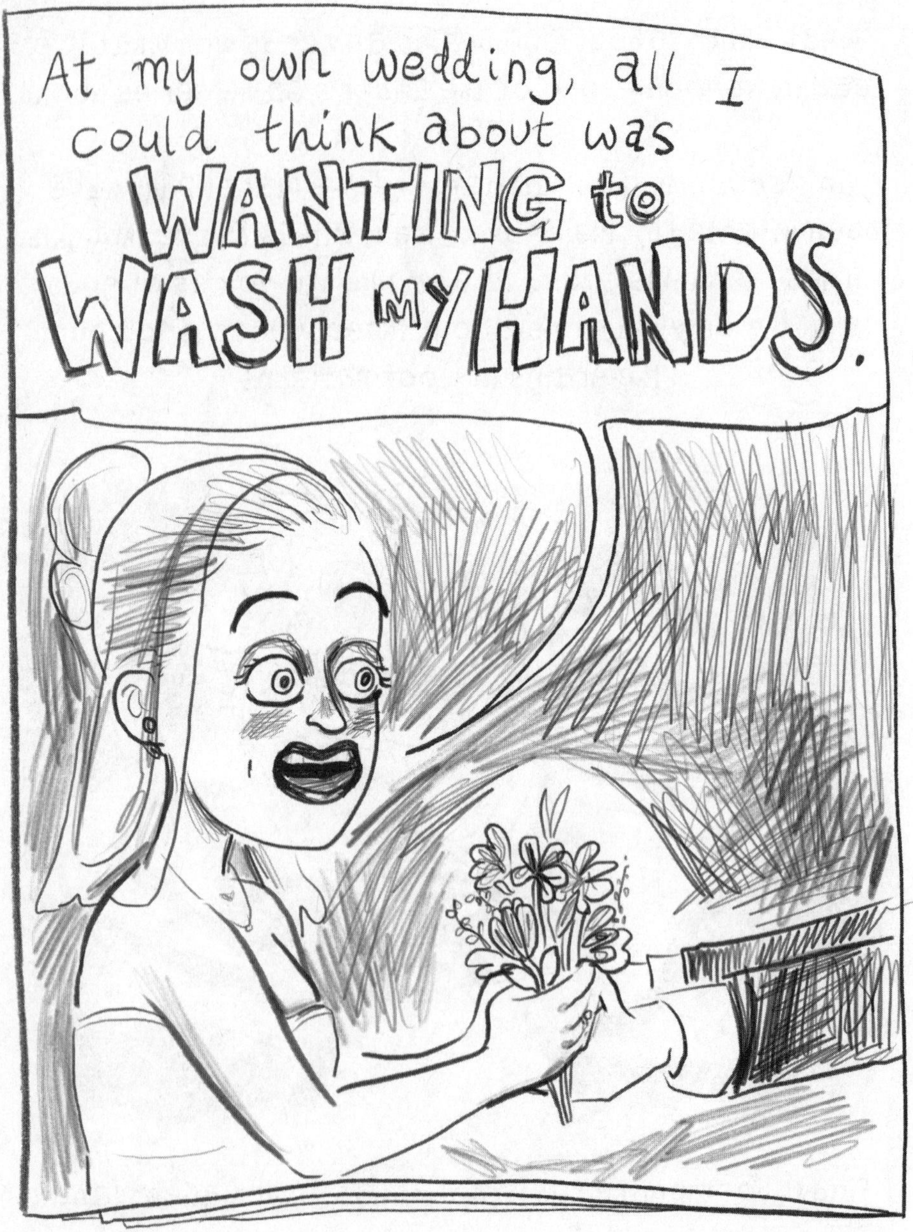
At my own wedding, all I could think about was
WANTING to WASH my HANDS.

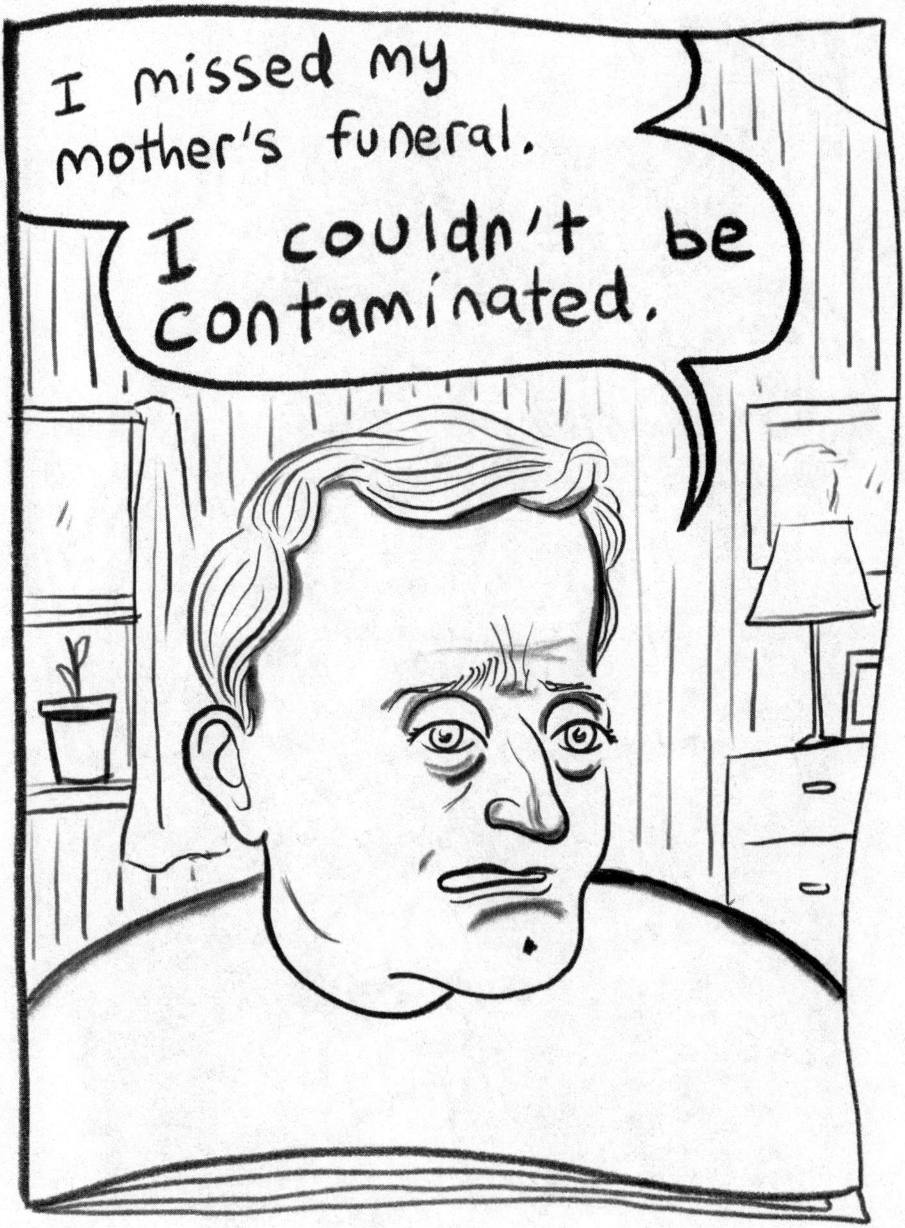
I missed my mother's funeral.
I couldn't be contaminated.

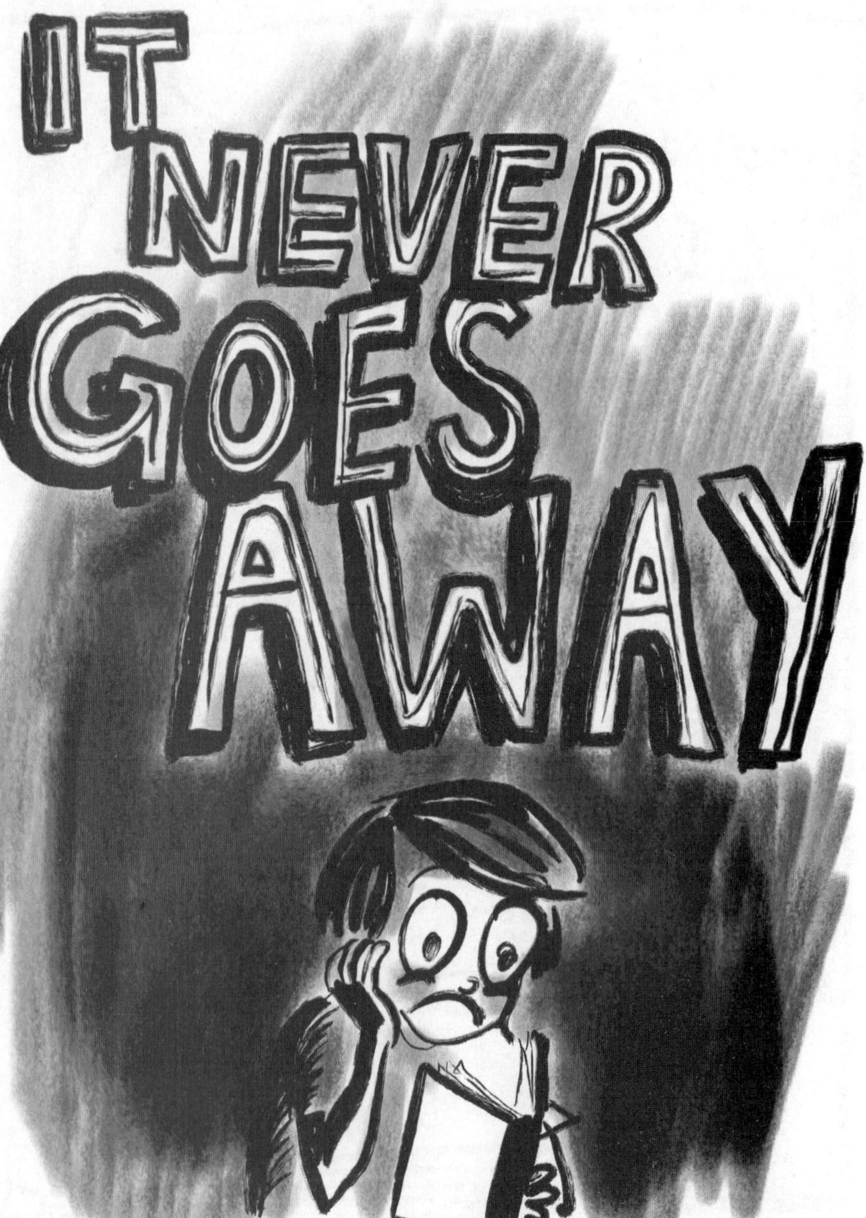
IT
NEVER
GOES
AWAY

I learn that OCD is an inflammation of the amygdala, the part of the brain in charge of interpreting threats.

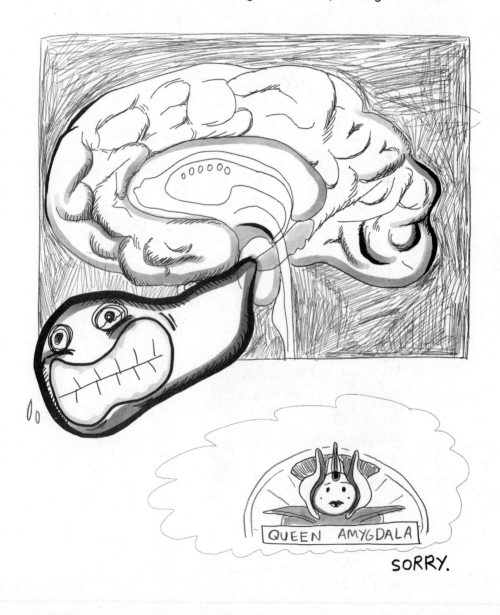

QUEEN AMYGDALA

SORRY.

It's a loop that begins with a thought. The thought is distressing, and it plays over and over again, overpowering other thoughts, distracting me, sapping all of my energy.

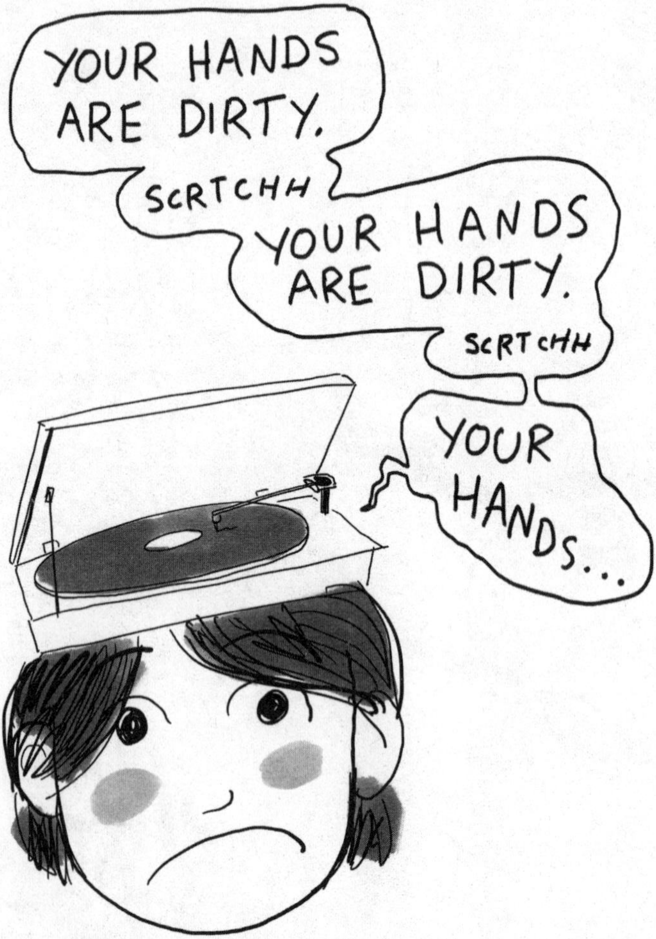
YOUR HANDS ARE DIRTY.
SCRTCHH
YOUR HANDS ARE DIRTY.
SCRTCHH
YOUR HANDS...

This is called the obsession.

I get desperate for relief...

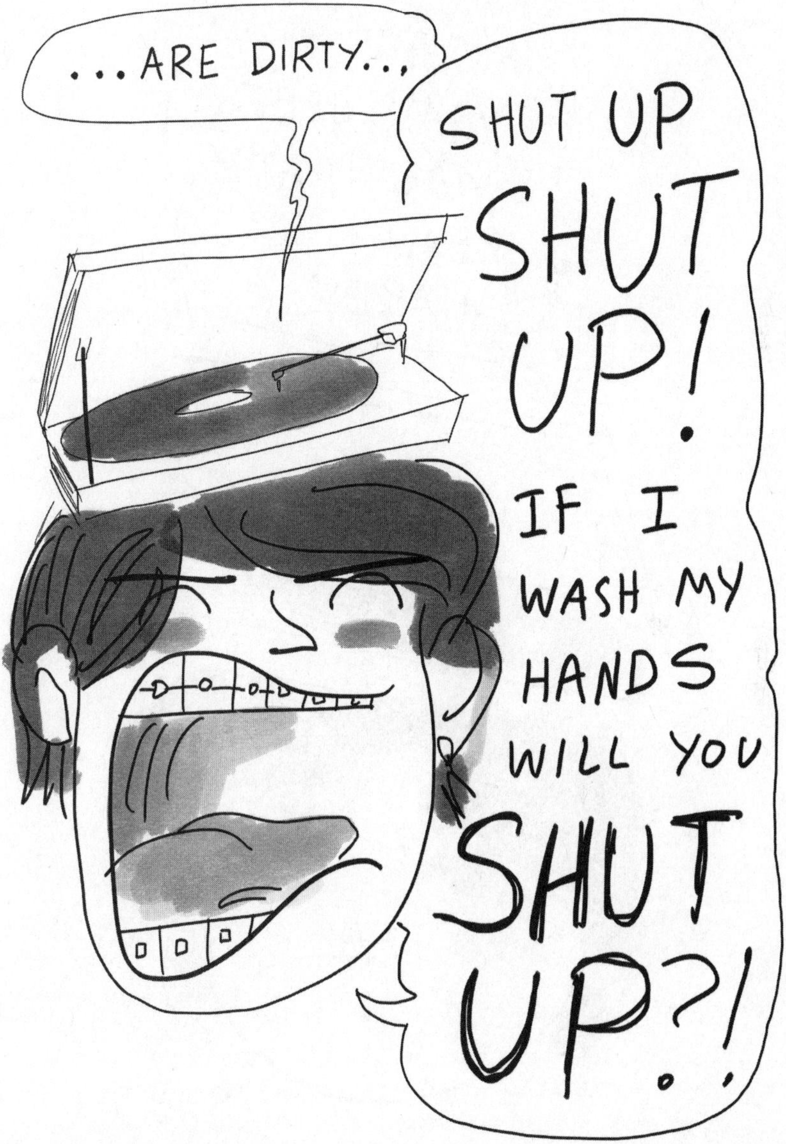
...ARE DIRTY...,
SHUT UP SHUT UP!
IF I WASH MY HANDS WILL YOU SHUT UP?!

. . . and I find it. I perform the compulsion.

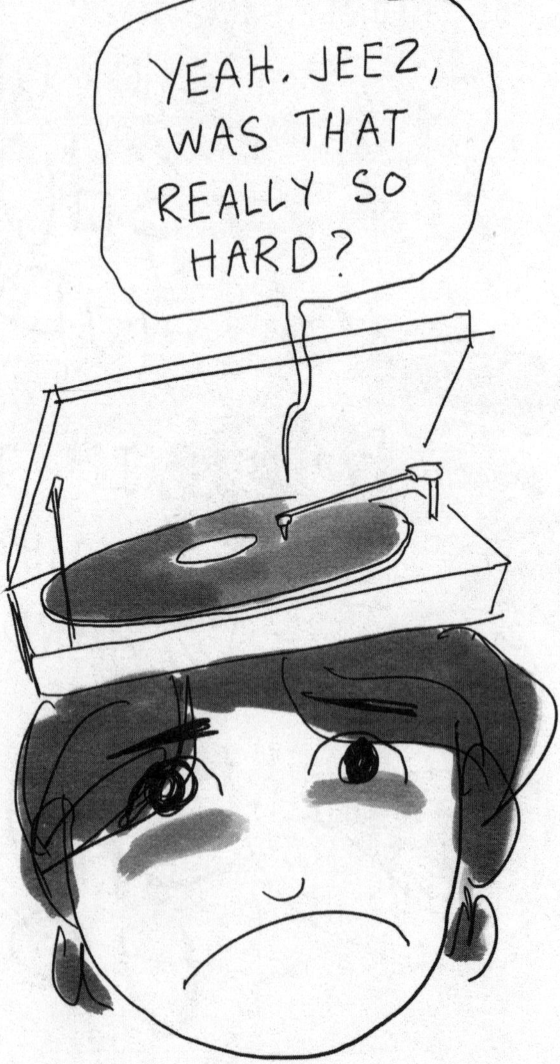
YEAH. JEEZ, WAS THAT REALLY SO HARD?

In the short-term, this works.

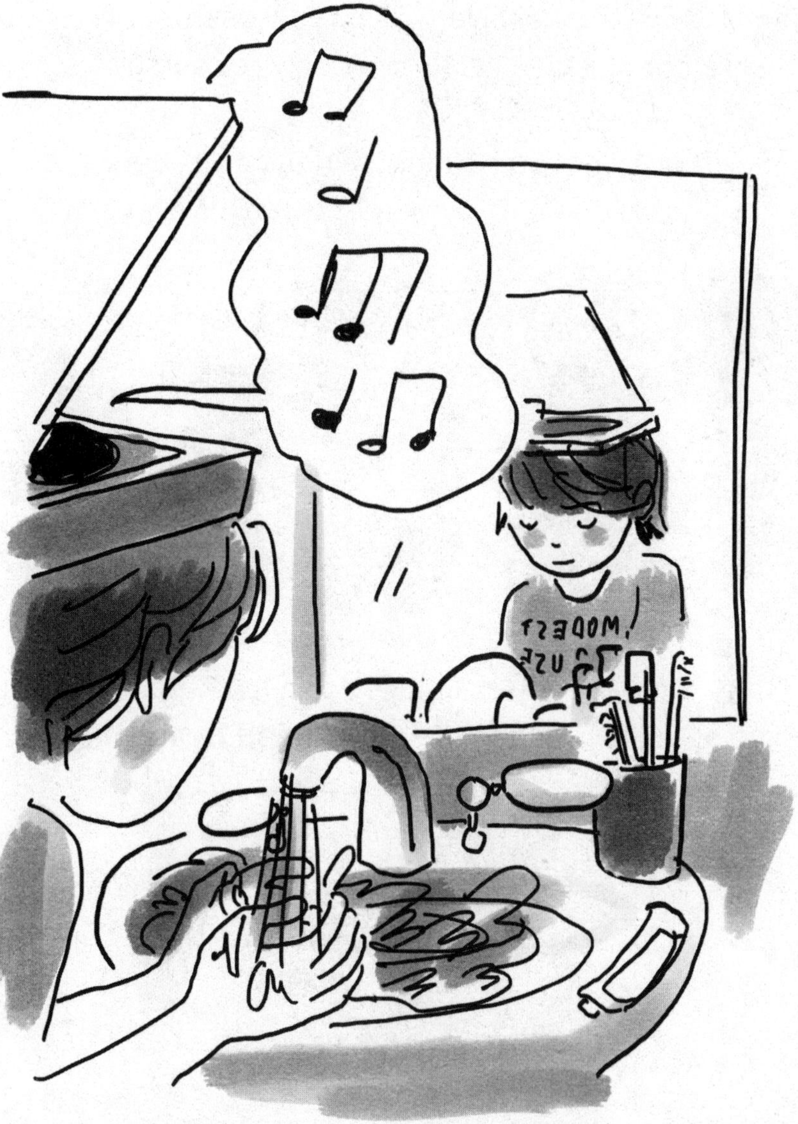

But the problem is that I've added significance to my obsession. I've taught my brain that the emergency signal it sends with an obsessive thought represents a real danger, and the compulsion I perform my only recourse to stay safe.

It may not be rational, but in my dream I feel compelled to compliment the woman's cat.

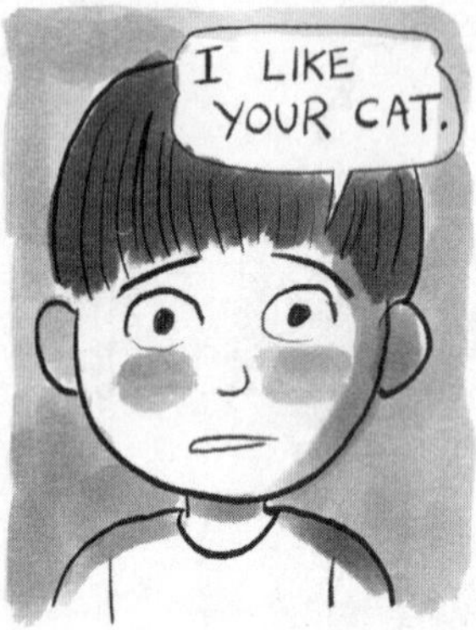
I LIKE YOUR CAT.

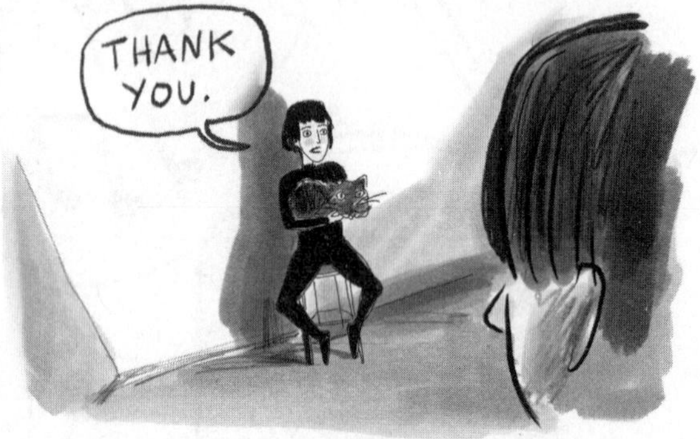
THANK YOU.

It keeps me safe, but as soon as I do it I'm back outside the room. I know I need to go in again.

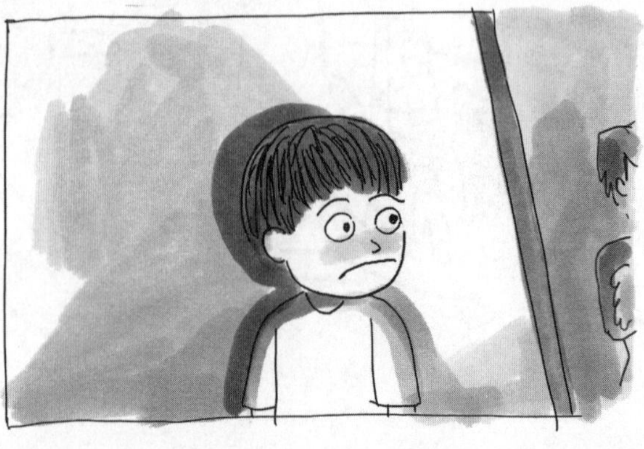

I try to get out of the loop. I bite my tongue this time.

I feel impending dread. I can't tell you exactly what I think will happen, just that it feels like a nightmare.

I have one way to save myself.

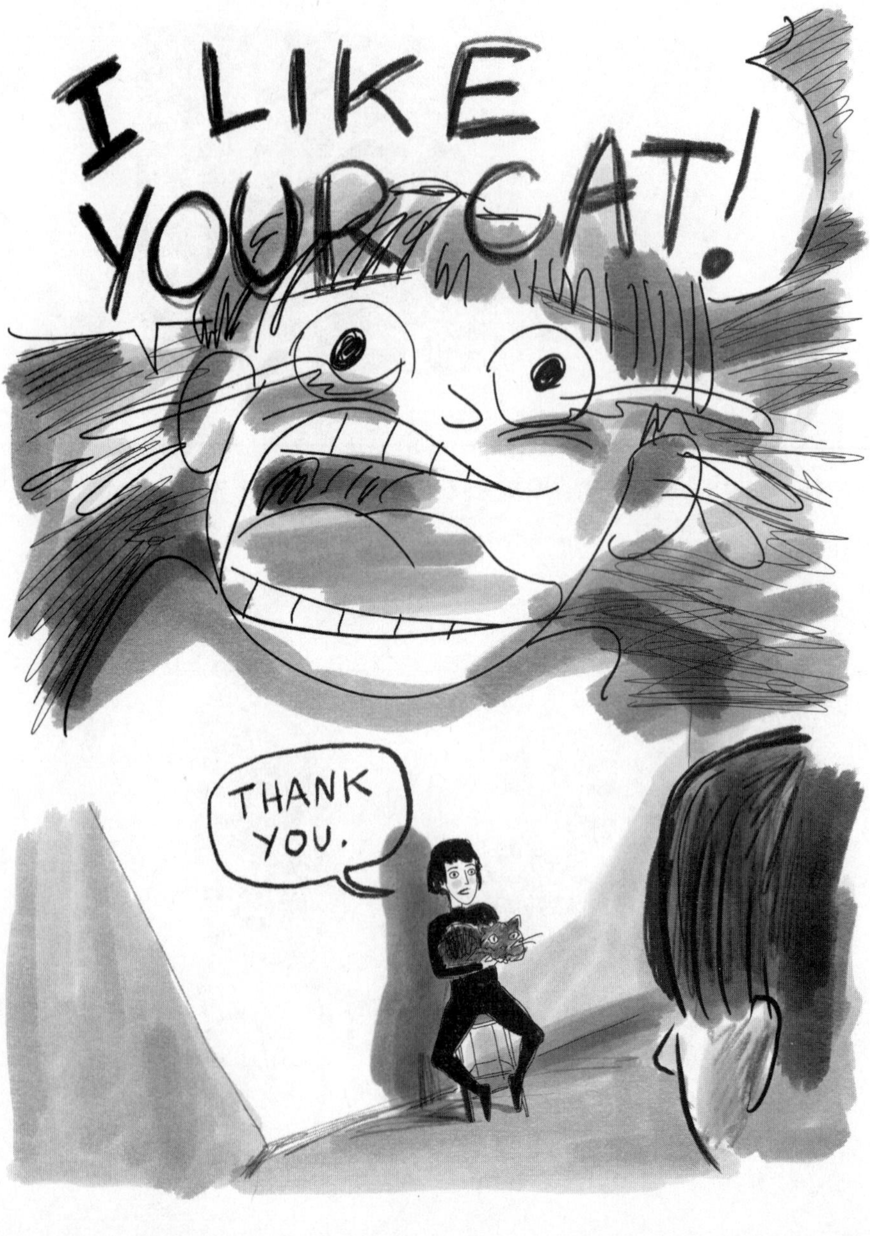
I LIKE YOUR CAT!
THANK YOU.

Then I'm always back outside the room again.

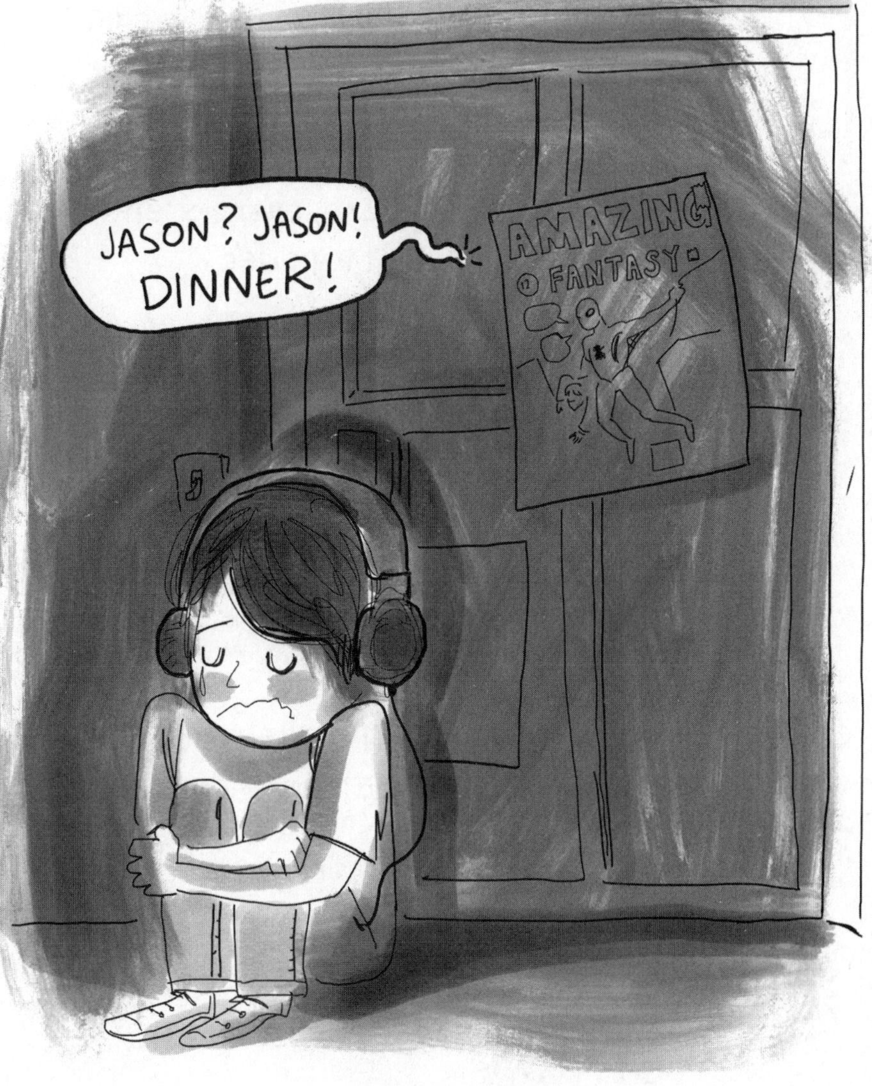
JASON? JASON!
DINNER!
AMAZING
FANTASY

I retreat into myself.

I have a diagnosed mental illness, and even as I begin to understand my strange behaviors as compulsions, I keep behaving compulsively.

I can't admit this to anyone, even myself, but I enjoy a shift in power.

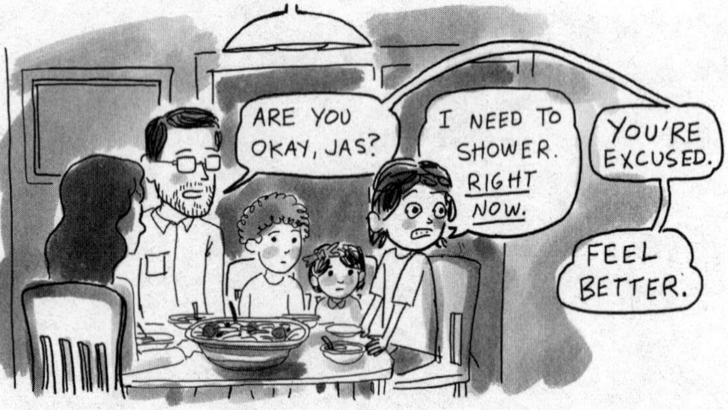
ARE YOU OKAY, JAS?
I NEED TO SHOWER. RIGHT NOW.
YOU'RE EXCUSED.
FEEL BETTER.

At home, rules that were ironclad become optional to accommodate my "needs."

There's a limit on this enjoyment, though, because I truly do feel at the mercy of these "needs." They hold me hostage.

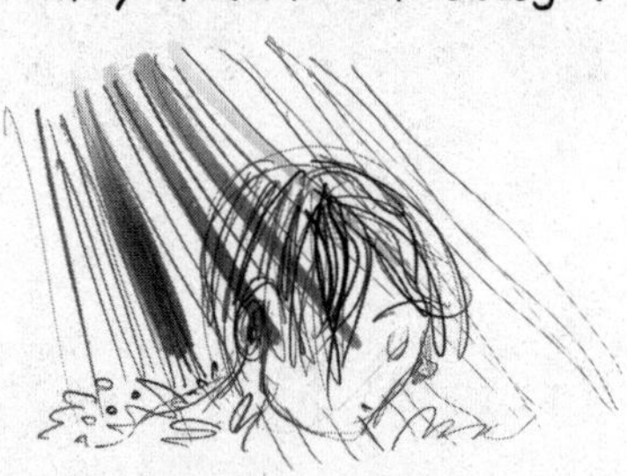

In public I learn to tell white lies to avoid contamination. I obsess about being dirty.

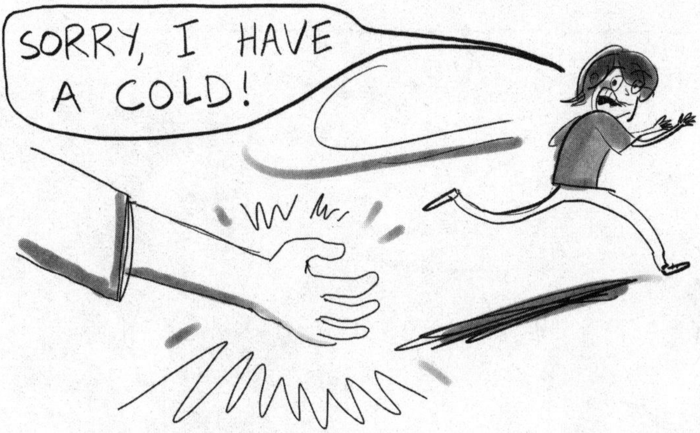
SORRY, I HAVE A COLD!

Now that I know what's wrong, I go through the motions of trying to improve. My parents send me to a cognitive behavioral therapist.

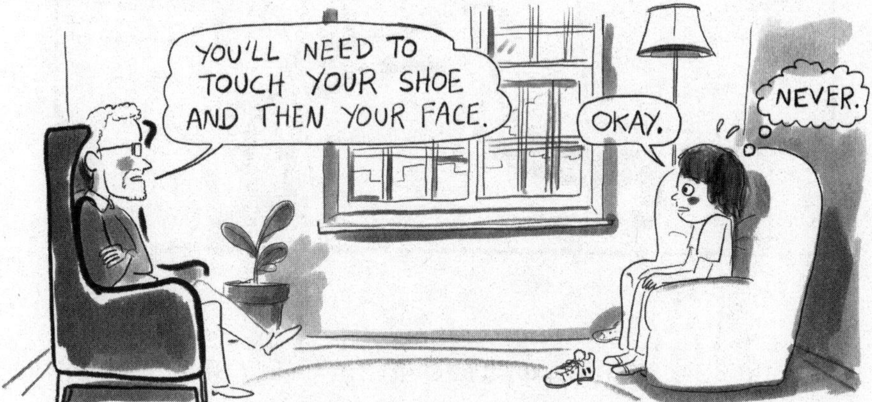
YOU'LL NEED TO TOUCH YOUR SHOE AND THEN YOUR FACE.
OKAY.
NEVER.

I don't do the homework.

At home I feel best working on big, surrealist paintings and listening to Pixies songs.

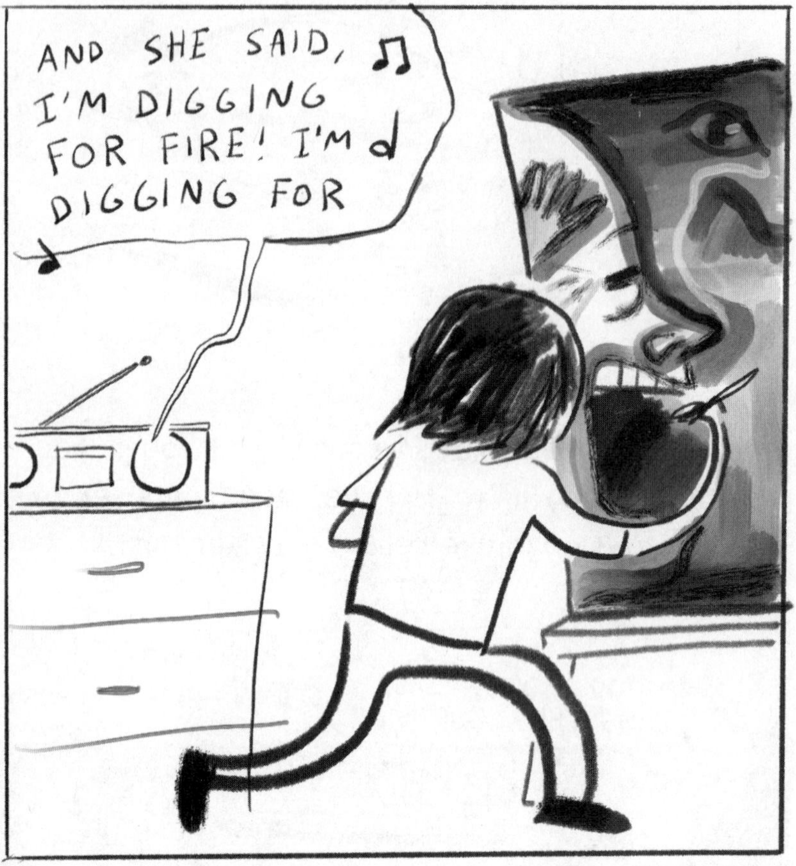
AND SHE SAID, I'M DIGGING FOR FIRE! I'M DIGGING FOR

Sometimes I plan on what to paint. Other times I follow accidents on the canvas and "find" images.

I fall in love with the paintings of Salvador Dalí.

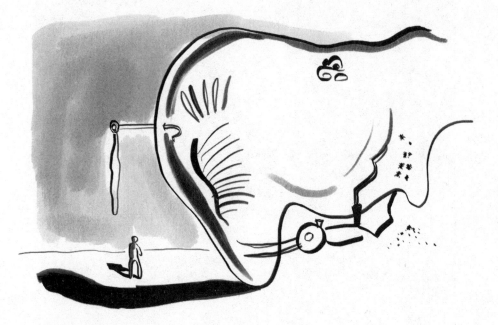

He paints his nightmares. There are signs and symbols in these paintings that only make sense to Dalí, but when I look at them I feel full-body terror. I feel the contamination of the ants that swarm his landscapes.

I want to send out messages like this, dispatches from my interiority that make no sense to anybody else, but move them anyway.

I try to make my own surrealist paintings.

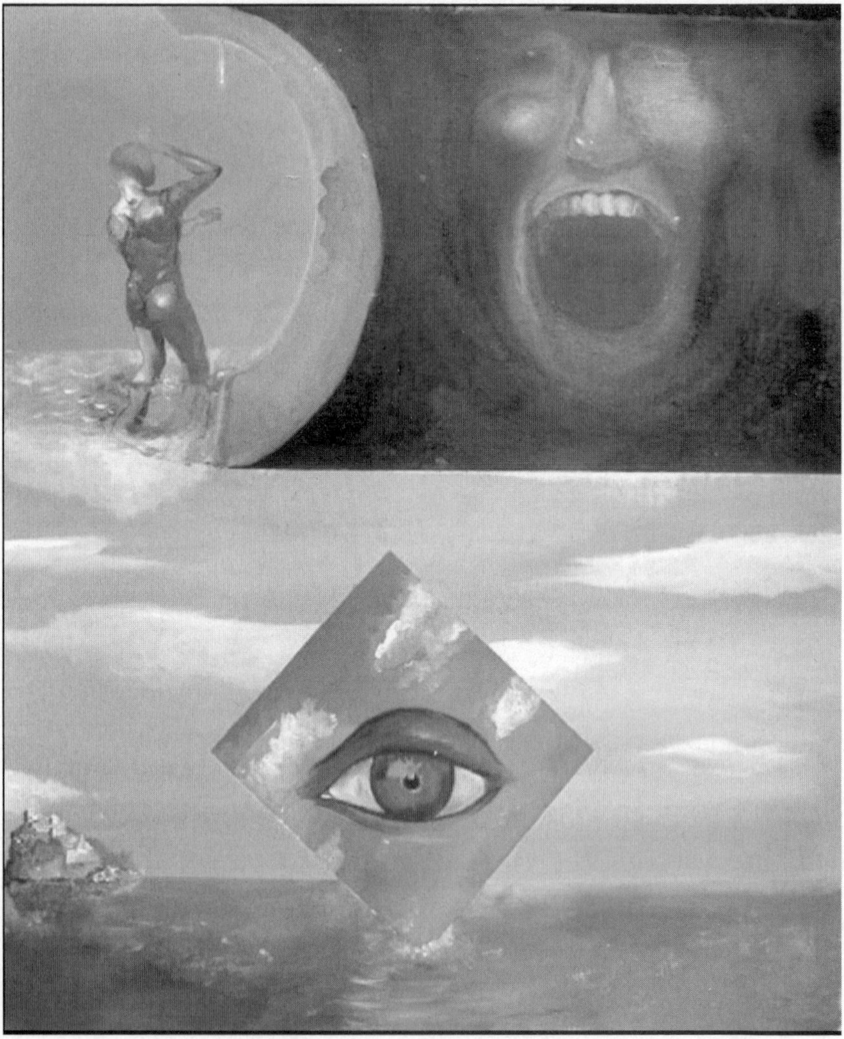

The result is equal parts Seventies prog rock poster and cry for help.

That summer, life imitates art.

Every night I brush my retainer with my sugary kid toothpaste, and one morning:

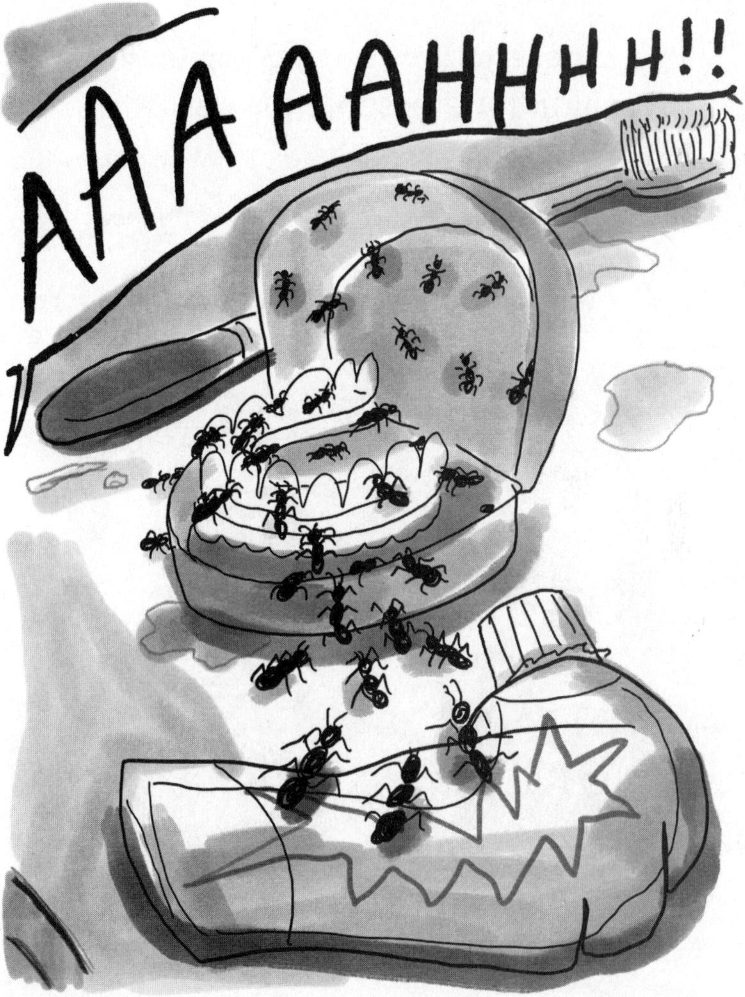
AAAAAHHHH!!

Retainers are expensive; I'm not getting another one. My mom says, "Soak it in vinegar, brush it again; and it'll be fine."

I neither want to put this thing in my mouth ever again, nor do I want crooked teeth.

I choose to take care of my teeth. I contaminate myself. I am disgusting.

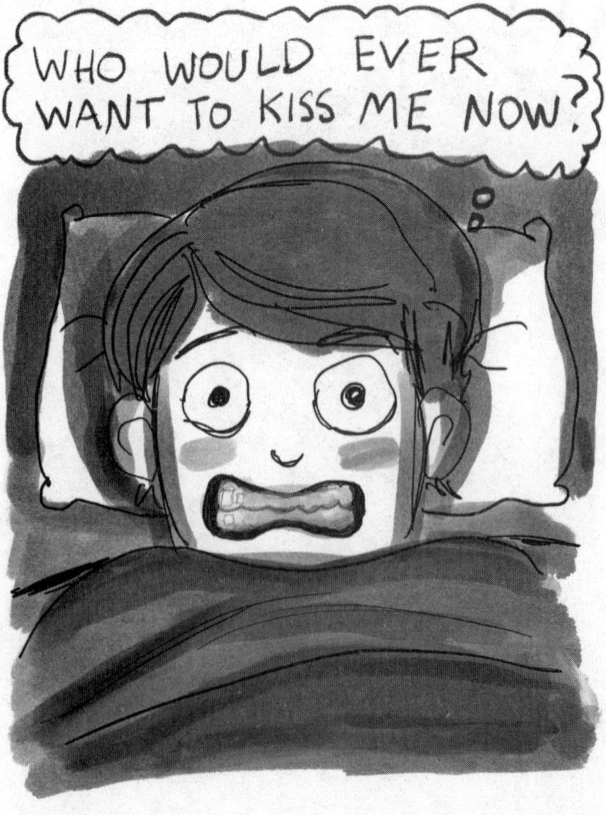
WHO WOULD EVER WANT TO KISS ME NOW?

In school, when I try to have conversations:

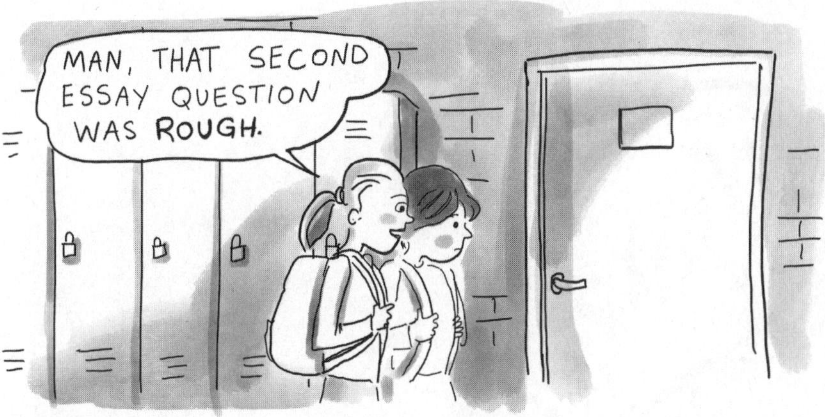
MAN, THAT SECOND ESSAY QUESTION WAS ROUGH.

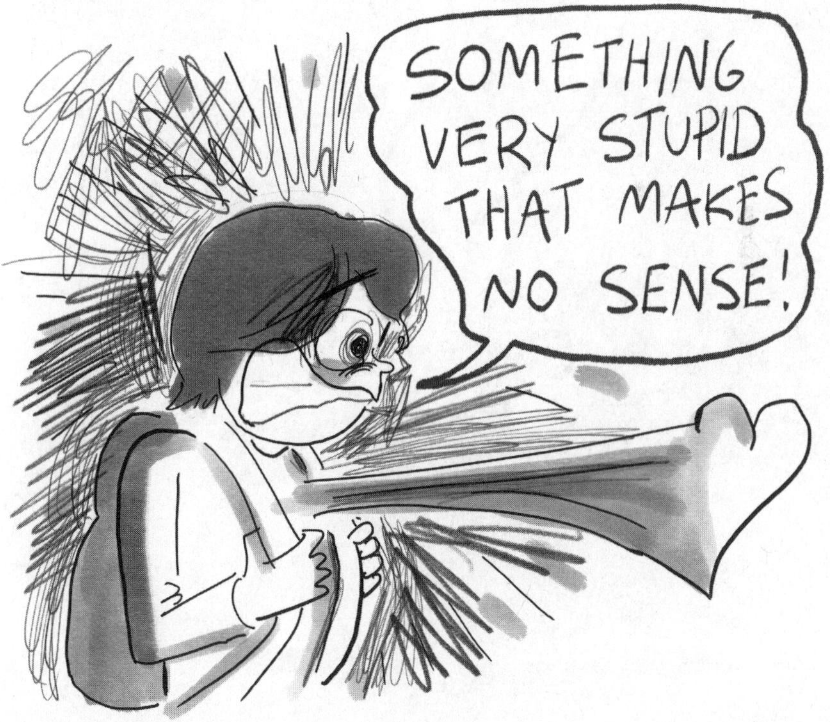
SOMETHING VERY STUPID THAT MAKES NO SENSE!

I spend the rest of the day going over the very stupid thing I said that makes no sense.

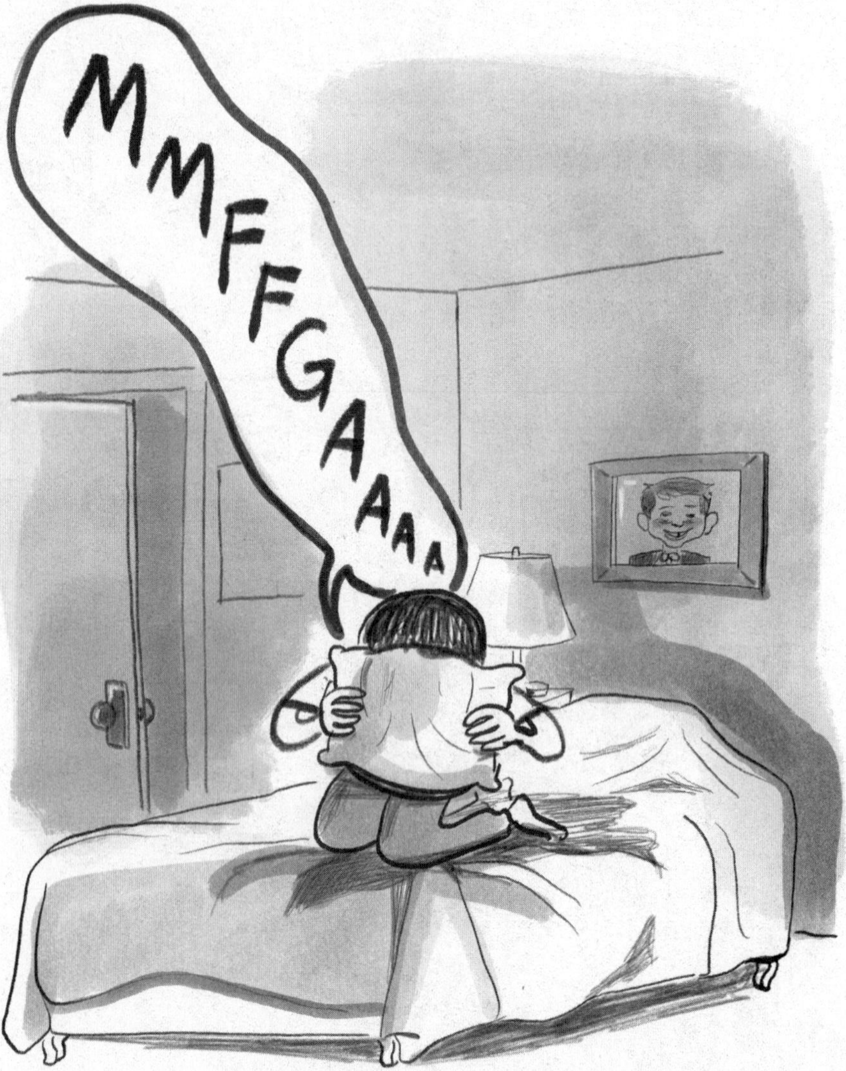
MMFFGAAAA

I apply to the CalArts summer program with
my portfolio of paintings and I get in.

Studio hours are strict. We draw and paint
all day. At night we sit on the little hill by our
dorm, and the smokers smoke too much.

I make only bad art and it's the best summer I've ever had.

I forget some of my shyness. I have a summer romance with a photographer named Patty.

When the program ends and she goes back to San Francisco and I go back to Los Angeles, we decide to try long distance.

We talk on the phone or videochat on AOL Instant Messenger for two hours every night.

One weekend a month I stay with her in San Francisco, or she stays with me in Los Angeles.

Maybe I'm reproducing a dynamic I'm used to, going back and forth between two places.

DAD'S HOUSE

THE GETTY

←(I JUST LIKE IT)

ME, FURIOUS

MOM'S HOUSE

I get used to feeling not all there in any one place. I feel comfortable communicating from a distance.

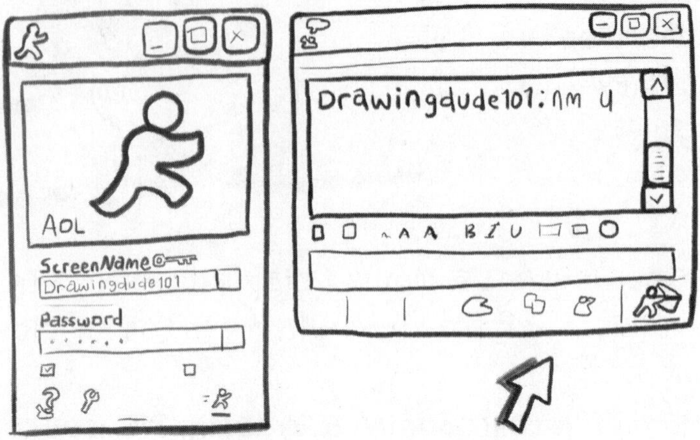
AOL
ScreenName
Drawingdude101
Password
Drawingdude101: nm u
B I U

Here's a too-literal self-portrait I paint around this time:

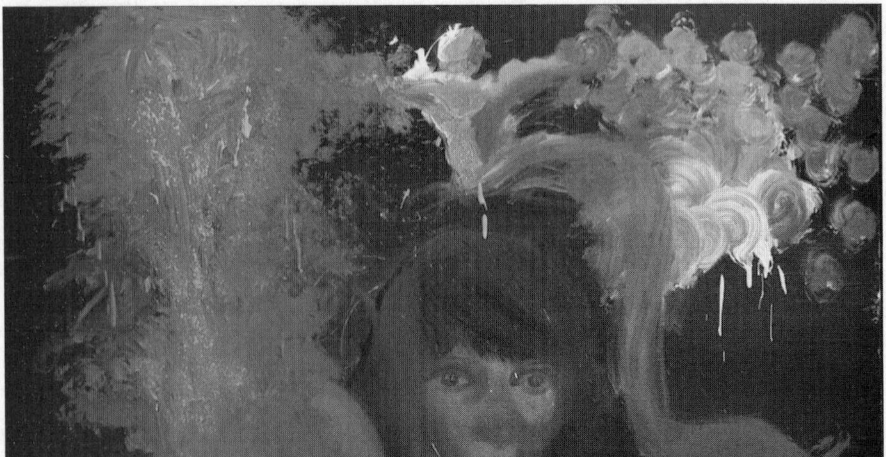

When Patty and I break up, it's over the phone. And it isn't really a breakup, because we can blame distance and still see each other but call it something different. We do this, on and off, for two years.

Tunnel of Getting Back Together
Tunnel of Breaking Up

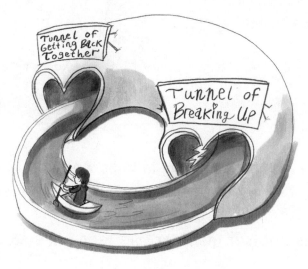

It's comforting to be in a relationship and also to not be. To trust someone completely is to give them the opportunity to hurt me when I least expect it.

Maybe they'll send a child development specialist to deliver the blow.

If I get too close to somebody, I may hurt them. That is unacceptable to me.

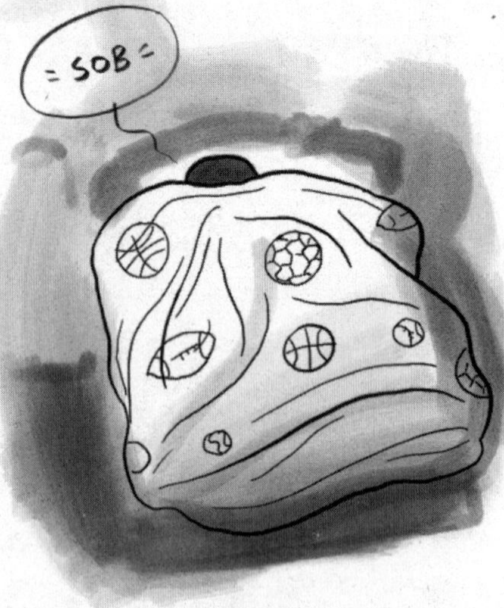
= SOB =

The safest option, then, is to be completely alone. Also, my biggest fear is being completely alone.

As another insufferable teen once said:

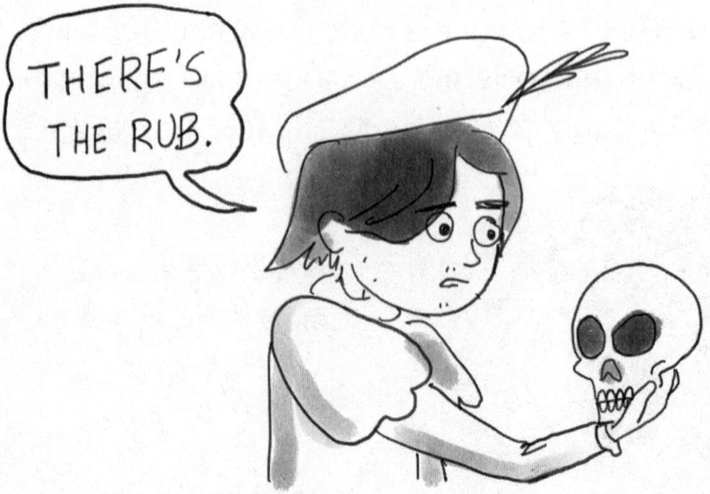
THERE'S THE RUB.

I want the controlled intimacy I feel with life drawing.

I move my pencil as if I'm touching the edge of what I'm observing.

I feel its weight and texture.

I'm engaged with my subject, but I don't affect it.

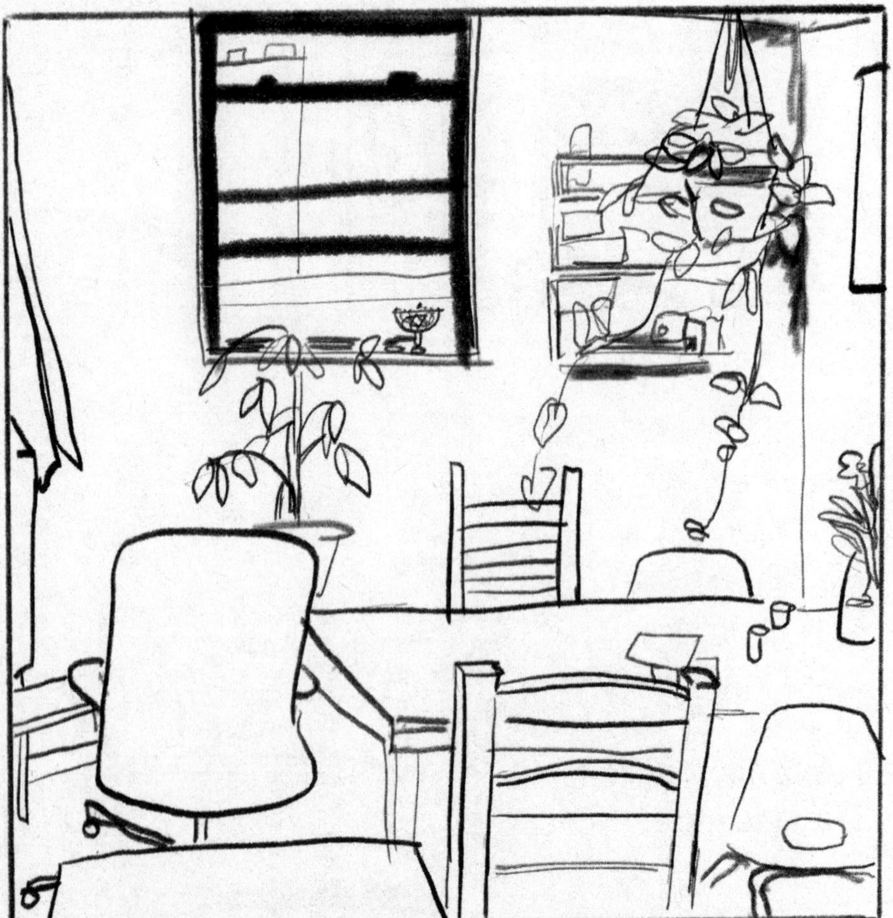

I want to touch nothing and no one. I want to live under nobody's roof and nobody's rules, to be irresponsible, unaccountable. Gone.

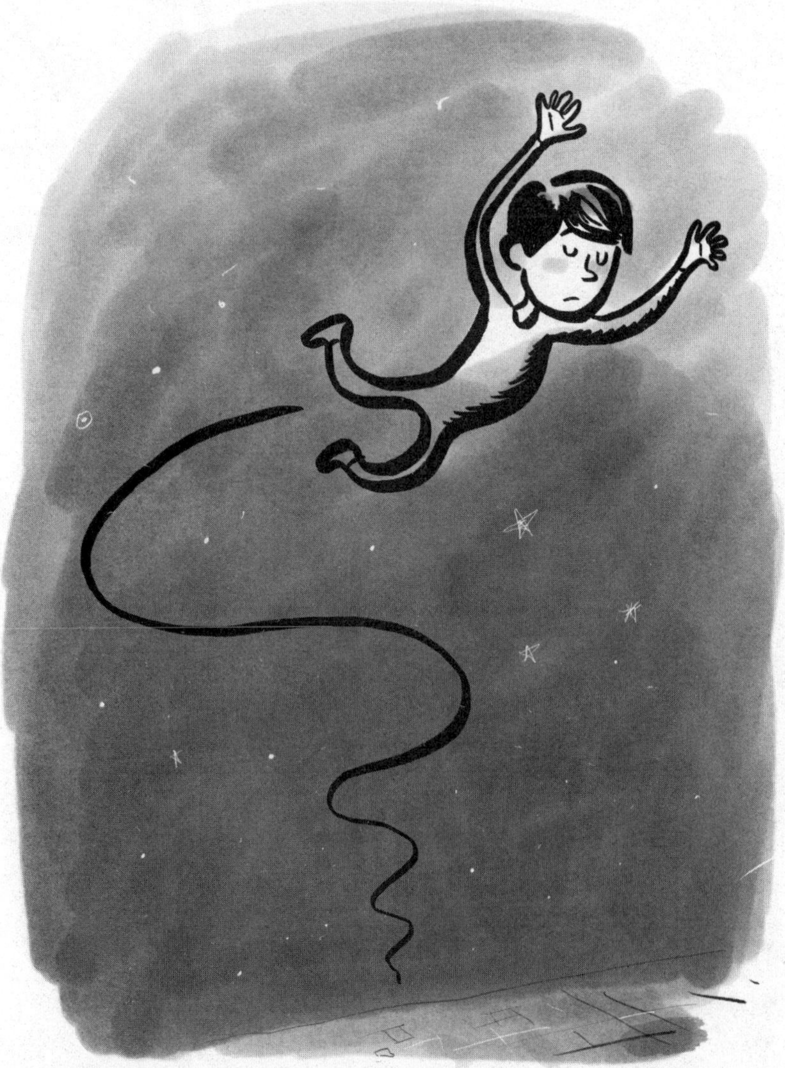

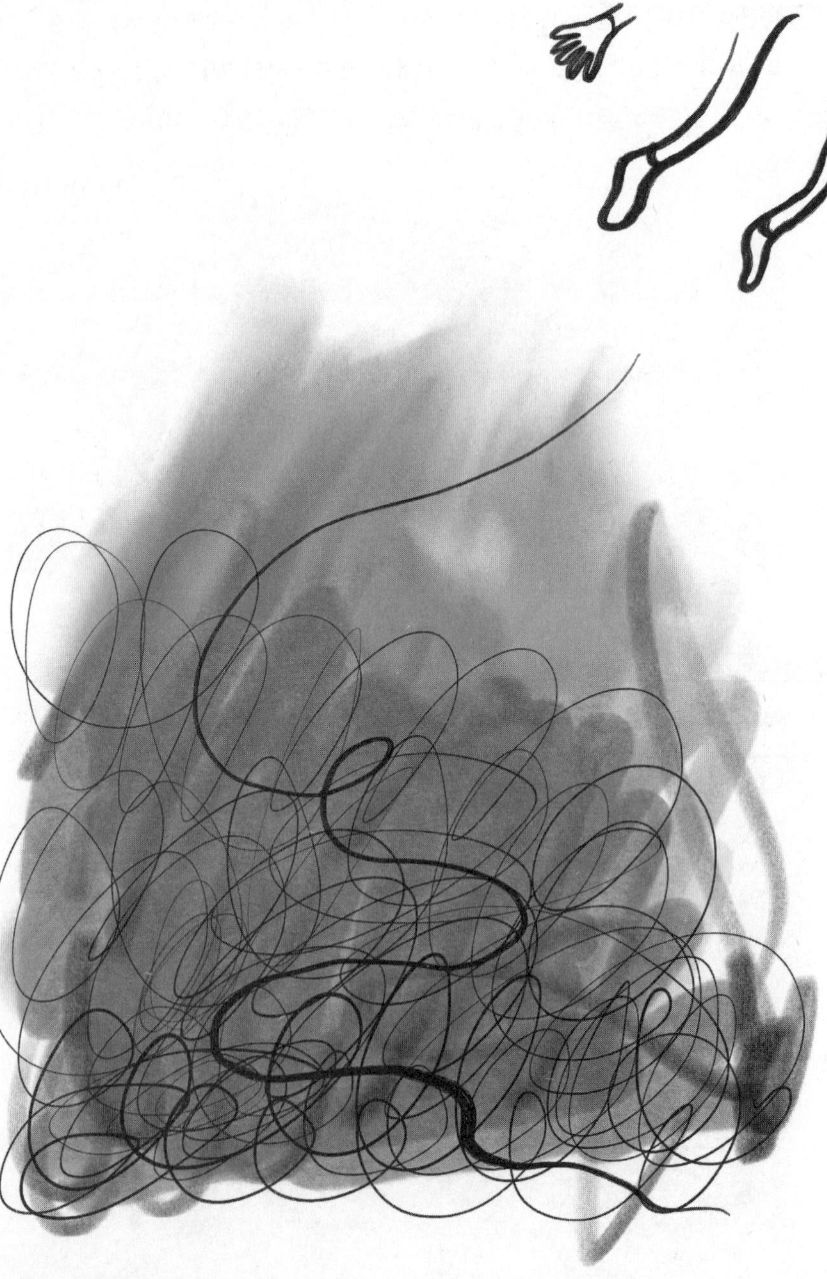

In high school, unacceptable thoughts begin to find me.

The worst images I can imagine play on a loop in my mind.

In these images I'm violent. I attack friends and family. I kill the people I love.

The intrusive thoughts might appear at any time, at an unguarded private moment or at a party.

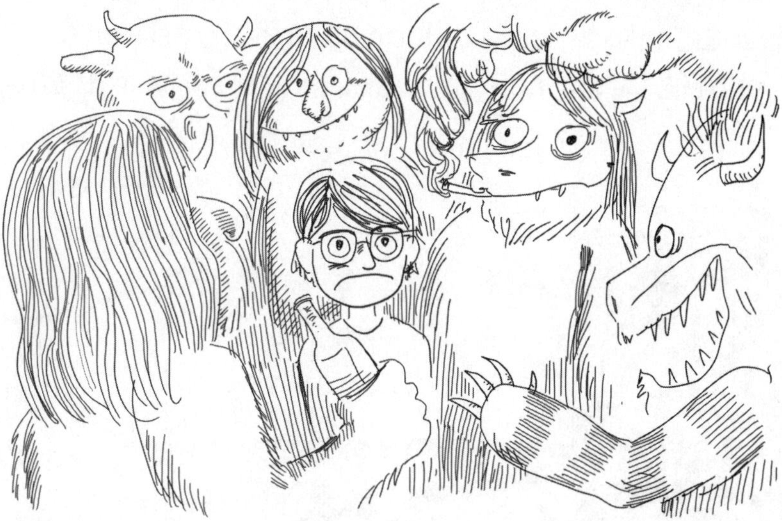

They might loop for minutes, hours, or days.

Some part of me deep down is dreaming up these torture images. I'm fighting a brain battle with myself.

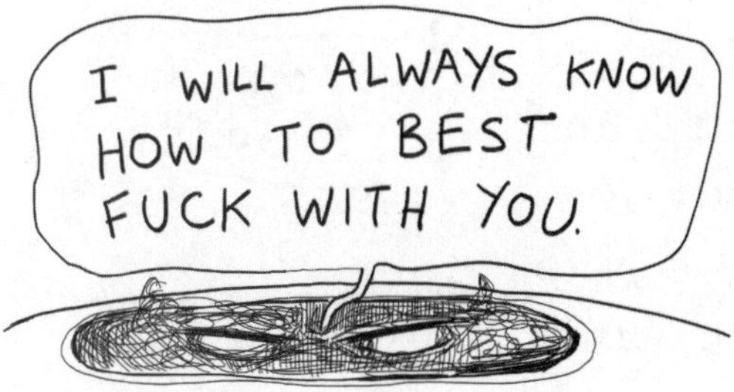
I WILL ALWAYS KNOW HOW TO BEST FUCK WITH YOU.

I'm getting my ass kicked.

The intensity of the obsessions ebbs and flows.

When I get to college, I feel an overwhelming sense of euphoria. In those early autumn days, the freshmen all sit on the main hill, which feels so much like that summer at CalArts.

The obsessions I do feel are muted, and I mostly keep them at bay with the white lies I've gotten used to telling and small compulsive behaviors.

TRY MY DRINK! IT'S GOOD!

...

I WOULD, BUT I'M GETTING SICK!

The communal bathroom is a challenge. I begin fixating on "contaminated" items of clothing.

When I feel most dirty, and I'm sure nobody else is looking, I throw away pairs of my underwear.

Winter comes, students hole up, classes kick my ass.

Some of that euphoria fades, and the intensity of my obsessions ramps again.

I discover a new coping mechanism.

Getting high makes me feel like I'm floating
above myself, watching the movie of my life.
My problems feel cerebral and remote.

I start doing it every day, and will continue
the habit through my early twenties.

That summer, I apply to *MAD Magazine*'s editorial internship program, with a sample article called "Terrifying Thoughts for Today's Youth" that contains perfectly crafted masterpiece lines like "Thanks to Viagra, your recently divorced dad is getting more action than you."

Their editors make a terrible decision:

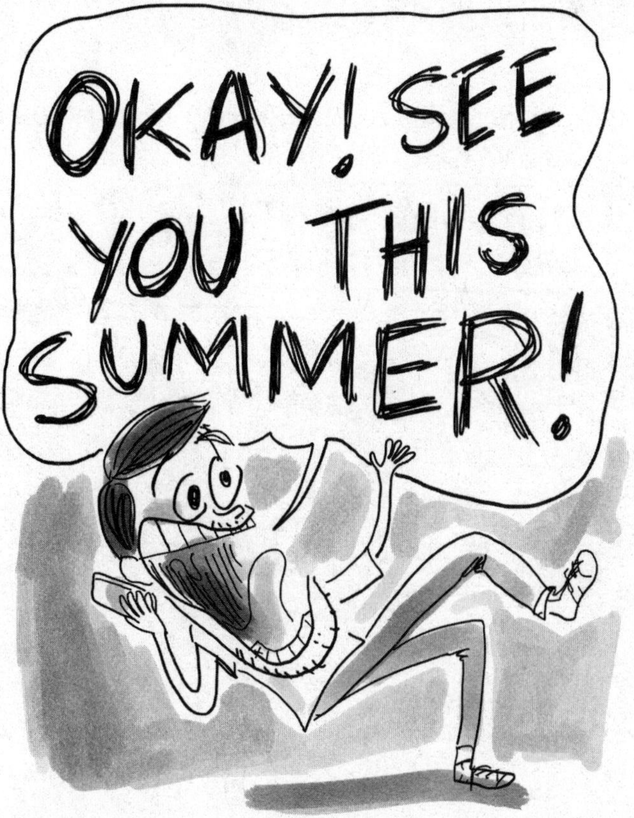
OKAY! SEE YOU THIS SUMMER!

The other summer intern is named Jason. He's quite tall. The editors give us nicknames to distinguish us.

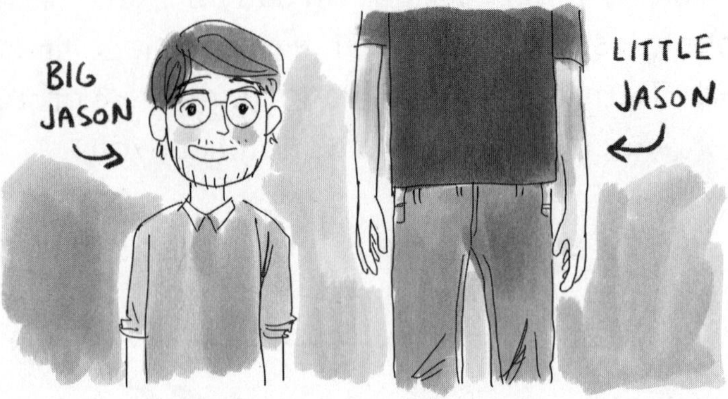
BIG JASON
LITTLE JASON

A lot of the job is sitting around trying to come up with puns.

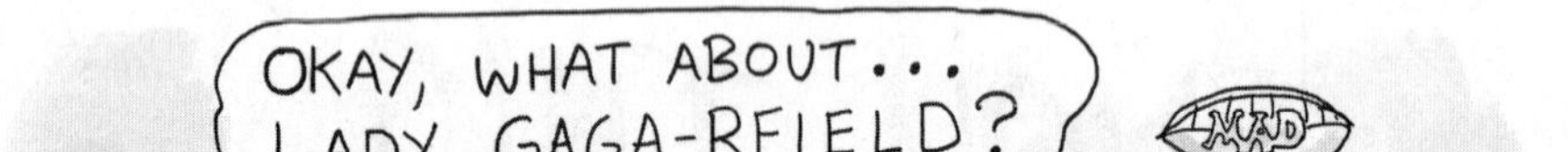
OKAY, WHAT ABOUT... LADY GAGA-RFIELD?
POTRZEBIE
ARTHUR
MAD
A
B
MELVIN WUZ HERE

This is the greatest experience of my life.

When I return to campus, my contamination compulsions get worse. I throw away the expensive jacket my mom bought me, and shiver that spring.

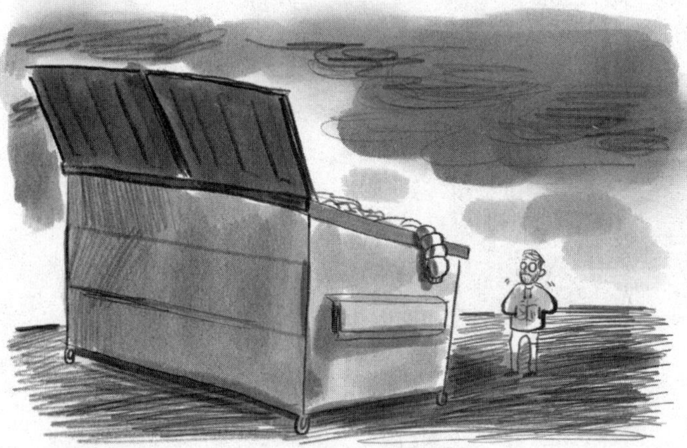

I go to the health center, where they tell me there isn't anyone on campus qualified to deal with OCD, but refer me to a therapist in Hartford, who tells me:

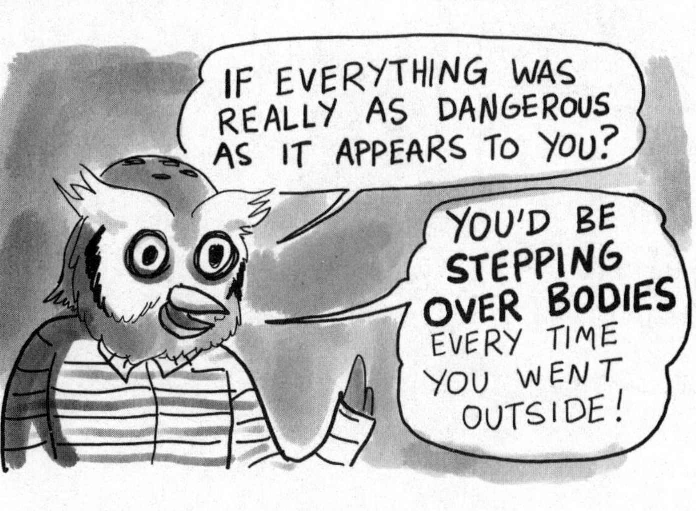
IF EVERYTHING WAS REALLY AS DANGEROUS AS IT APPEARS TO YOU?
YOU'D BE **STEPPING OVER BODIES** EVERY TIME YOU WENT OUTSIDE!

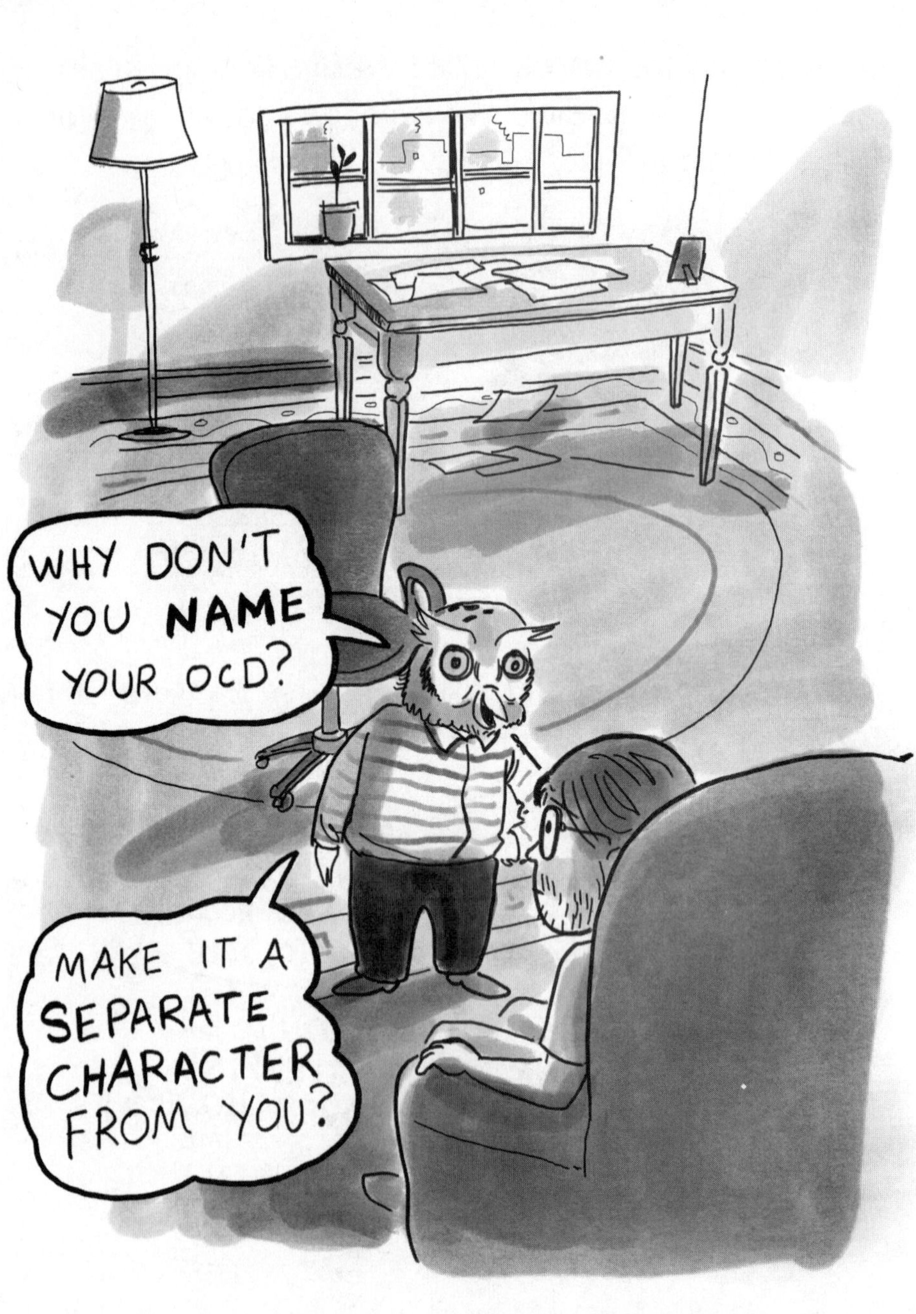
WHY DON'T YOU NAME YOUR OCD?
MAKE IT A SEPARATE CHARACTER FROM YOU?

Ever the overachiever, I create FOUR characters:

CONTAMINATION

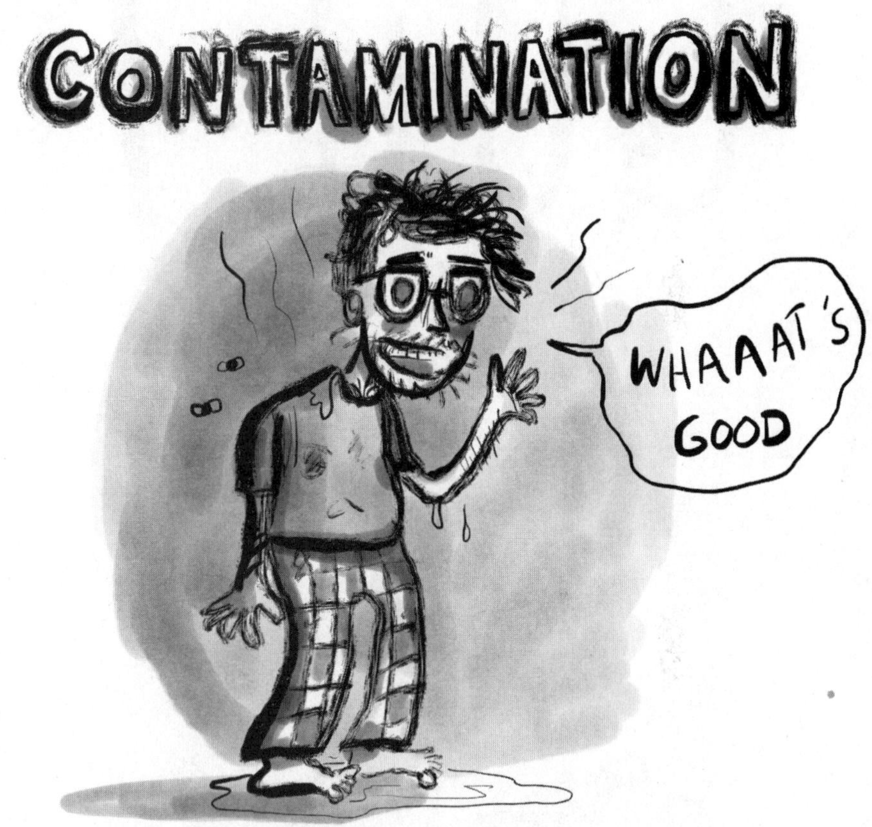
WHAAAT'S GOOD

I'm dirty. It's because of something I touched, or it's just something innate about me. I'm repulsive. I smell, I look bad, people see me and run the other way.

GUILT

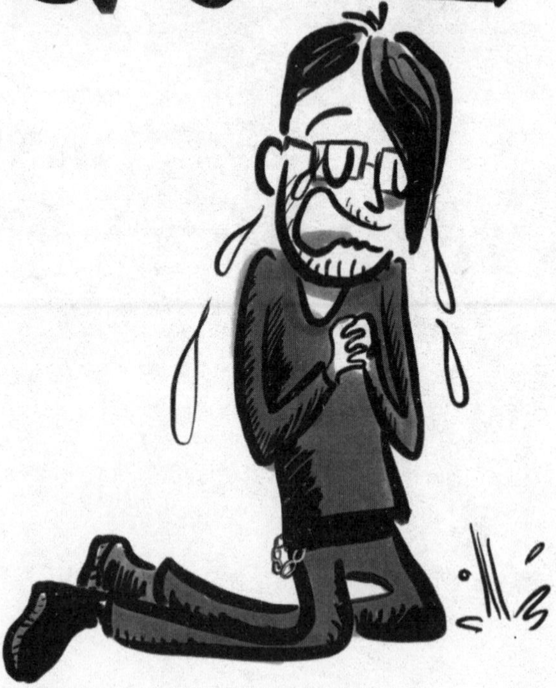

I'm a monster and bad things should happen to me.
I can never atone for all the terrible things I've done.

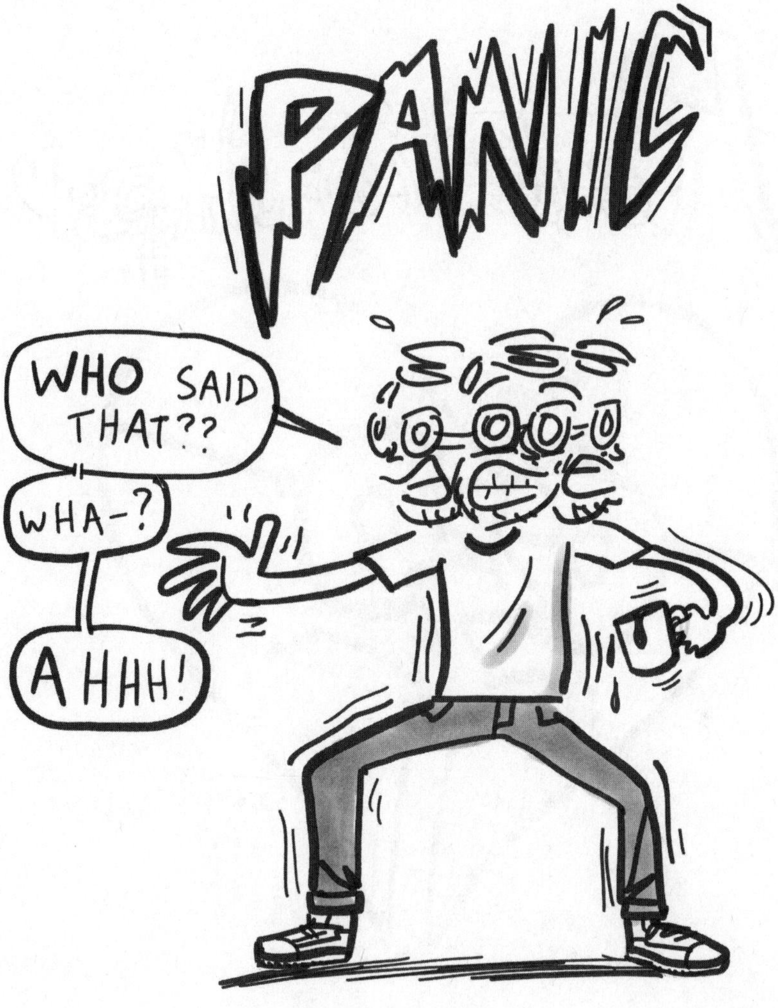
PANIC
WHO SAID THAT??
WHA-?
AHHH!

I NEED TO GET OUT OF HERE RIGHT NOW.
THERE'S NO ESCAPE? I'M TRAPPED. TRAPPED!

Relationships

Is this really love? Is love enough? How much more is this person going to learn about me before realizing that they shouldn't love me? Or, are they already faking it?

I am in college, so in addition to feeling constantly terrified and internally broken, I commit to a steady diet of partying, drinking too much, reveling in an insane myopia. Sometimes this helps me forget my anxiety.

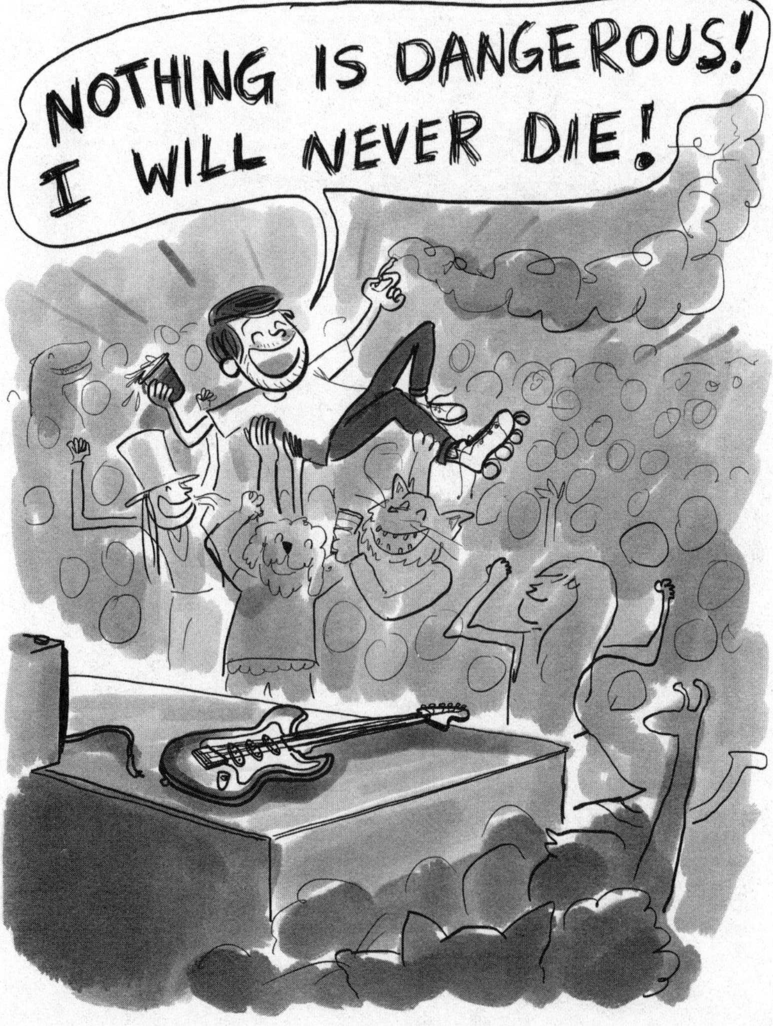
NOTHING IS DANGEROUS! I WILL NEVER DIE!

In my senior year, at a party, I take ecstasy.

I come up in waves, tiny earthquakes of enjoyment that make my teeth chatter. I want to tell everyone the truth. I qualify things with "This isn't just the drugs, but . . . "

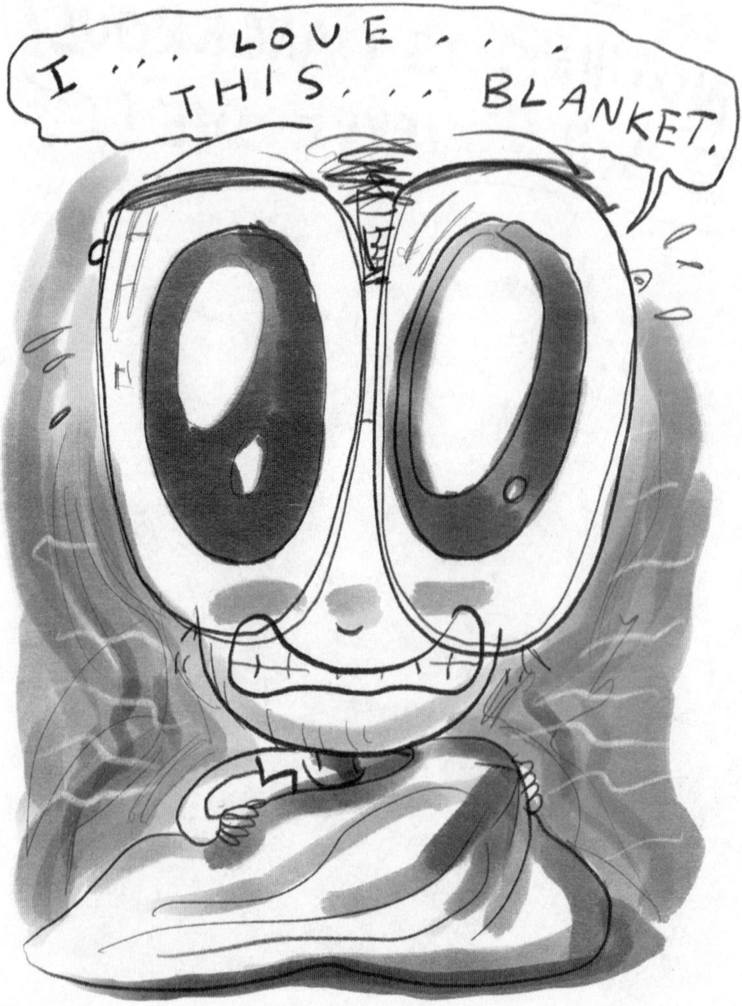
I . . . LOVE . . . . THIS . . . BLANKET.

There's one part of this night that will stay with me. It begins in my body all at once, before I can name or interpret it.

Difficult things have happened; difficult things will happen. I remember everything bad that ever happened to me and how it all felt. I can anticipate everything I don't want to happen, guess at how everything horrific may feel. Still, everything is okay right now.

Between the bad shit that's happened and the bad shit to come is this moment where I'm safe. I have permission not to live in the shitty parts for one second.

And another second.

And I can put enough of these seconds together to make minutes. There are minutes when I'm allowed to feel okay, not despite everything that's happened or will happen, but in addition to it.

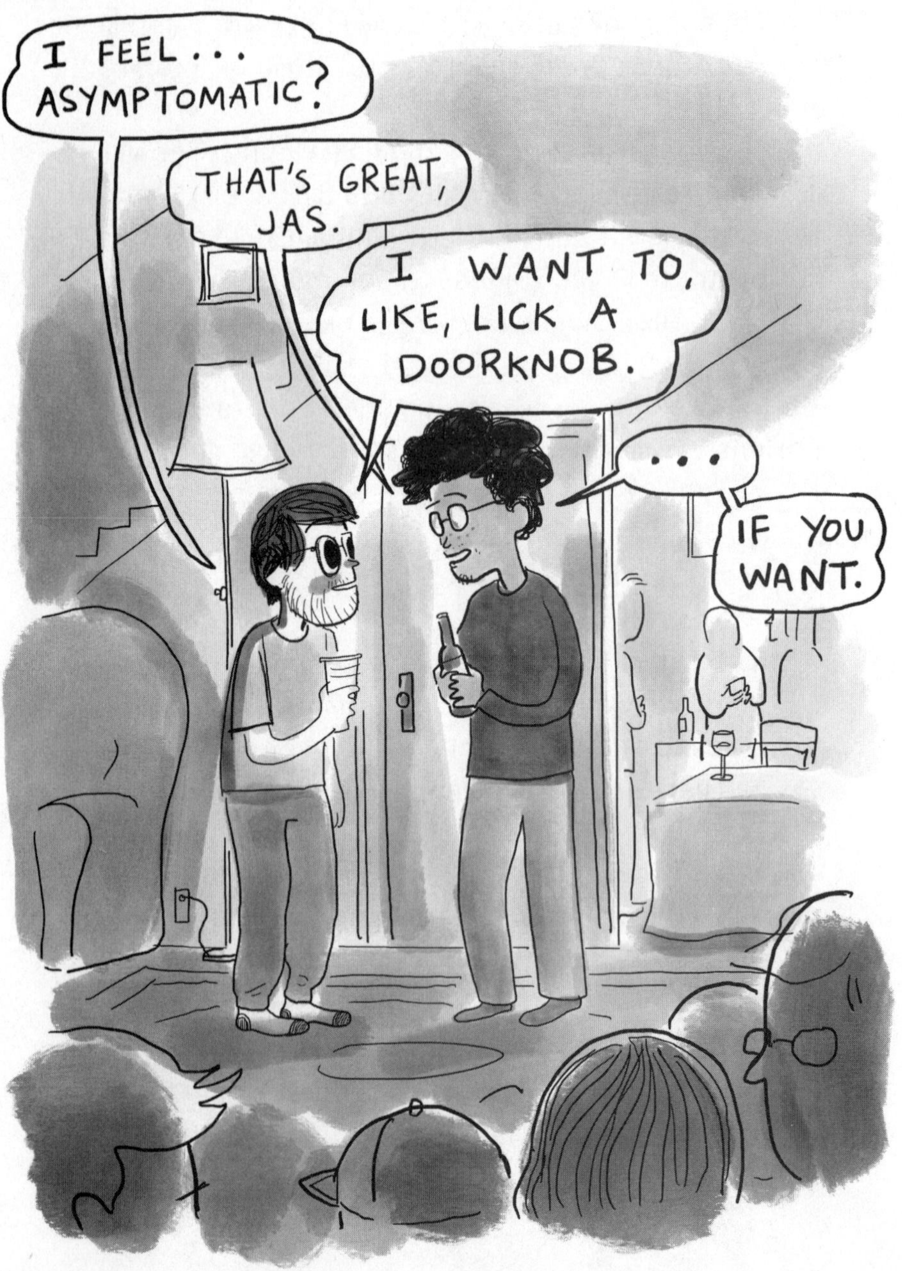
I FEEL...
ASYMPTOMATIC?
THAT'S GREAT, JAS.
I WANT TO, LIKE, LICK A DOORKNOB.
...
IF YOU WANT.

And reader,

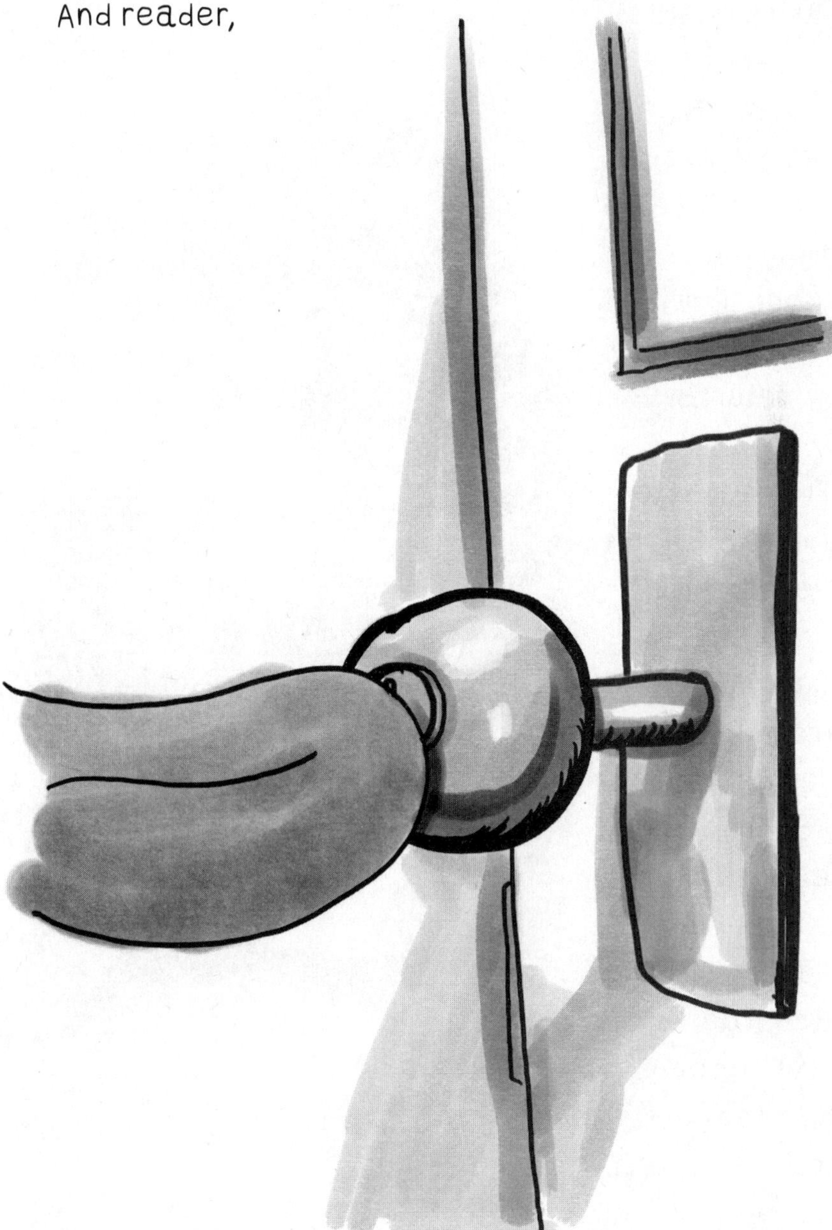

Taking ecstasy is not a sustainable lifestyle choice. I try it a few more times in college, with diminishing returns.

The day after is more difficult every time.

I keep a vestige from that first experience, a full-body epiphany that continues feeling simple and true: find the seconds that feel okay and live in them.

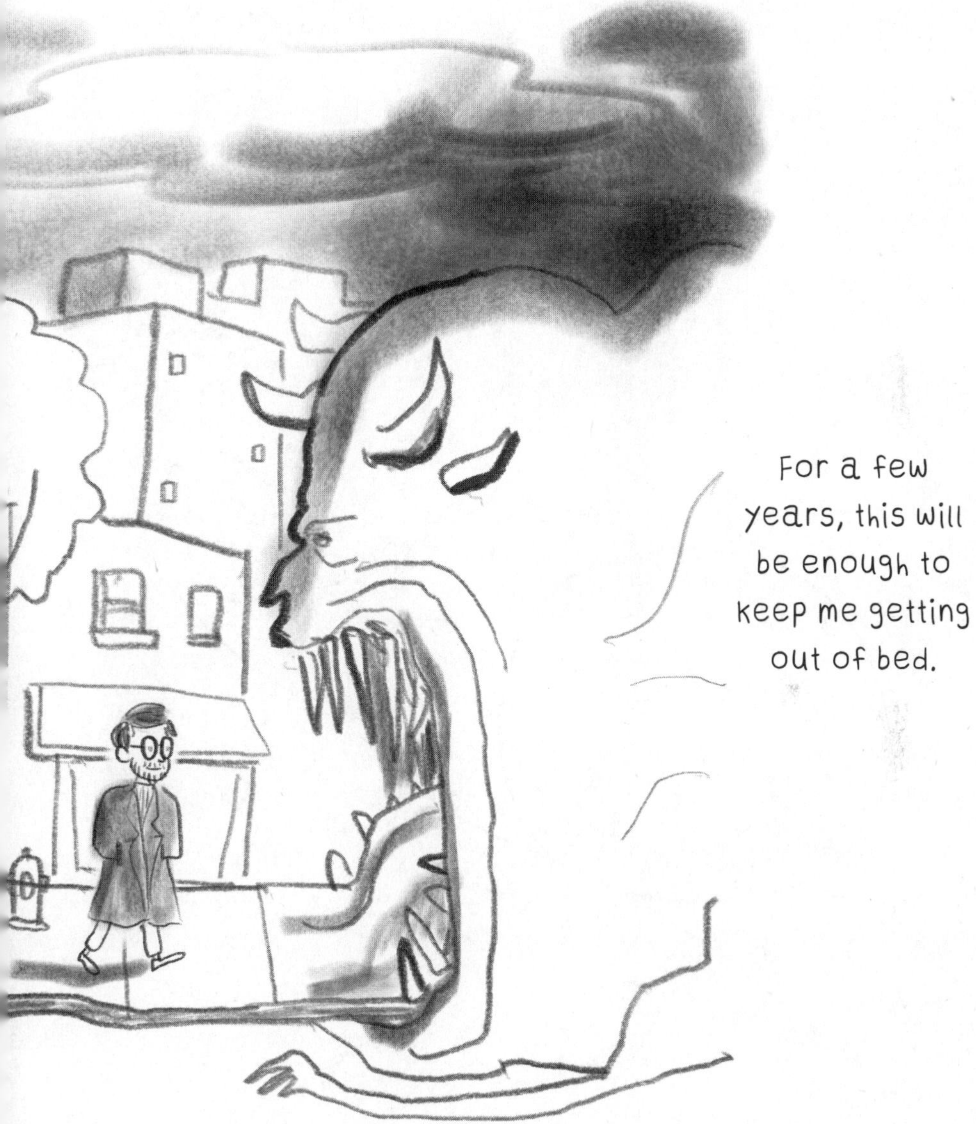
For a few years, this will be enough to keep me getting out of bed.

I'm home from school on my senior-year break. My latest compulsion is to wipe too much. Most of the time there's blood on the paper. This makes me wipe more, to get rid of the blood.

I clog the toilet, and when I try to plunge it I make it so much worse.

The bathroom tile is wrecked.

My stepdad, I think, is going to kill me.

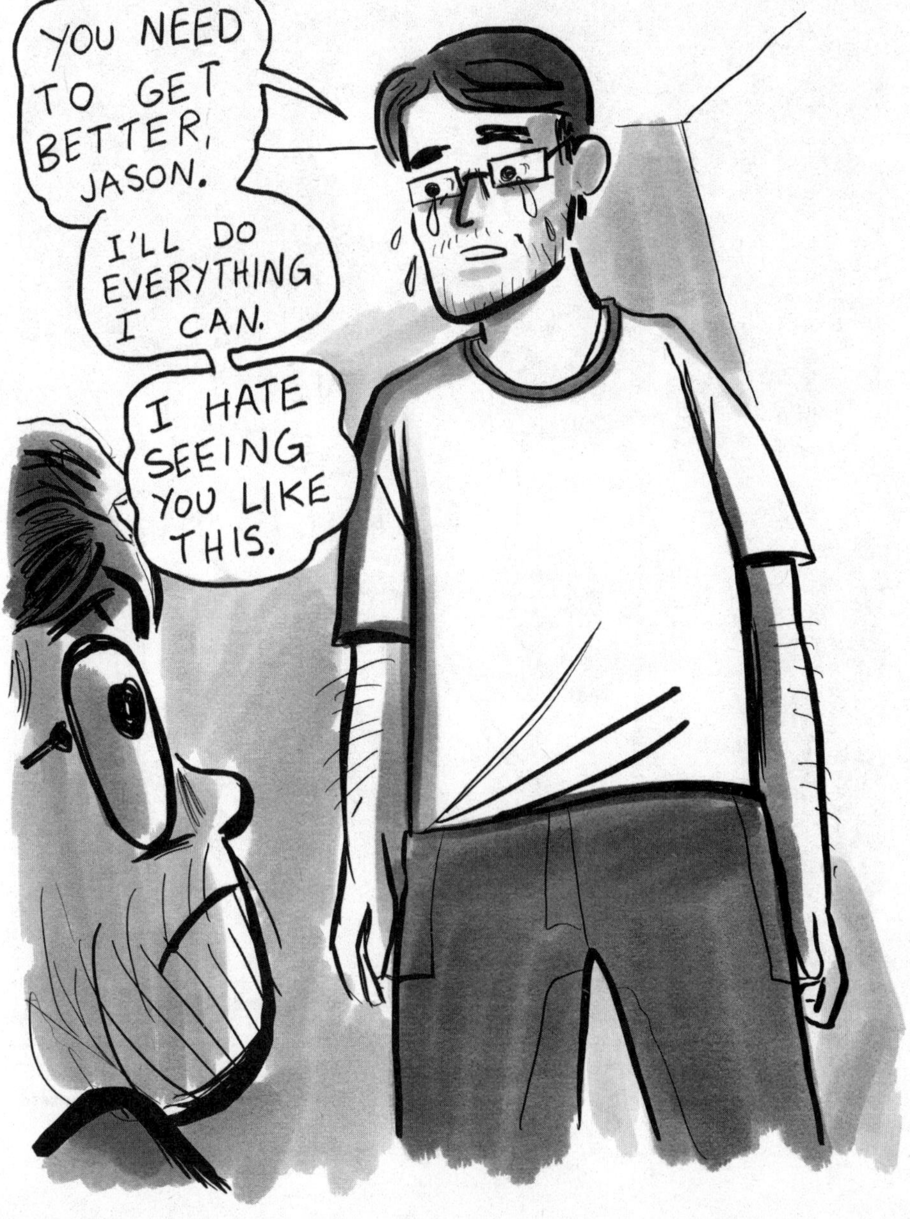
YOU NEED TO GET BETTER, JASON.
I'LL DO EVERYTHING I CAN.
I HATE SEEING YOU LIKE THIS.

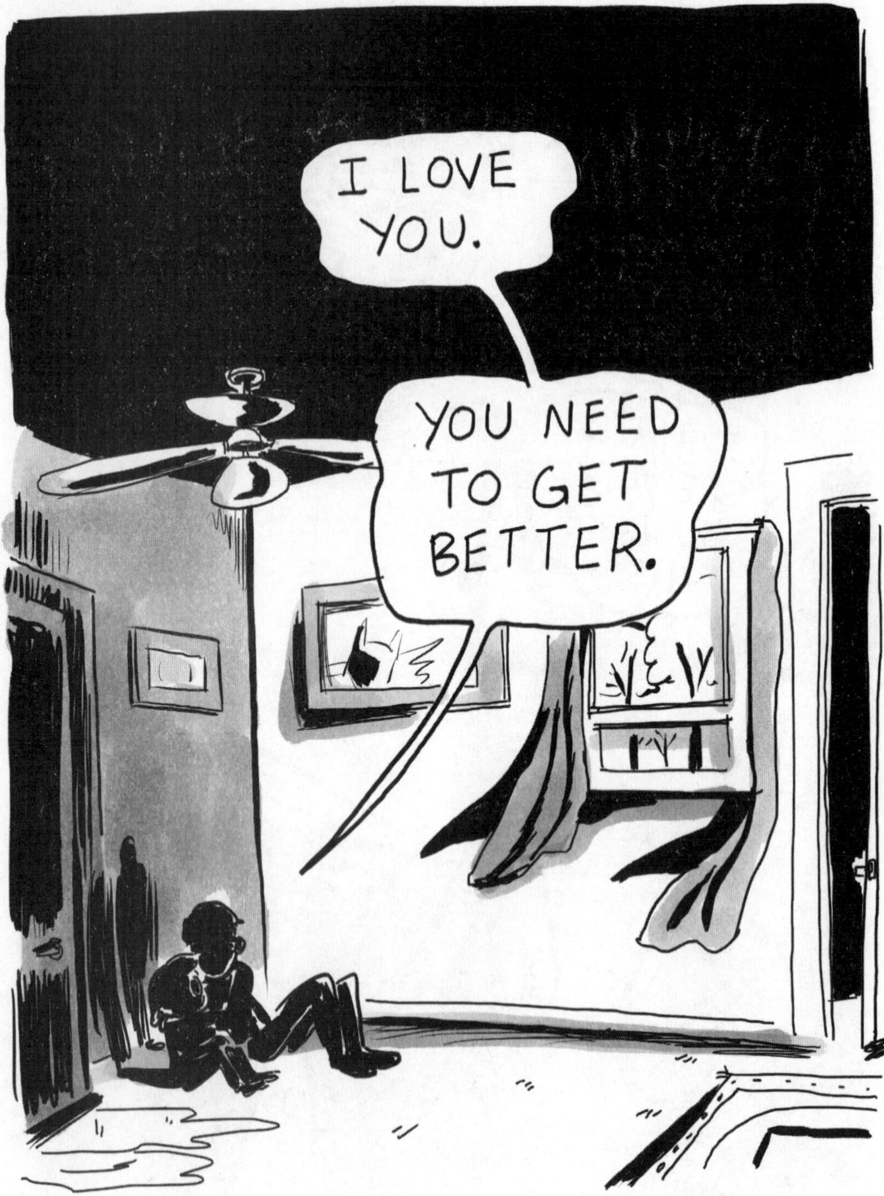
I LOVE YOU.
YOU NEED TO GET BETTER.

After college, I move to Brooklyn because that's what all my friends are doing. If they jumped off the Williamsburg Bridge, I'd follow. Despite the fact that everything that should be easy is difficult here, and even though the streets reek of trash and pee, notwithstanding there are three days of nice weather a year . . .

. . . I fall in love.

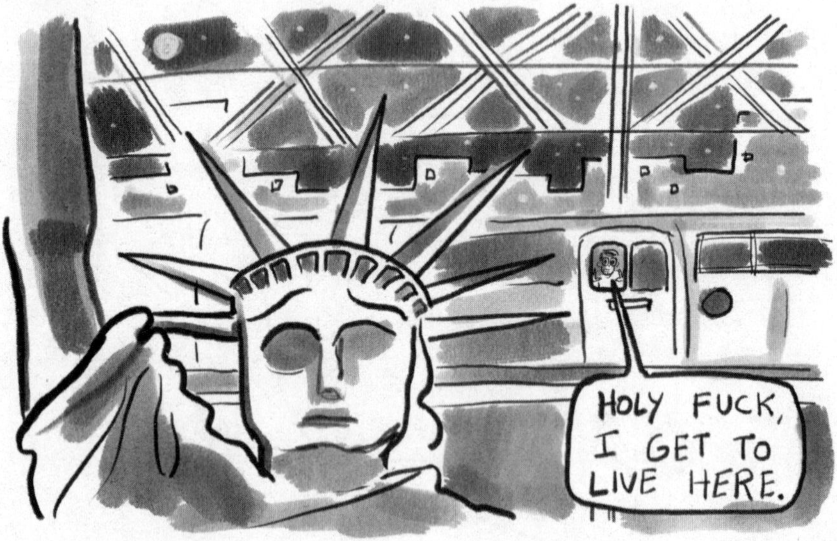
HOLY FUCK, I GET TO LIVE HERE.

OCD is very adaptive to its surroundings, and mine has become a New Yorker.

I find myriad opportunities to match my worries to my realities in Brooklyn.

CONTAMINATION

EVERY BATHROOM IN NEW YORK

I can't look out my window without seeing seven hundred emergencies.

GUILT/RESPONSIBILITY

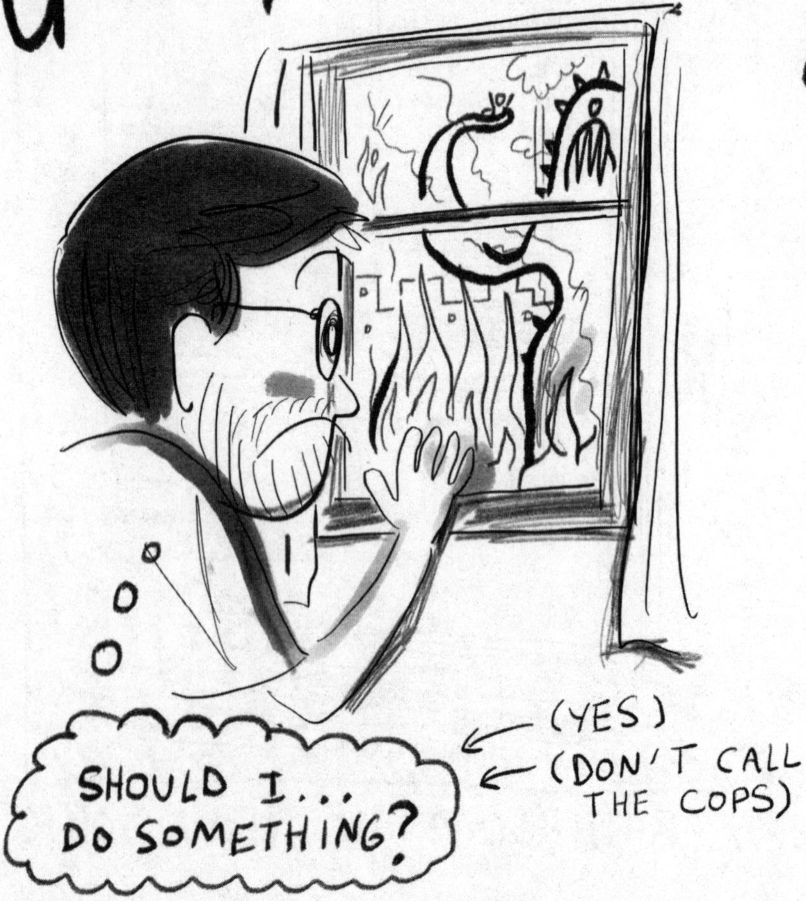
SHOULD I... DO SOMETHING?
(YES)
(DON'T CALL THE COPS)

I am frequently in crowded spaces without immediate exit opportunities.

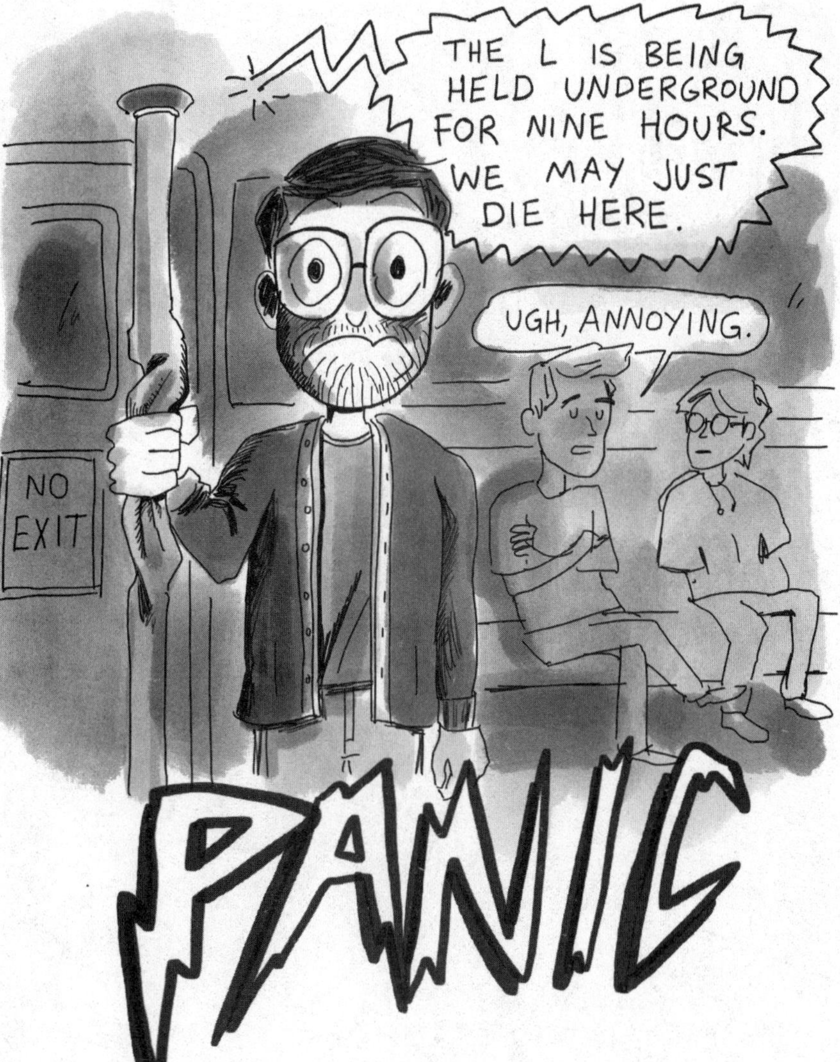
THE L IS BEING HELD UNDERGROUND FOR NINE HOURS. WE MAY JUST DIE HERE.
UGH, ANNOYING.
NO EXIT
PANIC

I have never dated a stranger before moving here.

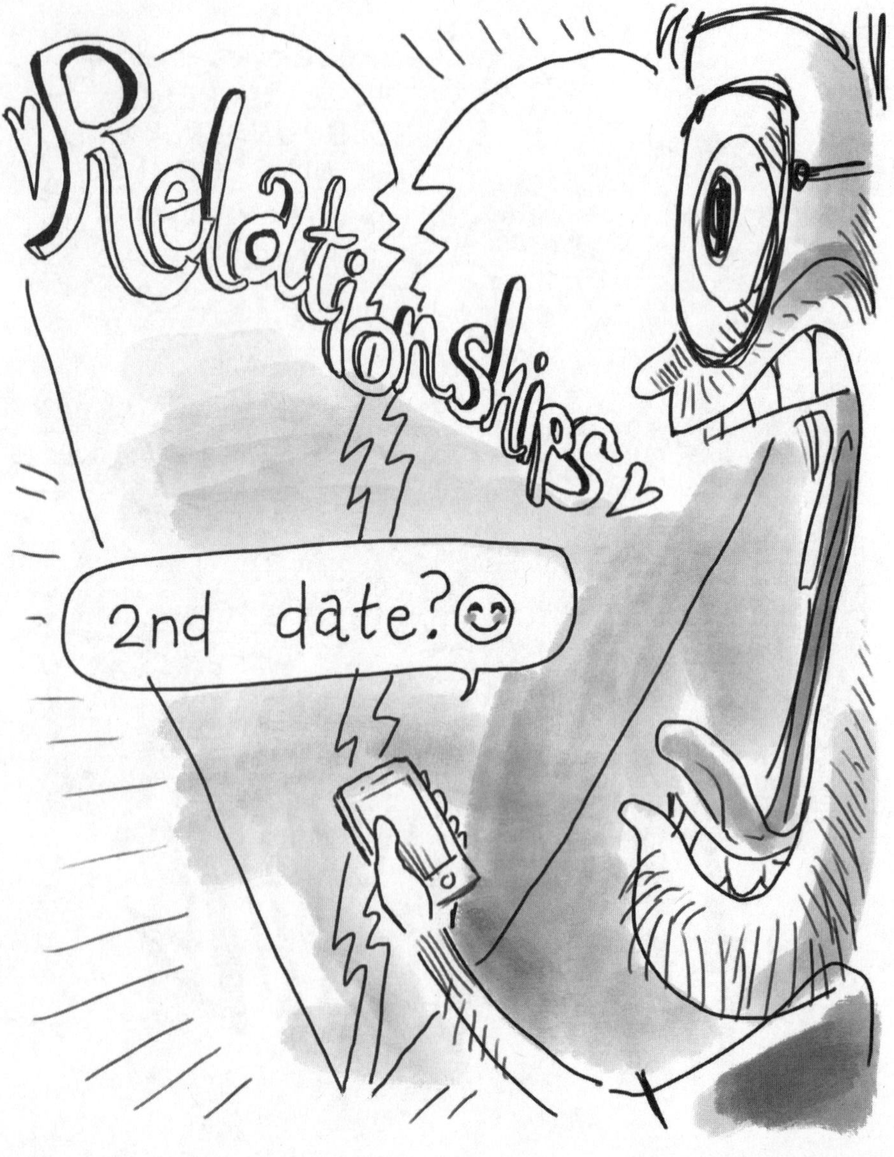
Relationships
2nd date?

In New York I can feel anonymous. I love when a movie ends by slowly zooming up and out until everyone walking on the sidewalk is a dot and I think, "You could zoom in on ANYBODY and it could be a whole movie."

<"DREAMS" BY THE CRANBERRIES PLAYS>

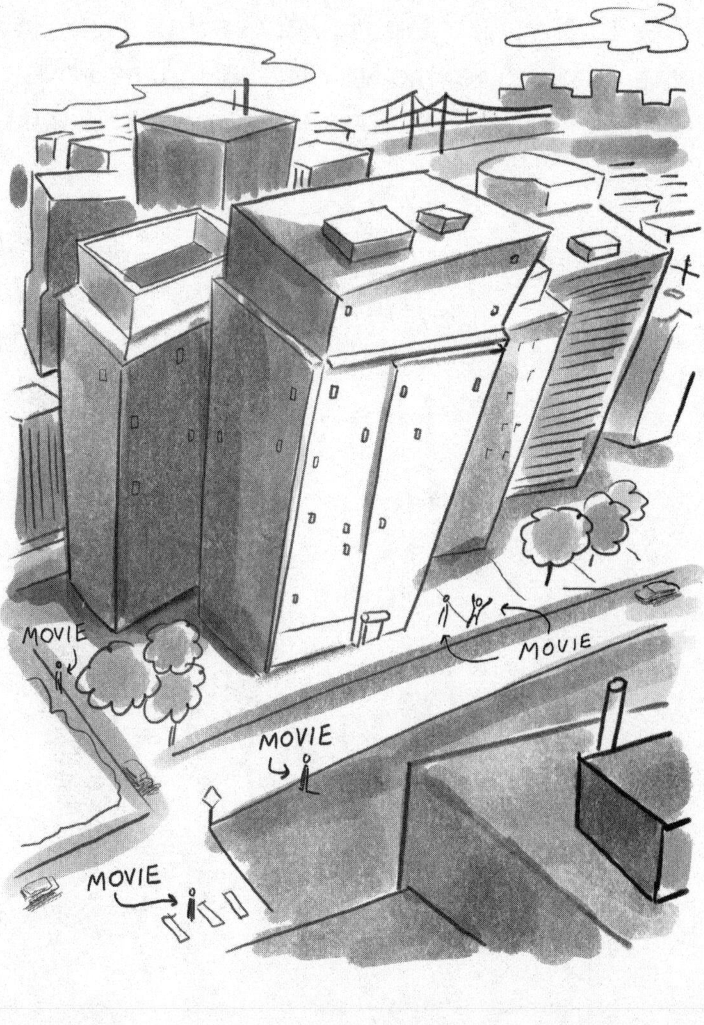
MOVIE
MOVIE
MOVIE
MOVIE

In New York, if I make my deadlines and say nothing's wrong when people ask, nobody needs to worry about me.

My best friends know about my OCD and they try to help.

They reason, pragmatically, that protecting me from my fears will make me feel better. They do my compulsions for me, the way my dad turned over my pillow. Sometimes it helps, sometimes it doesn't.

At a party in my apartment, I feel a wave of contamination fear and shut myself in my room.

A dear friend talks to me from the other side of the door.

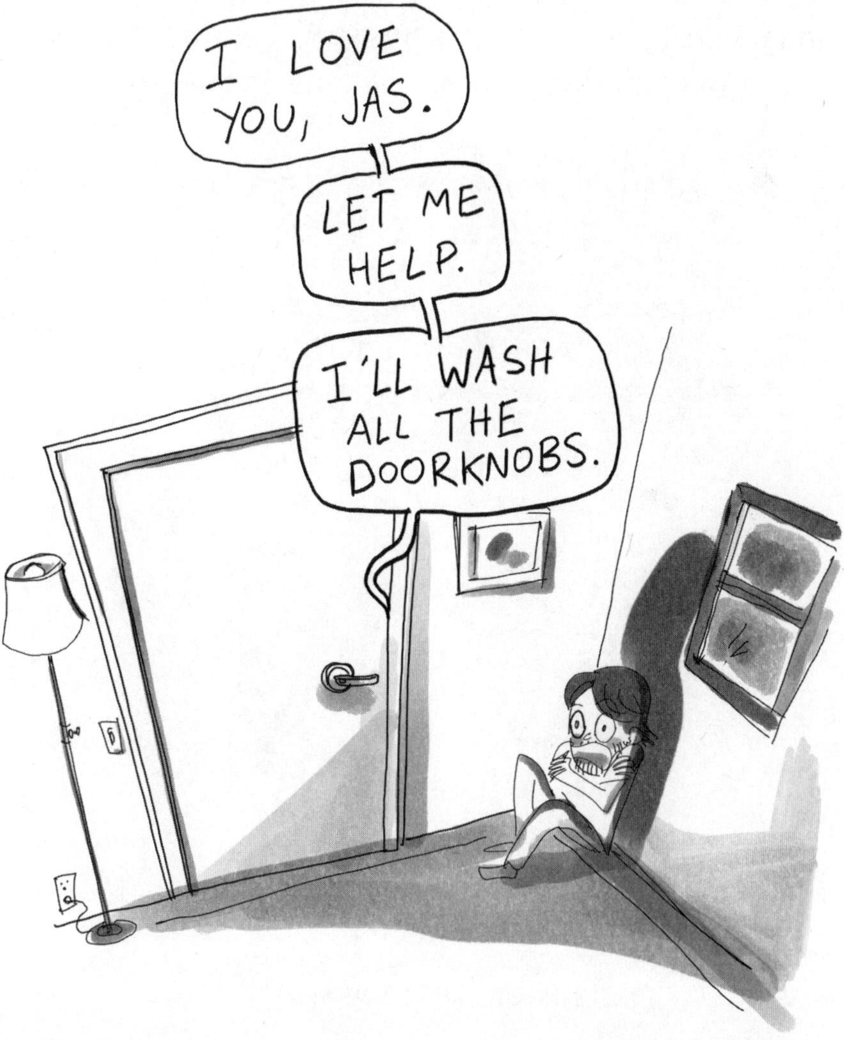
I LOVE YOU, JAS.
LET ME HELP.
I'LL WASH ALL THE DOORKNOBS.

Whenever it gets to this point, I'm ashamed. I shut my door and curl up. I know it's hurting the people I love to see me like this. I know it's frustrating them, too.

Imagine your best friend looped on the same irrational thought. Imagine trying to help them. They don't listen, and you watch them continue to suffer.

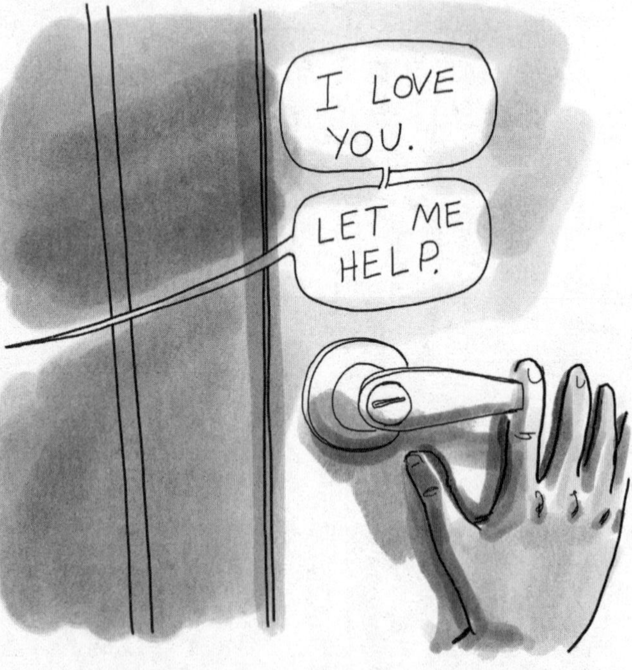
I LOVE YOU.
LET ME HELP.

I won't let anybody help me because I don't know how they can help.

I keep the door shut.

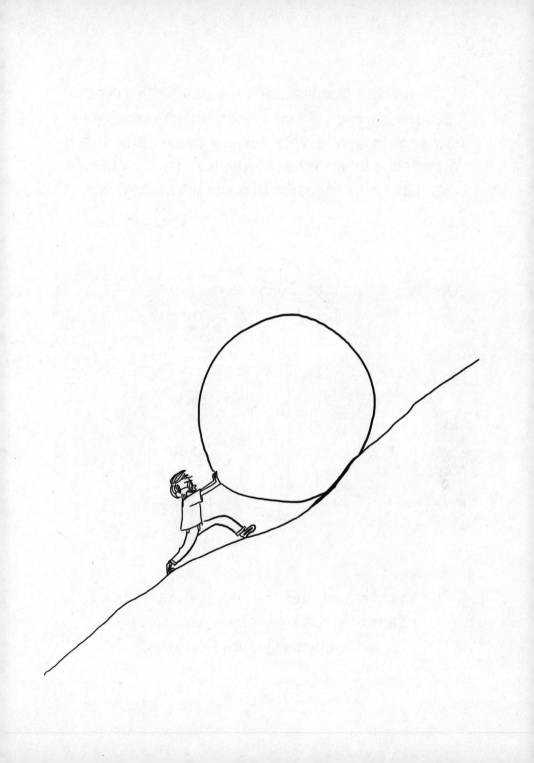

I'm on the billionth floor of a building in Times Square, surrounded by my cartoonist heroes and trying not to have a very public panic attack. I have a portfolio under my arm, and the one thing I know is that I'm an impostor who doesn't belong here.

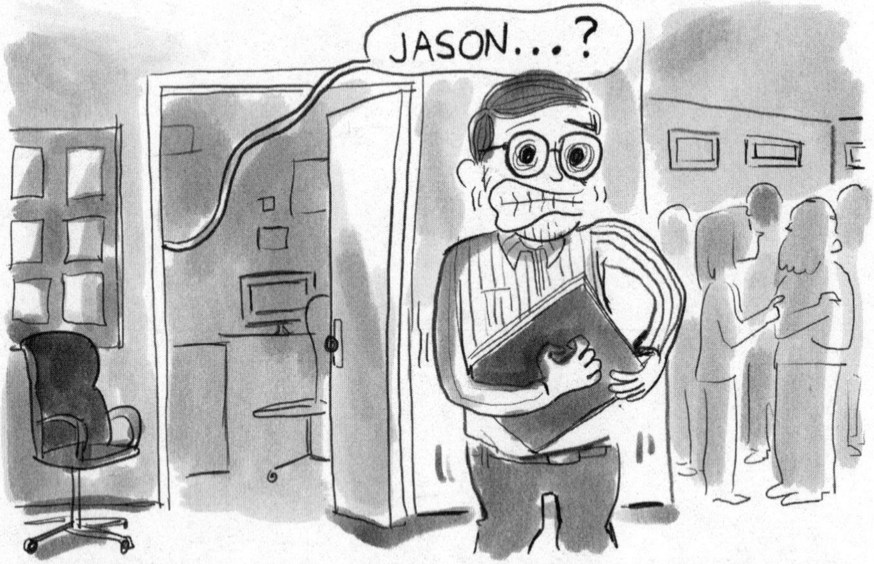
JASON...?

I have a mutual friend with a cartoon editor at *The New Yorker*, who saw my work and suggested I come in.

Every Tuesday there is a cartoon pitch meeting, and local cartoonists bring in a "batch" of cartoon sketches — the norm is about ten — to pitch in person to the cartoon editor. He looks at the batches, hands you back the ones he's rejecting, and holds on to the ones he's considering. If you sell, you get an e-mail that weekend with the subject line "OK."

He looks at my first batch.

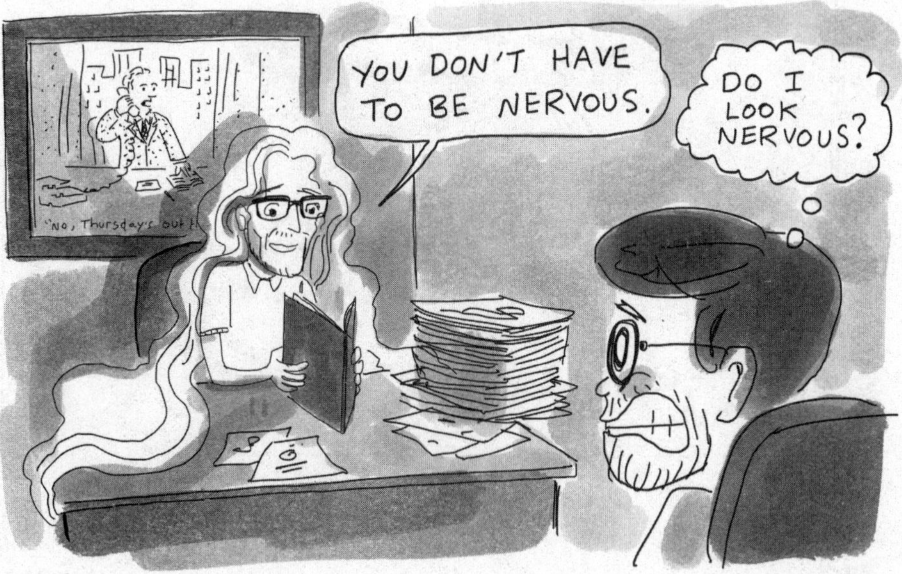
"No, Thursday's out
YOU DON'T HAVE TO BE NERVOUS.
DO I LOOK NERVOUS?

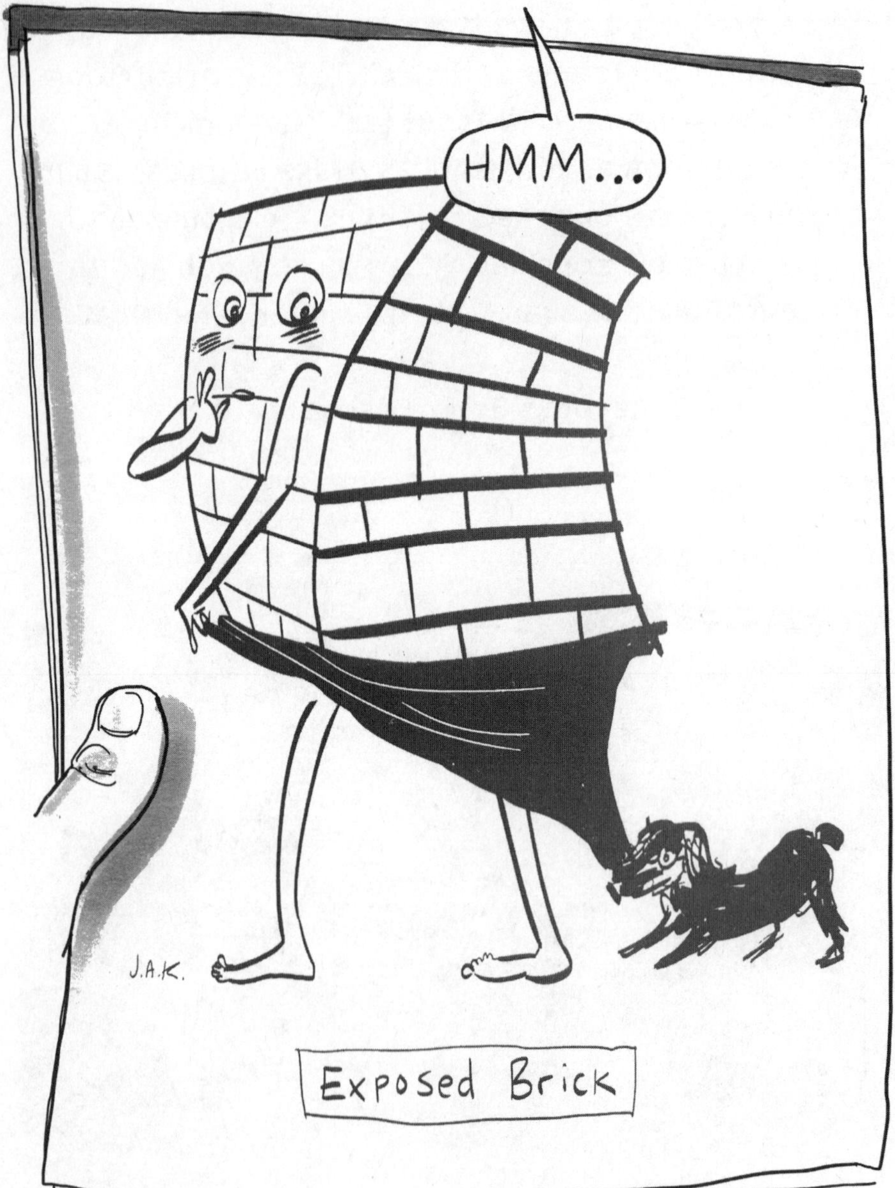
HMM...
J.A.K.
Exposed Brick

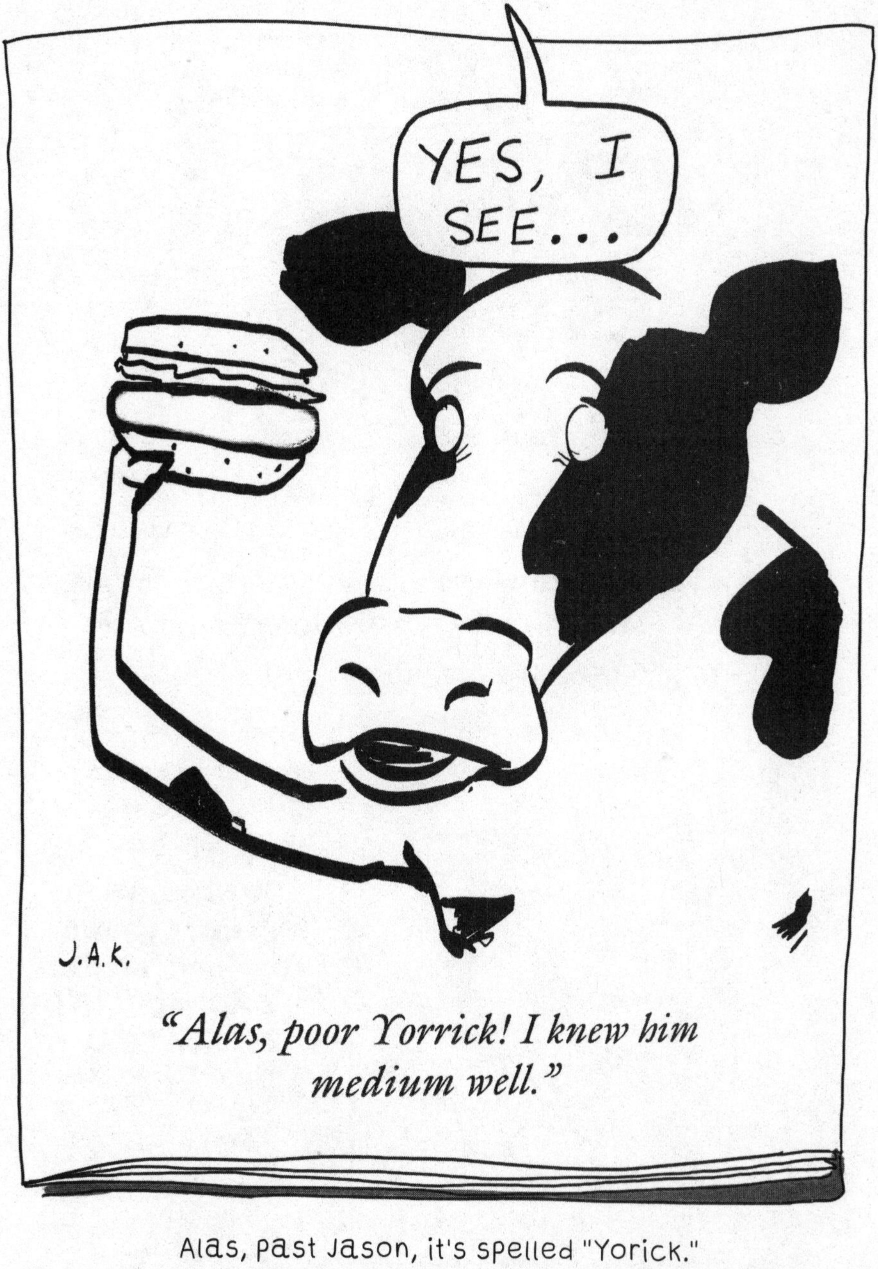
YES, I SEE...
J.A.K.

"Alas, poor Yorrick! I knew him medium well."

Alas, past Jason, it's spelled "Yorick."

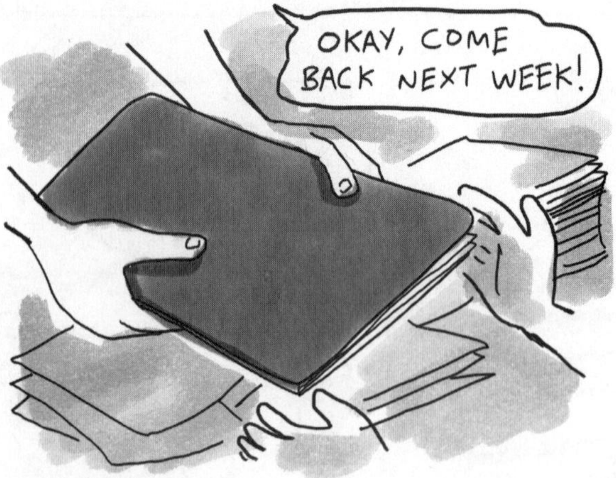
OKAY, COME BACK NEXT WEEK!

I come back next week, and week after week, I draw batches all summer. I look through the big book of *The New Yorker* cartoons and try to understand the engine of every joke.

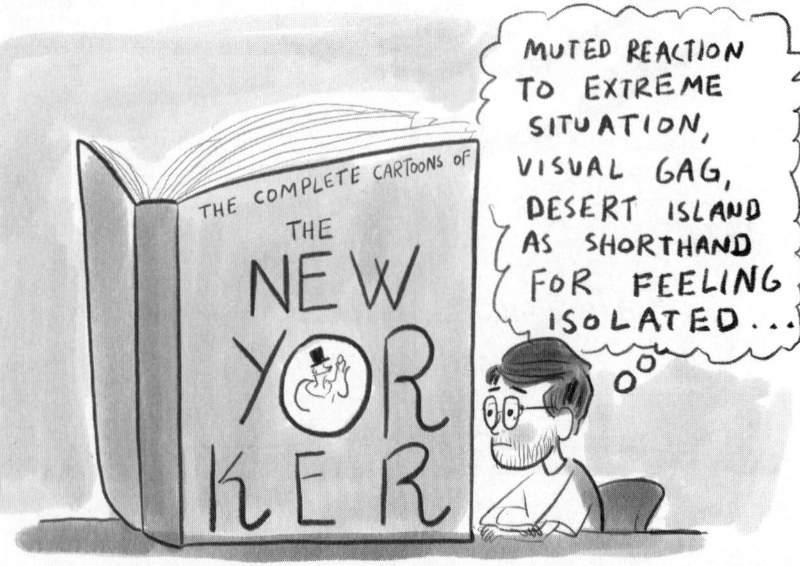
MUTED REACTION TO EXTREME SITUATION, VISUAL GAG, DESERT ISLAND AS SHORTHAND FOR FEELING ISOLATED...
THE COMPLETE CARTOONS OF
THE
NEW
YORKER

I hang my rejected cartoons in my coffee shop, and some mornings when I'm waiting on line . . .

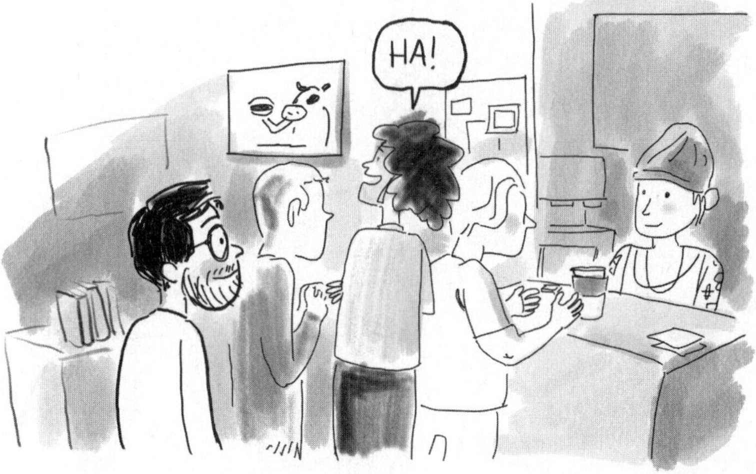
HA!

One Monday evening I'm in Fuck-It mode, and I put one last cartoon in the batch, surreal like the last sketch on *SNL*, not trying to make something I think could be in print, just trying to make myself laugh.

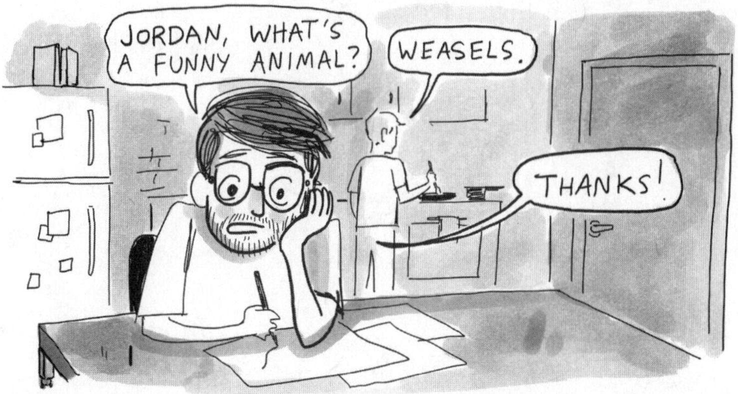
JORDAN, WHAT'S A FUNNY ANIMAL?
WEASELS.
THANKS!

Of course this is my first "OK," my first cartoon in *The New Yorker.*

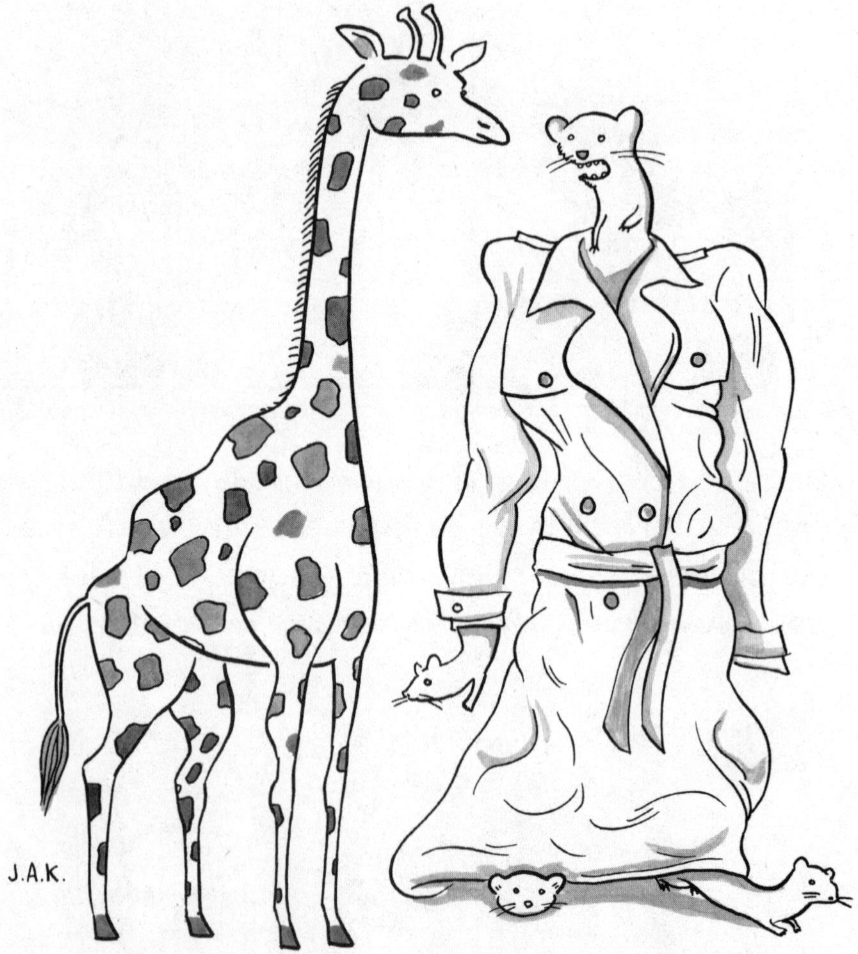
J.A.K.

"Now that we've fallen in love, I have a confession. I'm not a giraffe—I'm fifty-eight weasels in a trenchcoat."

This is the single coolest moment of my career. It feels unreal. It feels incredible.

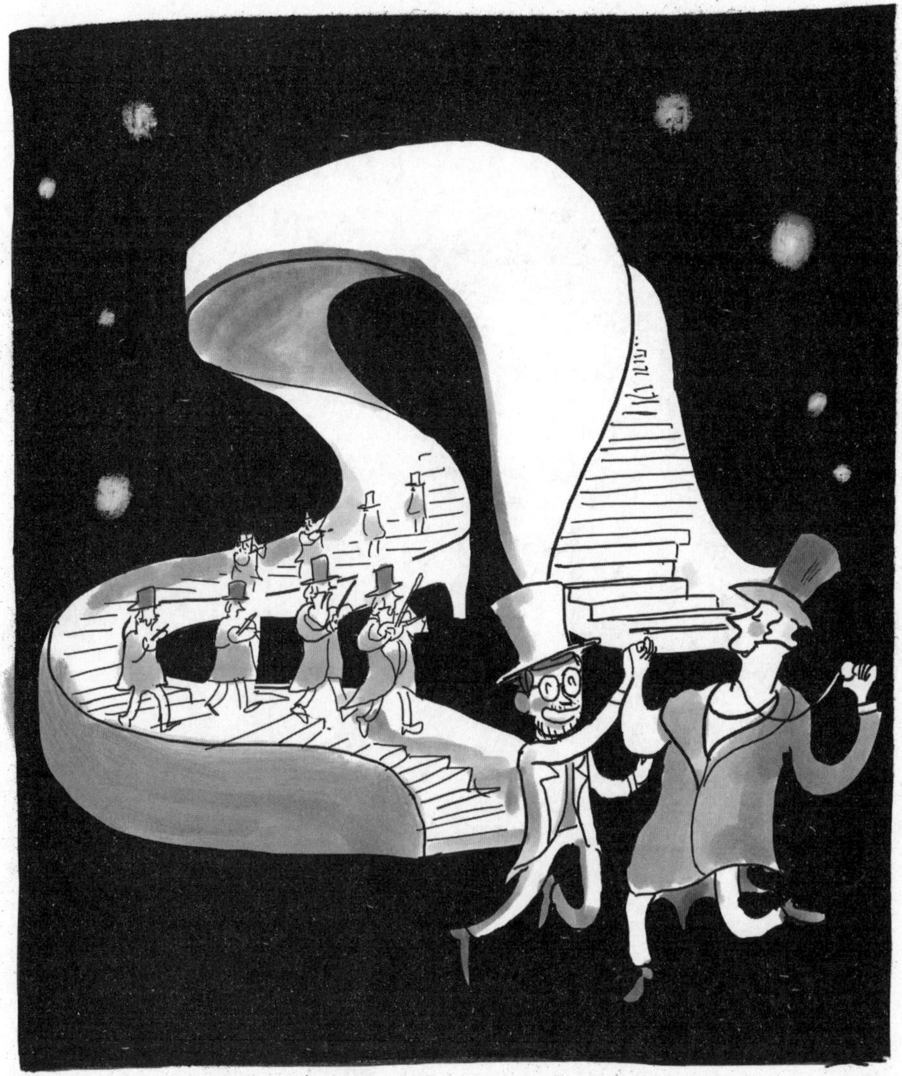

I'm surprised that every problem in my life is not immediately solved.

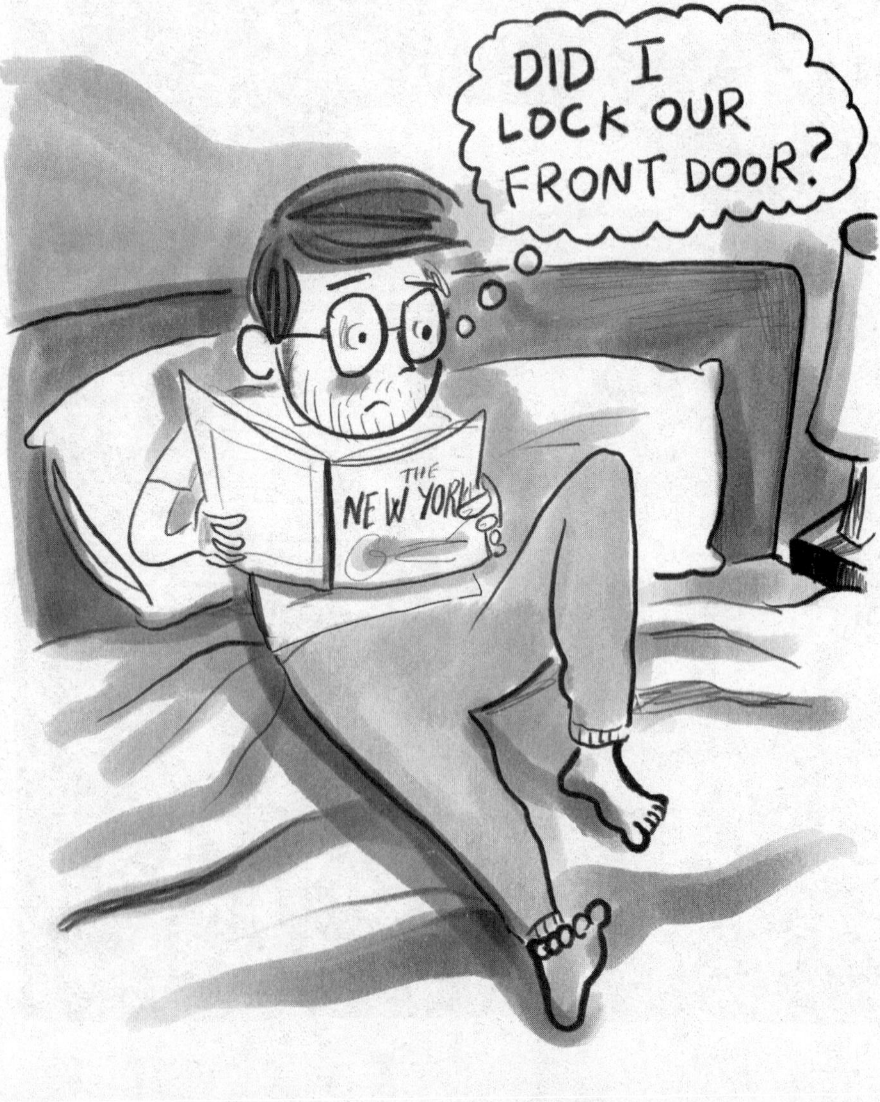
DID I LOCK OUR FRONT DOOR?
THE NEW YORK

In New York, I try to date. This goes like you might expect.

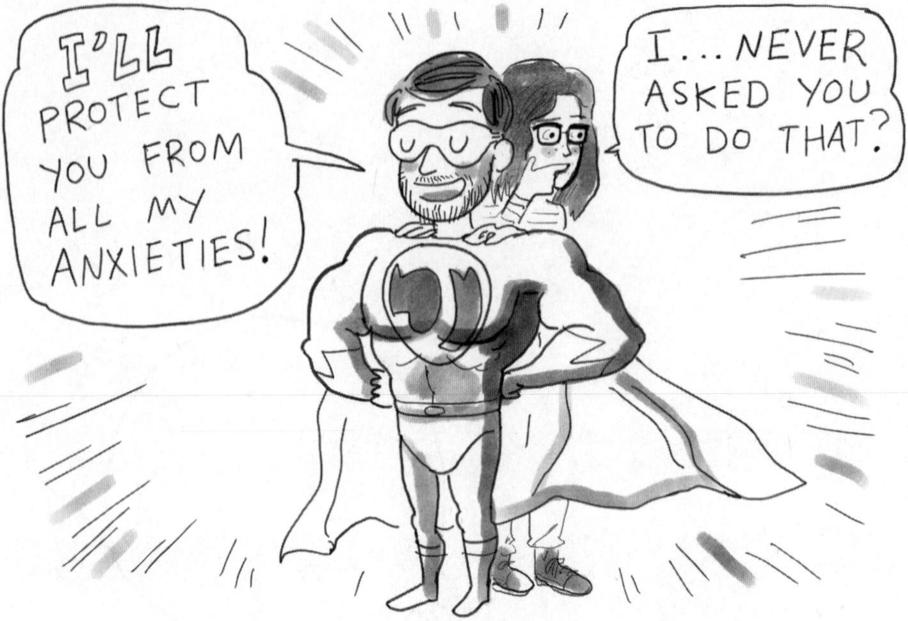
I'LL PROTECT YOU FROM ALL MY ANXIETIES!
I... NEVER ASKED YOU TO DO THAT?

Am I with the right person? Do I love them enough? Is this how it's supposed to feel? How do other people feel? Would we be better off apart? Is this healthy or codependent? Am I slowly ruining my partner's life? Am I making a mistake? Can I love? Can I be loved?

Valid questions, I guess. They don't have answers. This doesn't keep my brain from playing and replaying the questions, searching for any sign or symbol to confirm that this is the best or worst thing to ever happen to me.

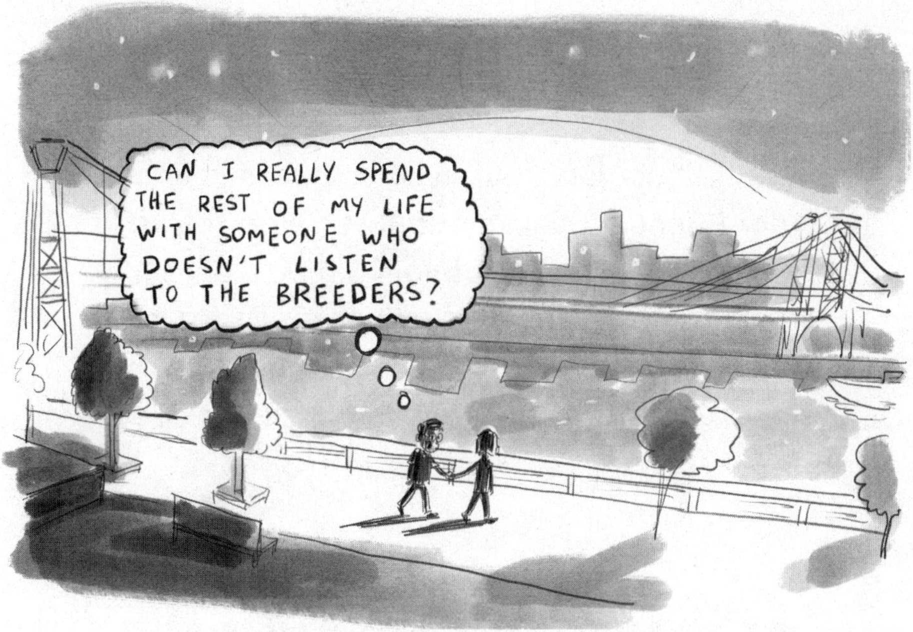
CAN I REALLY SPEND THE REST OF MY LIFE WITH SOMEONE WHO DOESN'T LISTEN TO THE BREEDERS?

It doesn't help that every movie I've ever seen and also this guy seem to be in agreement:

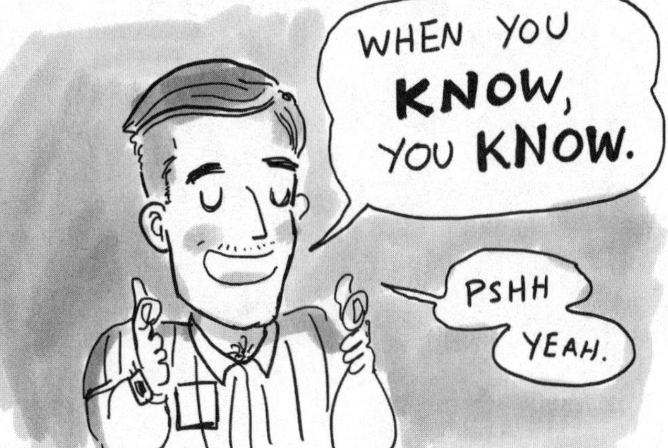
WHEN YOU **KNOW**, YOU **KNOW**.
PSHH YEAH.

At this point it should be clear that I do not KNOW when I KNOW.

Neither do you. You may know when you're confident enough about a decision you've made that you aren't going to waste time ruminating on alternate universes where you made a different choice. If so, you have my sincerest congratulations and also fuck you.

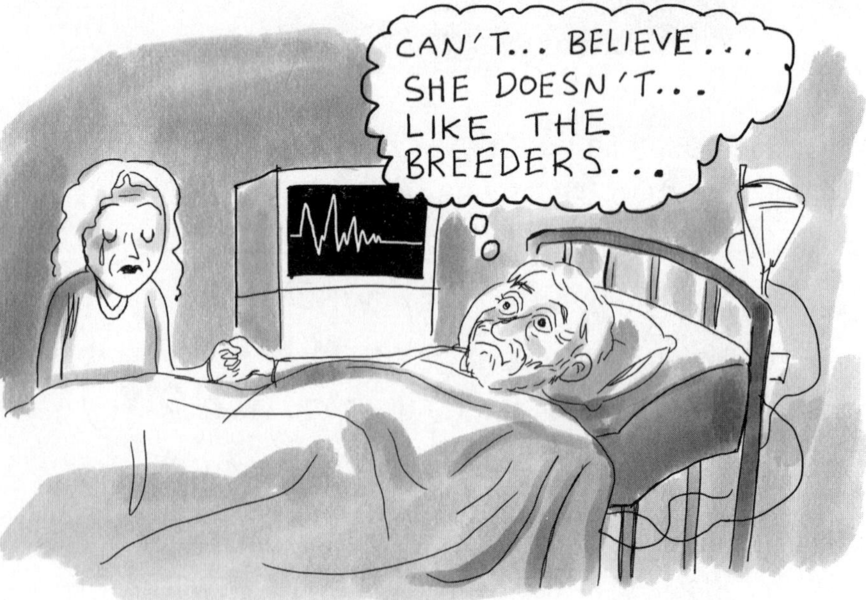
CAN'T... BELIEVE... SHE DOESN'T... LIKE THE BREEDERS...

On our first date, Ana stops me from taking a sip of a bodega coconut water that somebody has clearly opened and then put back.

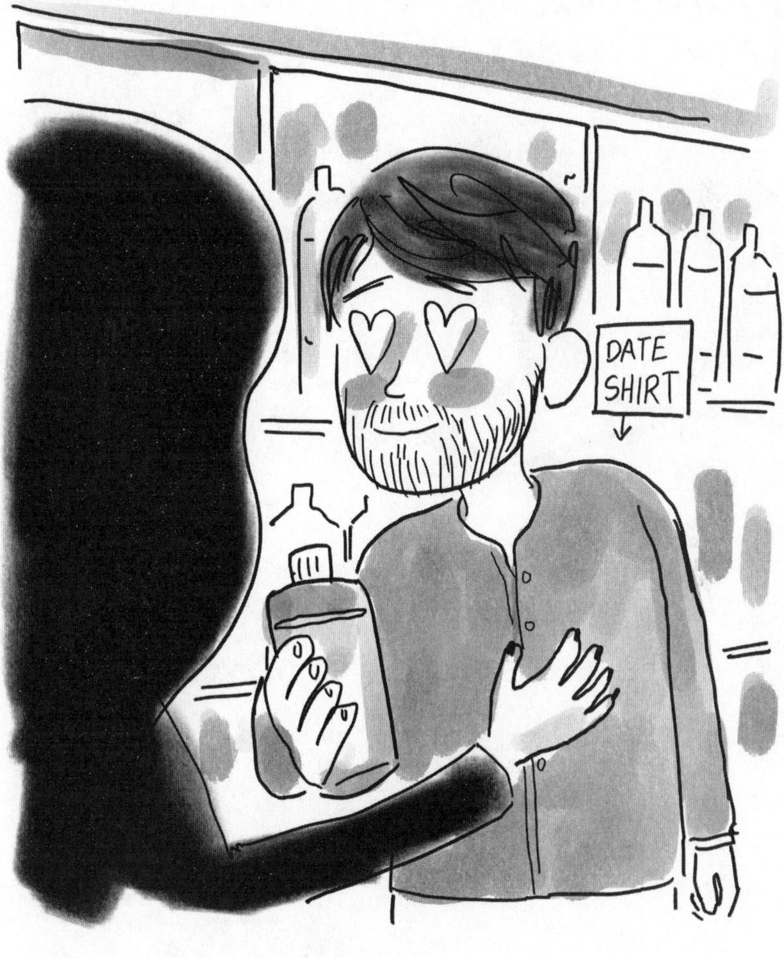
DATE
SHIRT

She is my hero.

On our second date, we start talking to each other like an imaginary old Jewish couple.

OH, MORDY, YER ALWAYS ANGRY ABOUT SOMETHIN'.
WHAT, CAN I HELP IT THAT THERE'S THIS MUCH TO BE ANGRY ABOUT?

This is when I begin to fall in love with her.

Our third date is the night of the 2016 election.

Do you still want to hang out even if...?

5:47 PM

Yes even if.

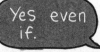

Ana's a journalist, and when they call it
she's sent to report outside the tower.

At 3 a.m. she comes over and we hold
each other and talk for hours.

Lots of couples are breaking up or getting
together tonight, and we're the latter.

Ana divides her time between New York and Washington, DC, until she eventually moves to DC to report on Capitol Hill full time. At her going away party, we say some famous last words:

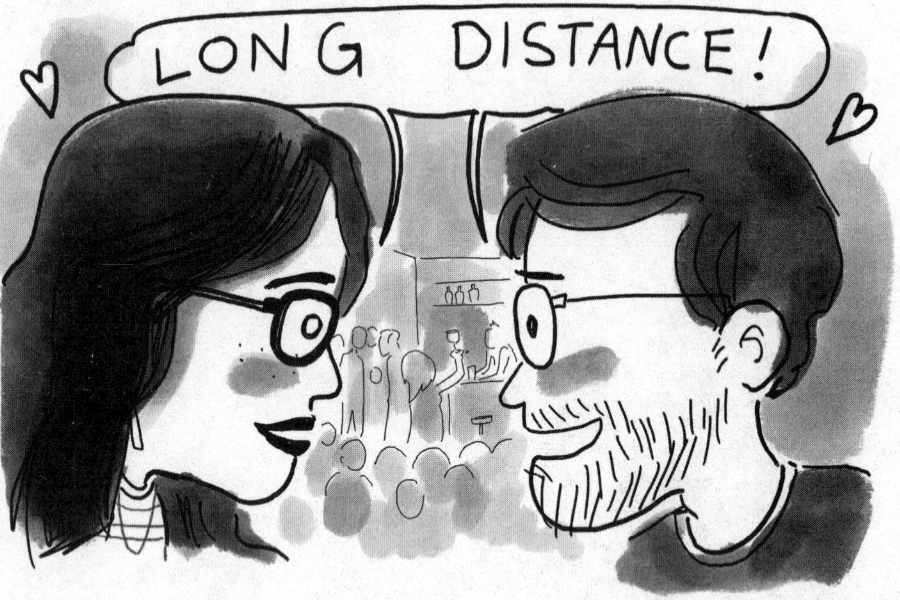
LONG DISTANCE!

"I didn't fall in love with someone who wouldn't take this job. We'll make it work."

I say all the right things, and I believe these things.

For a while it works. I take the train to DC — a city I hate — to see the person I love. We drink wine and watch movies on the porch of her beautiful house, while the fireflies flicker.

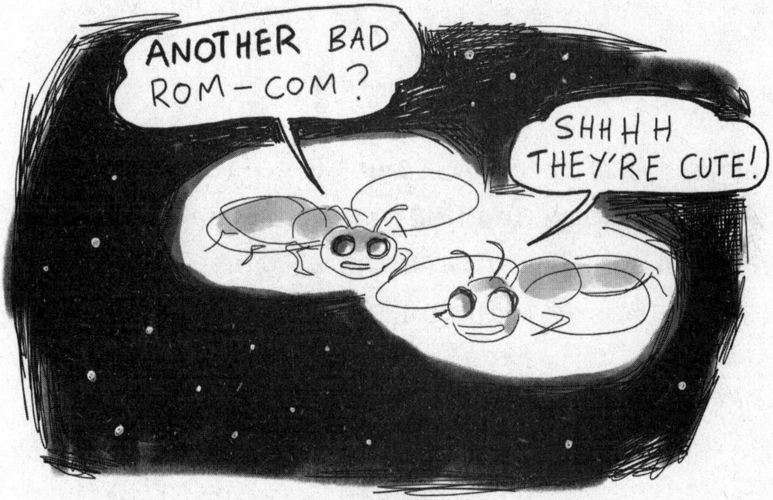
ANOTHER BAD ROM-COM?
SHHHH THEY'RE CUTE!

Ana wants me to let her in more.

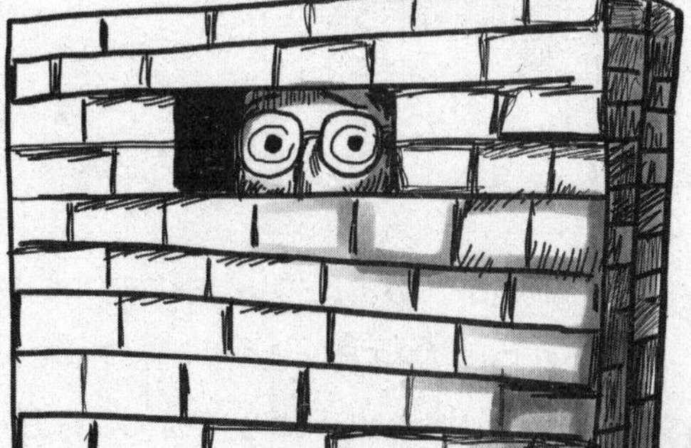

But I also believe something else . . .

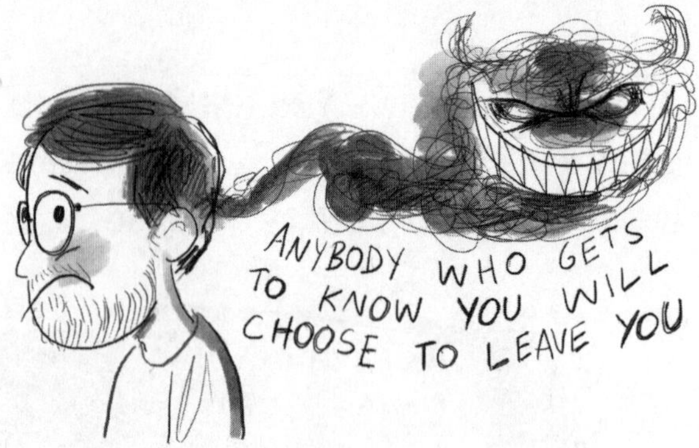
ANYBODY WHO GETS TO KNOW YOU WILL CHOOSE TO LEAVE YOU

One night in New York, I'm leaving a coffee shop where I've just hung my work, and I can't stop thinking about how the nails won't hold. Tomorrow people will work under my frames and the frames will fall on their heads and concuss them.

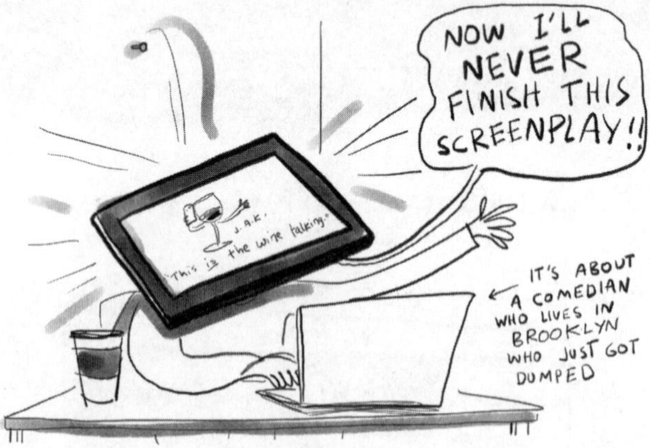
NOW I'LL NEVER FINISH THIS SCREENPLAY!!
J.A.K.
"This is the wine talking."
IT'S ABOUT A COMEDIAN WHO LIVES IN BROOKLYN WHO JUST GOT DUMPED

Reluctantly, I tell this to Ana over the phone. She tries to help me out of this spiral, and I argue with her as aggressively as I would with my own thoughts.

I make Ana cry.

I have familiar nightmare thoughts about her that terrify me.

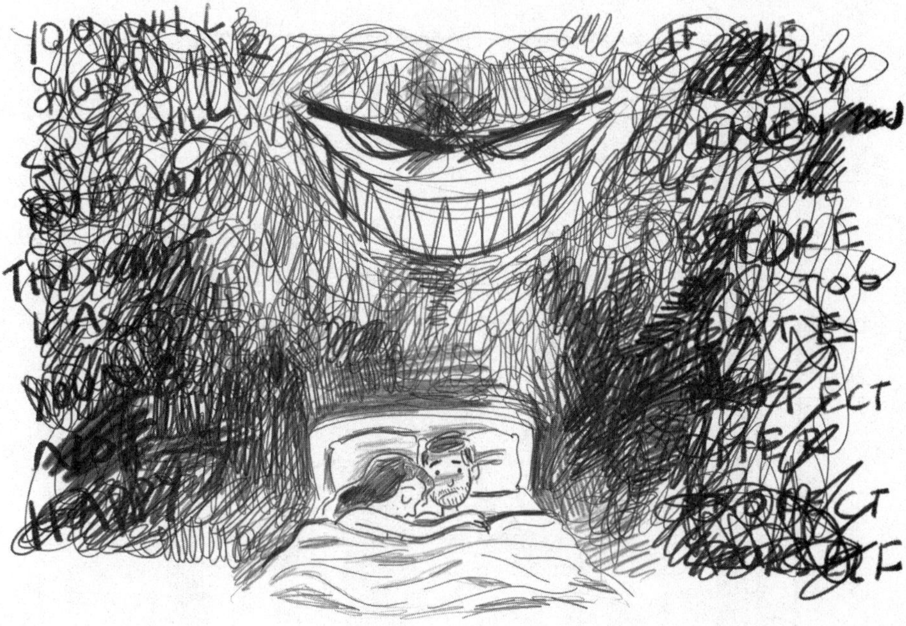

I'm exhausted.

I want relief.

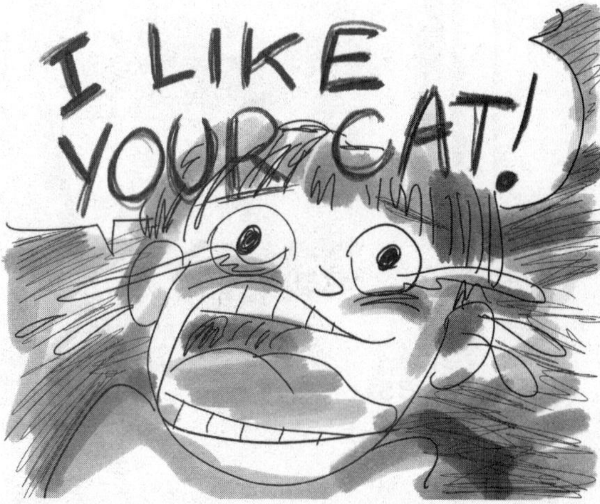
I LIKE YOUR CAT!

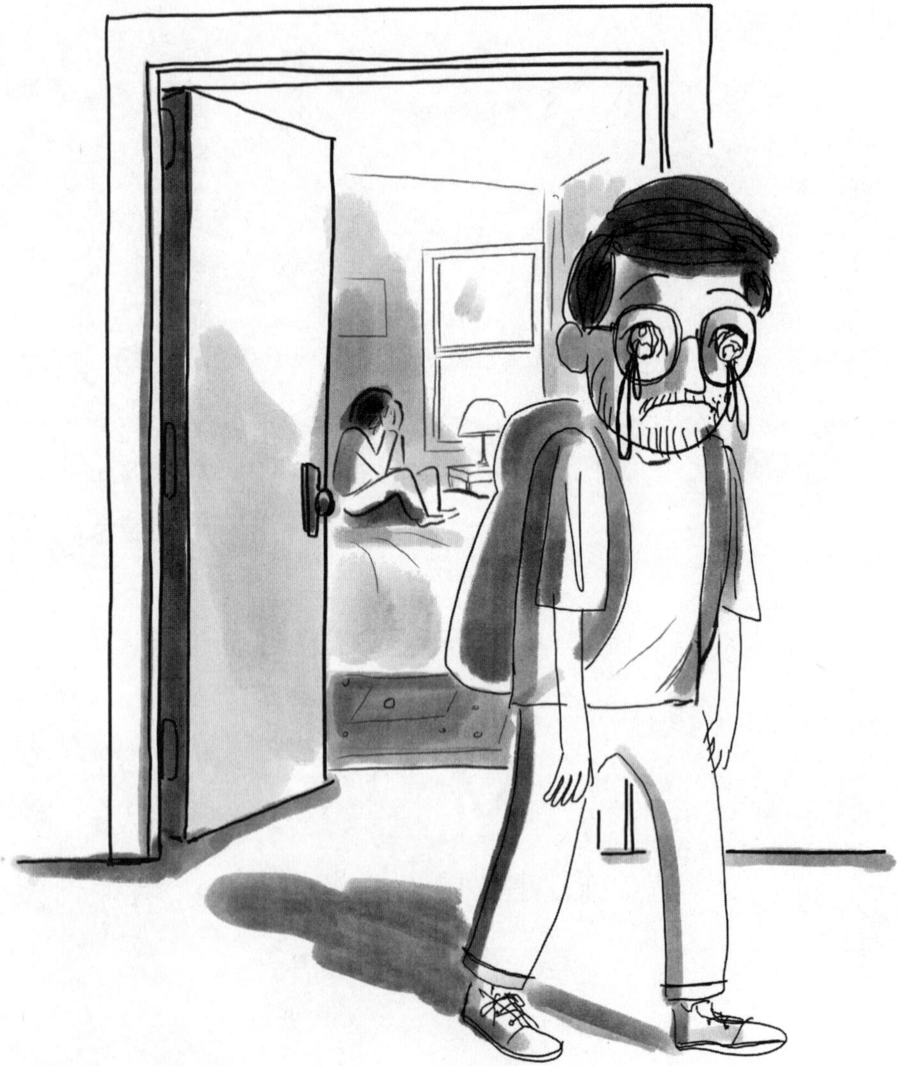

A year later, we see each other for a night in DC.

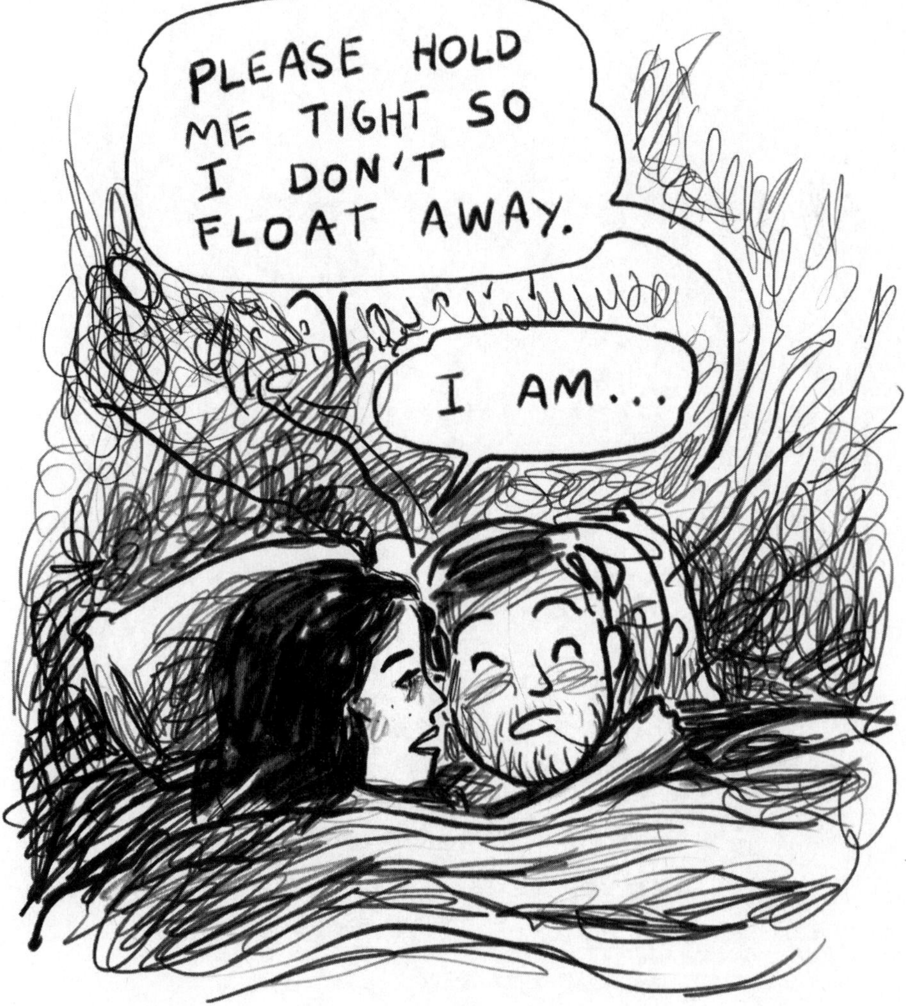
PLEASE HOLD ME TIGHT SO I DON'T FLOAT AWAY.
I AM...

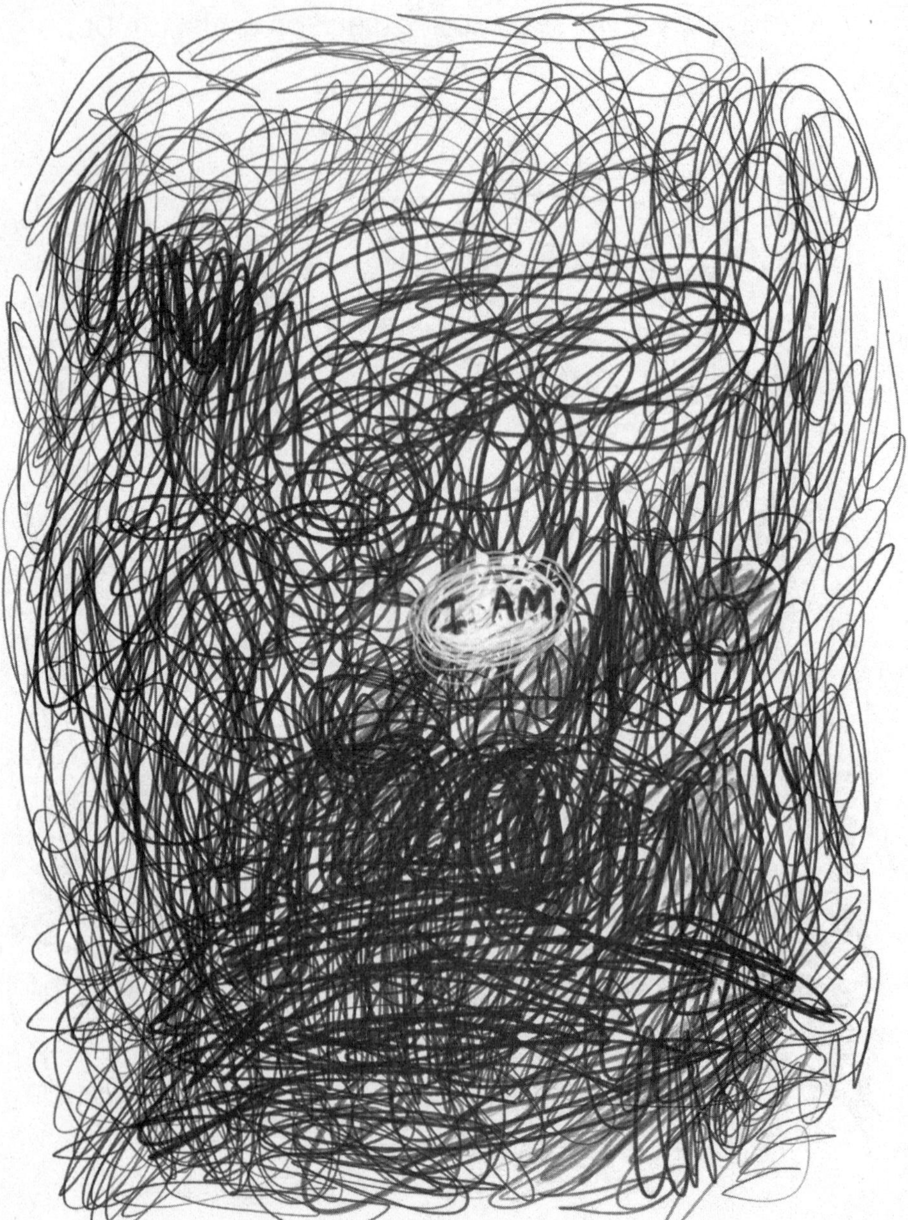
I AM.

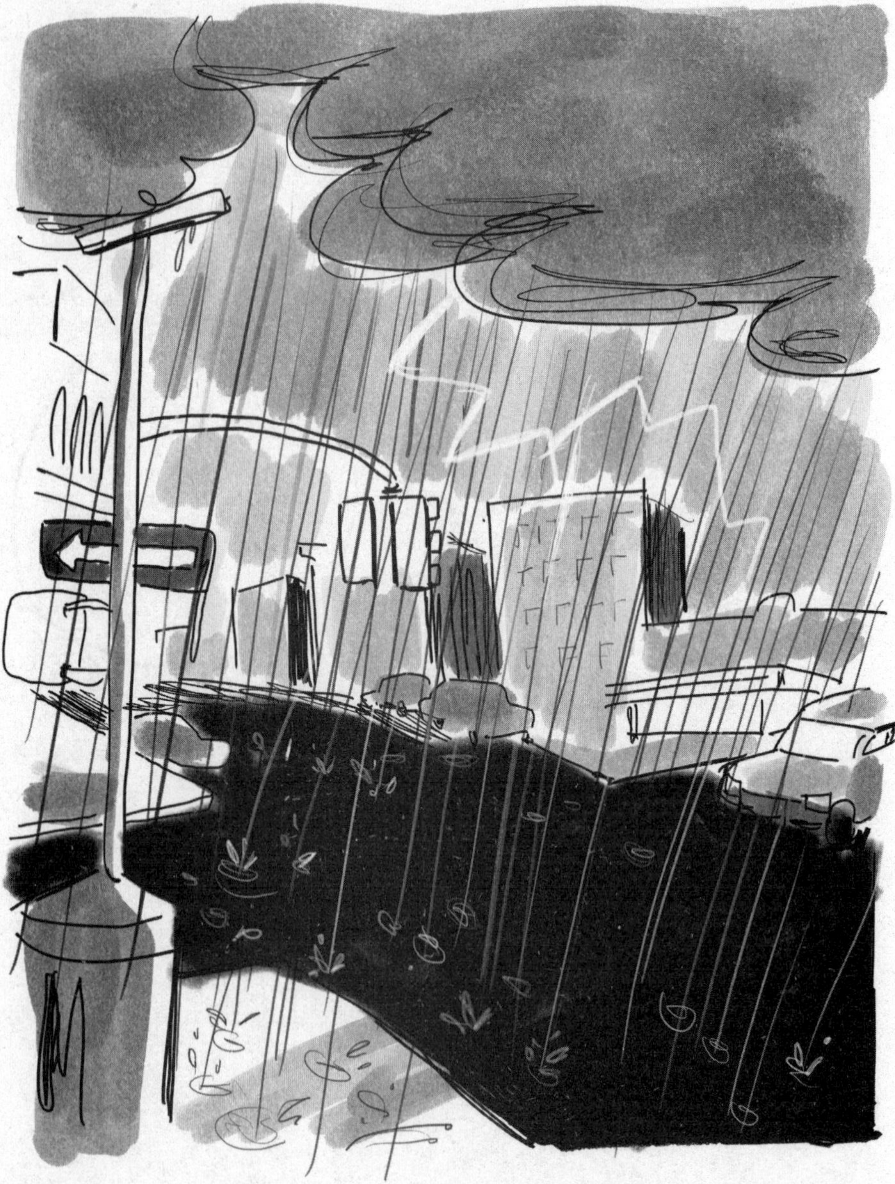

New York does its thing: a loud spring storm.

The next morning . . .

The kitten must have been afraid of the
thunder and run into our building.

The cat gets so flat under there,
and he won't come out.

I name him Stanley, after

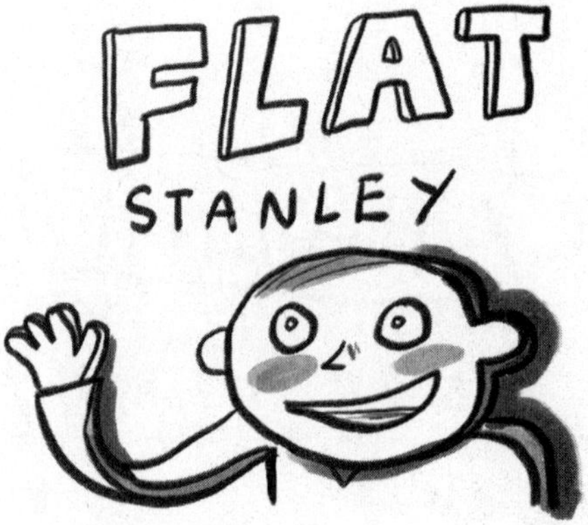
FLAT
STANLEY

He moves in.

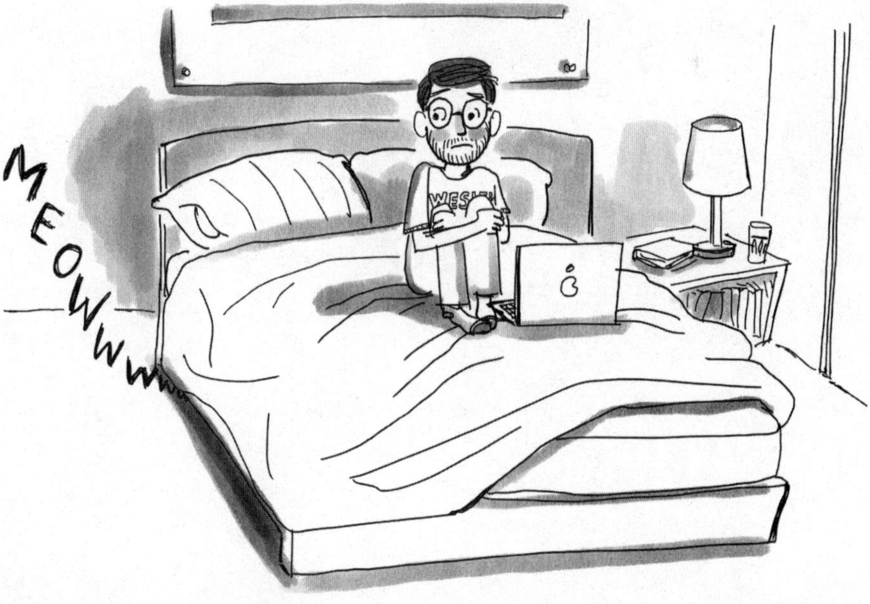
MEOWWWW

Stanley, it turns out, can't be left alone in my room.

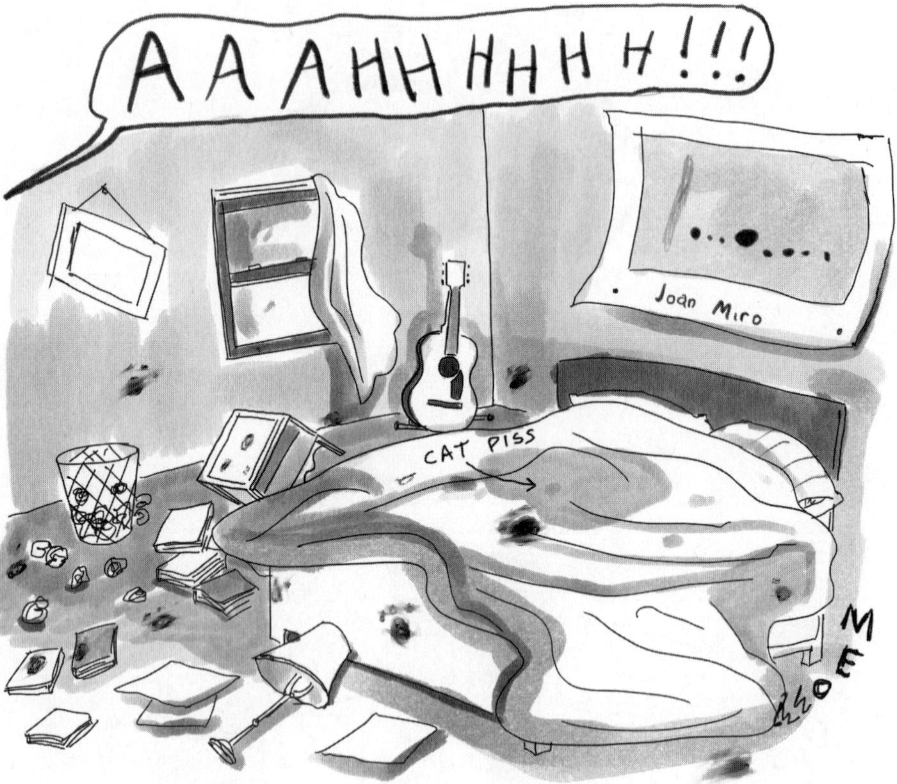
AAAHHHHHH!!!
Joan Miro
CAT PISS

My roommate finds me in our kitchen.

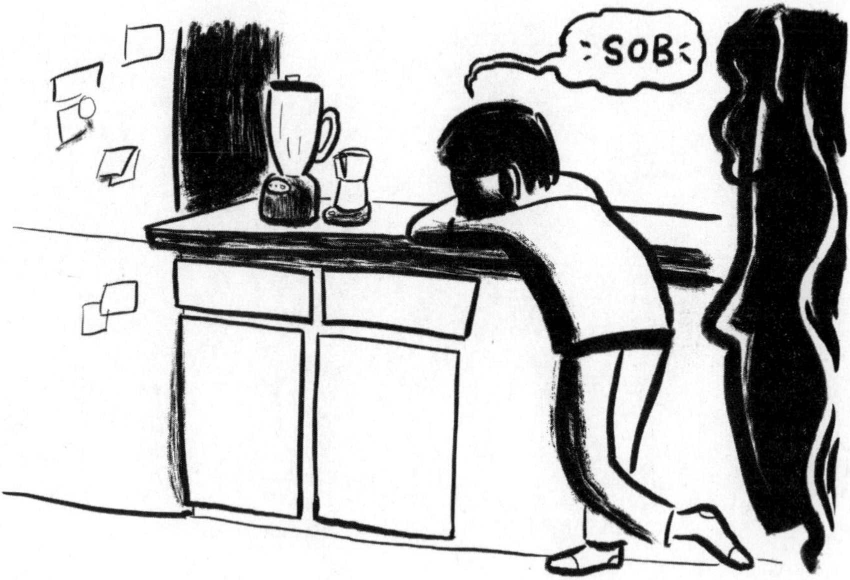
SOB

She helps me catch Stanley. By this I mean she catches Stanley while I hold the crate and curse.

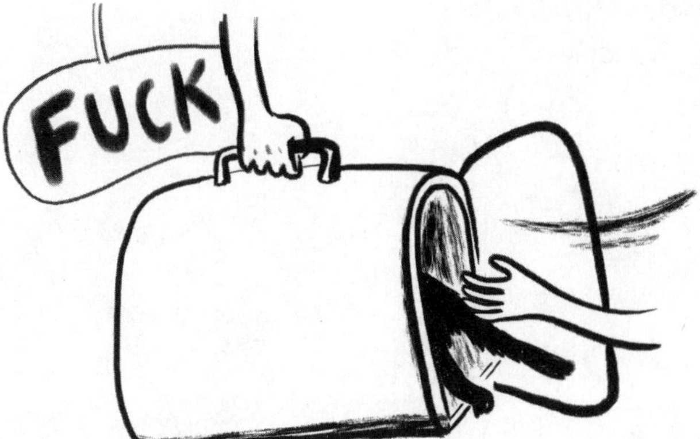
FUCK

I wait to see the vet.

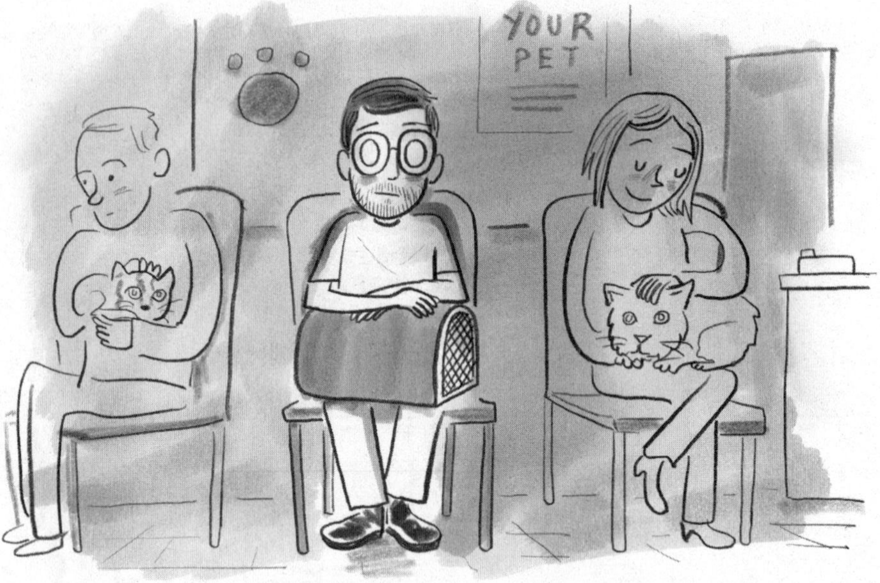
YOUR PET

I learn about my cat.

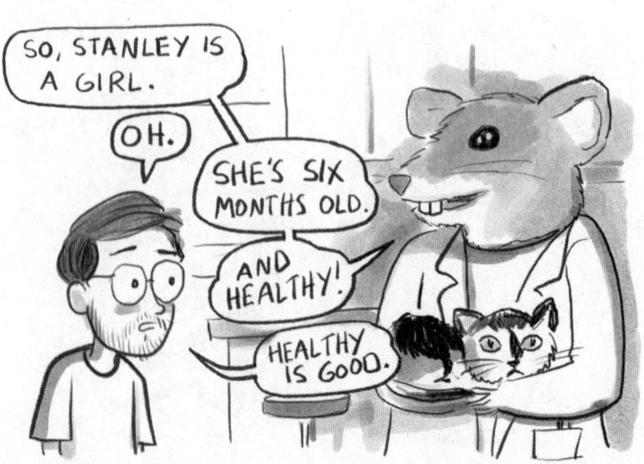
SO, STANLEY IS A GIRL.
OH.
SHE'S SIX MONTHS OLD.
AND HEALTHY!
HEALTHY IS GOOD.

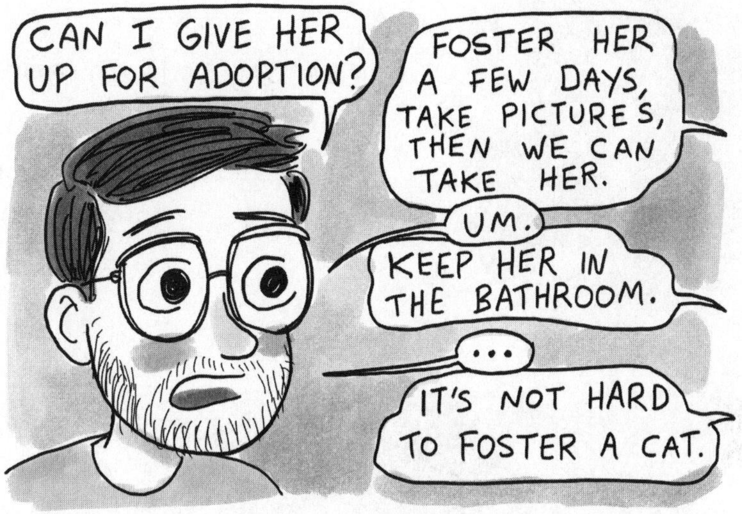
CAN I GIVE HER UP FOR ADOPTION?
FOSTER HER A FEW DAYS, TAKE PICTURES, THEN WE CAN TAKE HER.
UM.
KEEP HER IN THE BATHROOM.
...
IT'S NOT HARD TO FOSTER A CAT.

In television, the "Gilligan Cut" is when you cut from some proposition directly to the ironic resolution. I'll attempt the comics version now.

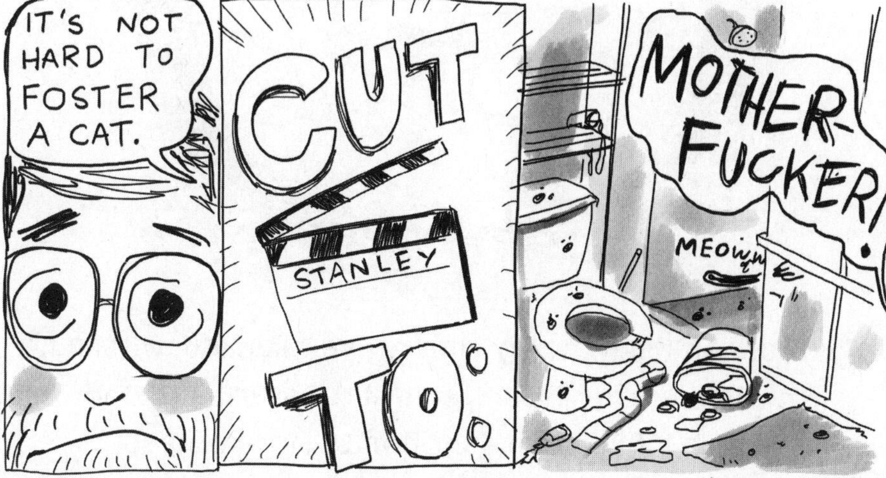
IT'S NOT HARD TO FOSTER A CAT.
CUT
STANLEY
TO:
MOTHER-FUCKER!
MEOWW

For as long as I can remember, I've dreaded some abstract terror that will destroy me.

I've held on tightly to my world. I've checked, washed, scrutinized, ruminated, sought reassurance, and avoided. I've been functional, more or less.

This kitten is my undoing.

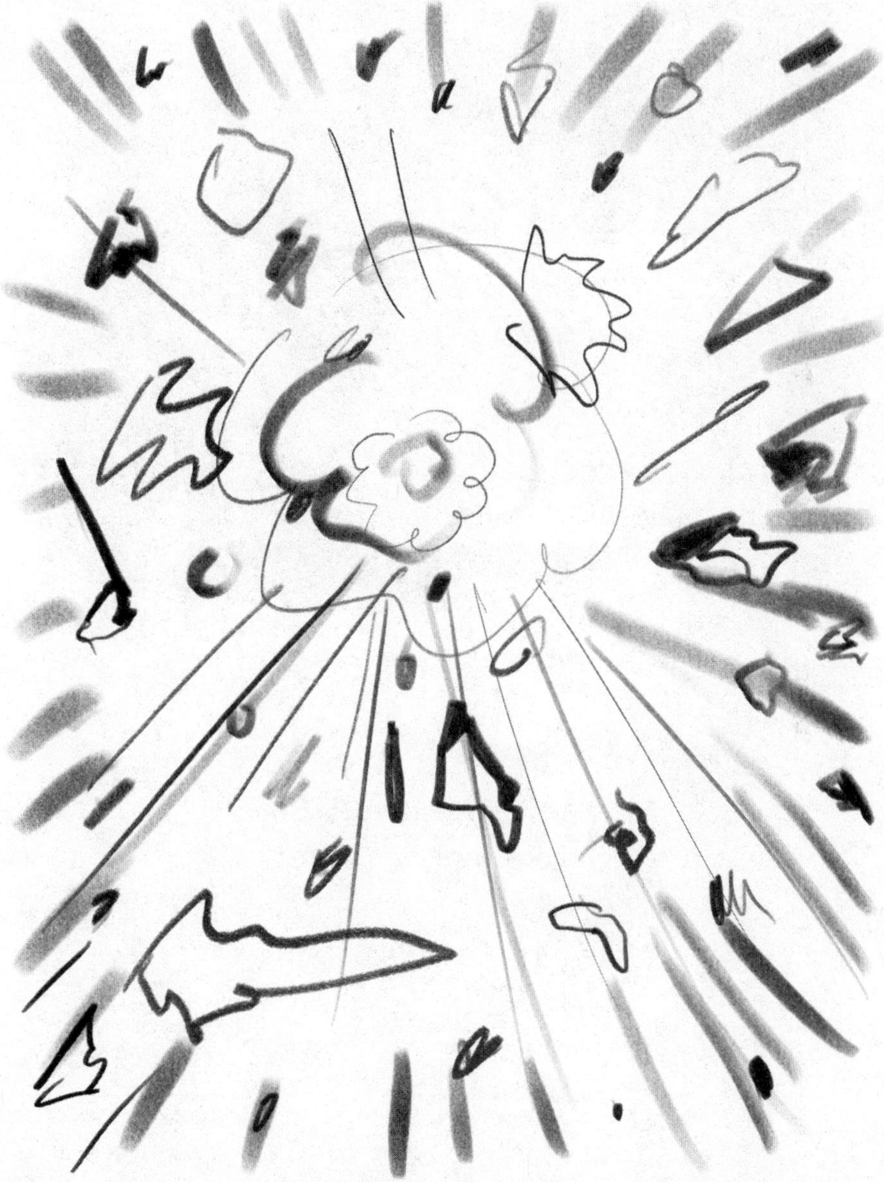

The next day, I take Stanley
to the adoption center.

The panic sticks around.

The L train is stopped somewhere between Bedford and First.

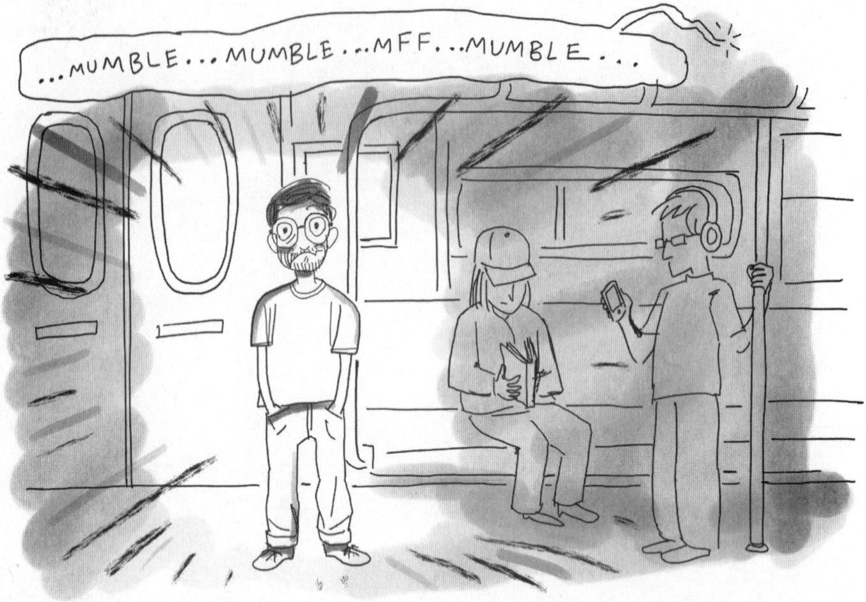
...MUMBLE...MUMBLE...MFF...MUMBLE...

I'm convinced this is how I die.

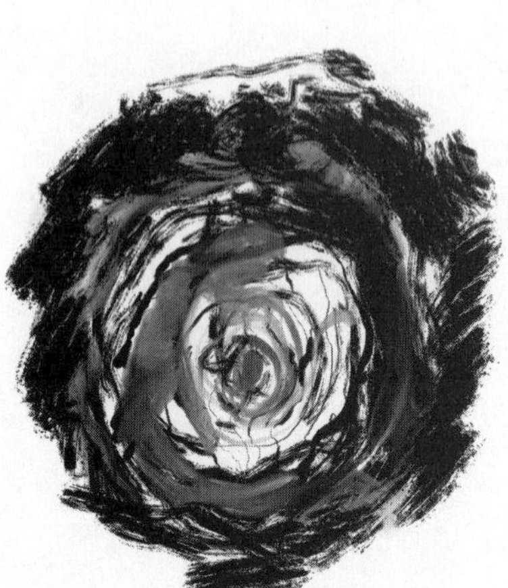

Or, not die, exactly. It's more like a feeling that some unnameable, terrible thing is going to happen, and I can't exist after it happens. It's not exactly death and it's not exactly pain, because those are nightmares that I can understand. It's somewhere inside me threatening to come out.

At first I only get this feeling in spaces
that are crowded, or dark, or loud.

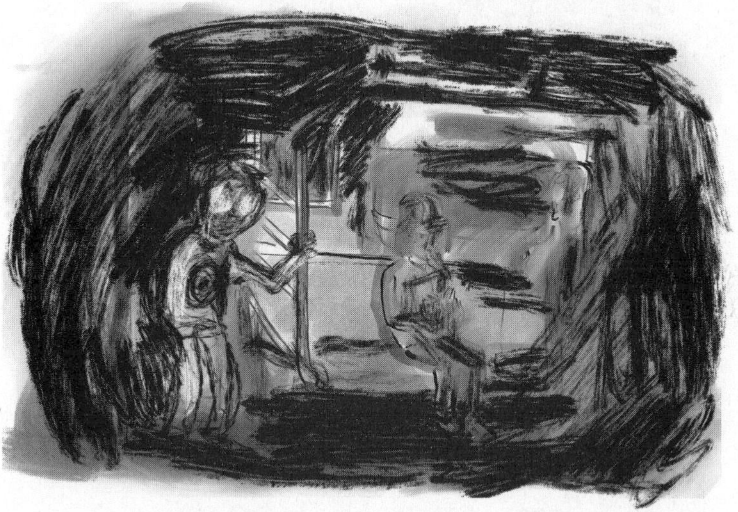

Then the panic attacks start happening more frequently.
I stop being able to predict where or why they'll happen.

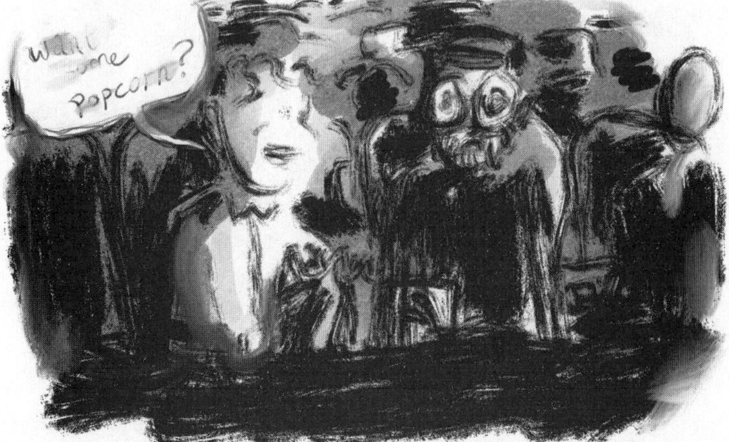
popcorn?

I'm visited even in the places I've always felt most safe.

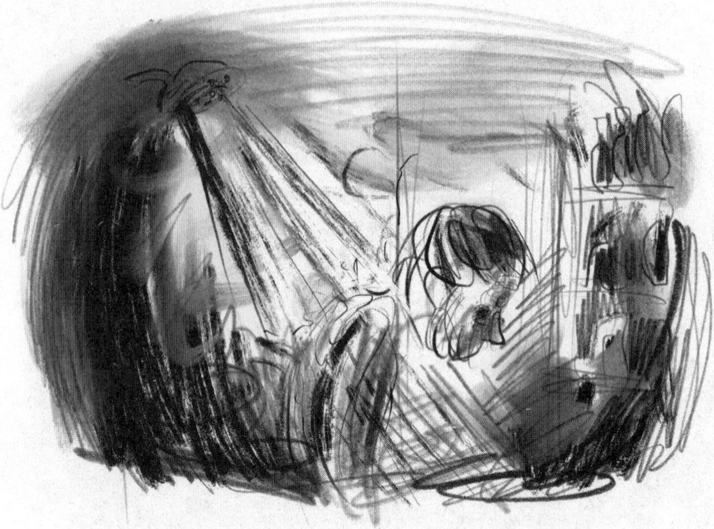

I rely heavily on my friends.

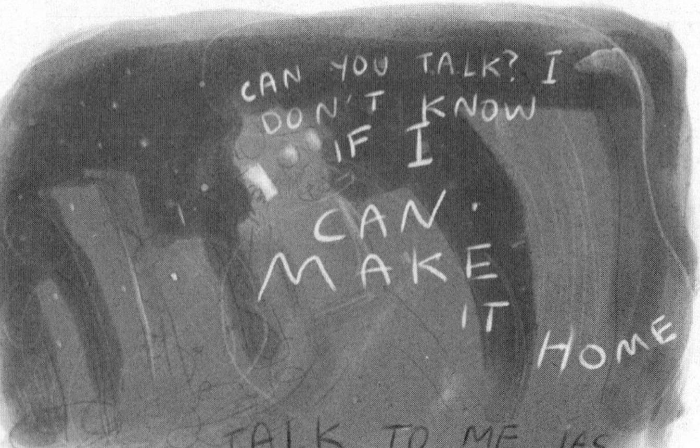
CAN YOU TALK? I DON'T KNOW IF I CAN MAKE IT HOME
TALK TO ME, JAS

My friends do their best.

Until:

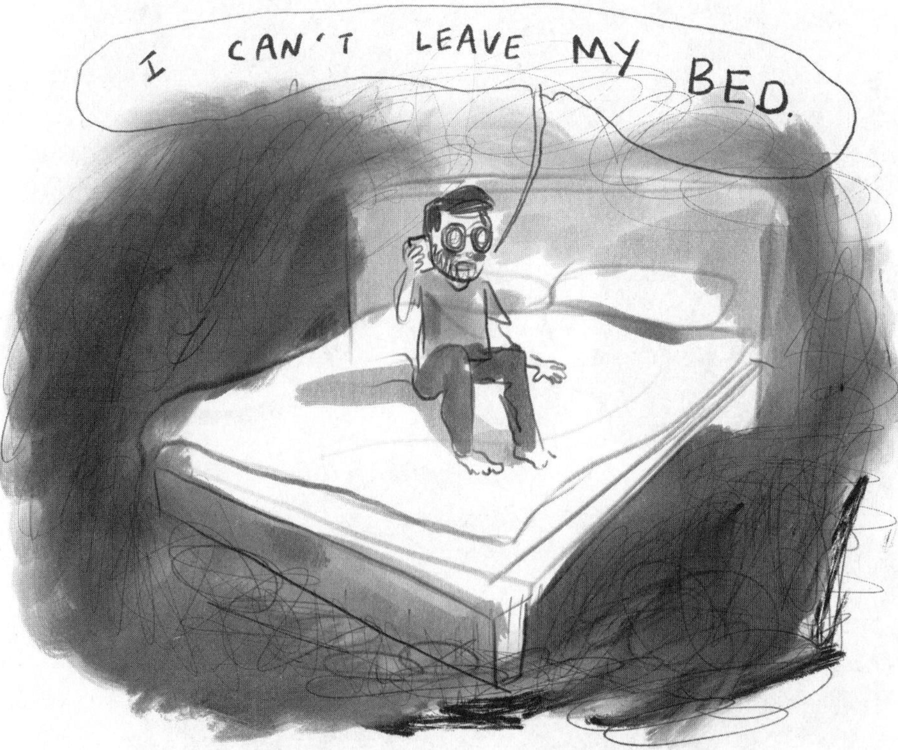
I CAN'T LEAVE MY BED.

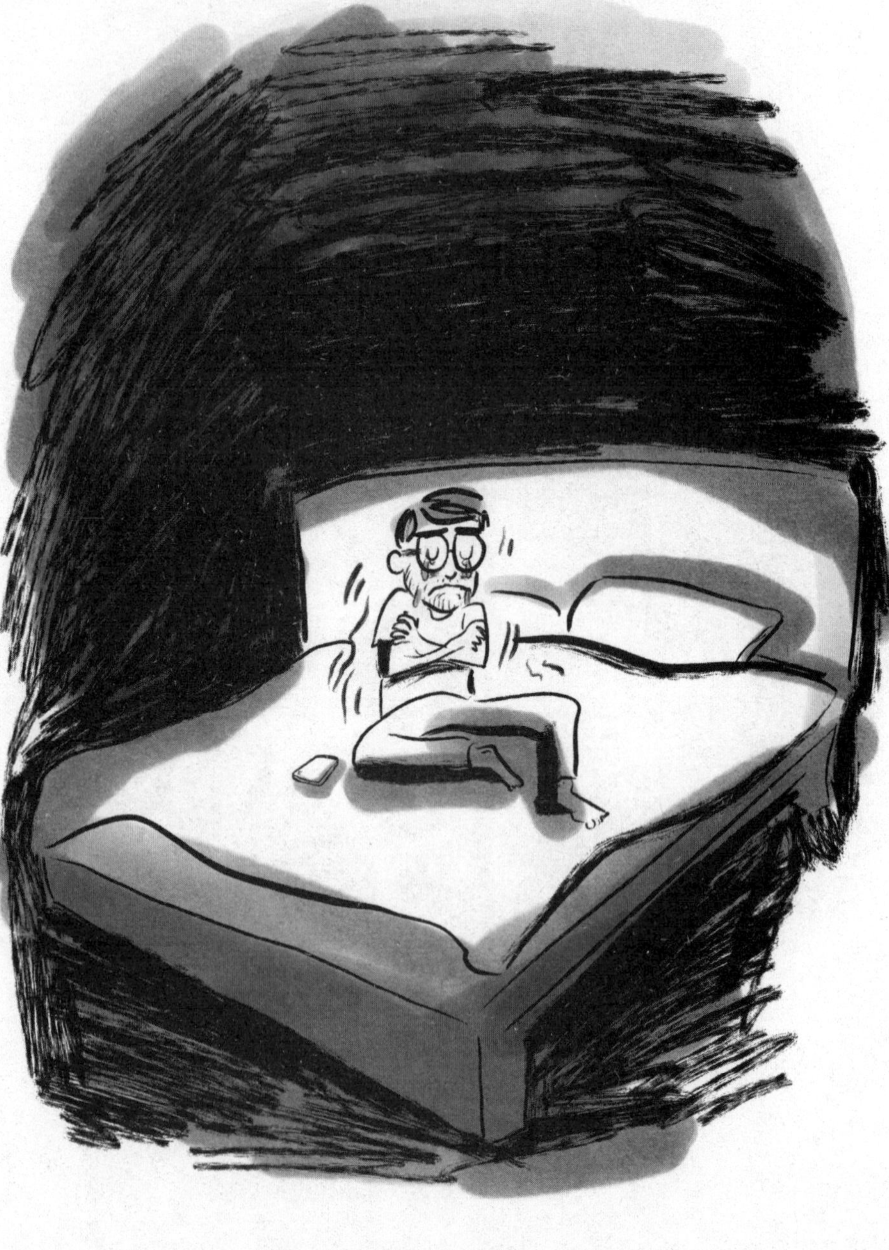

One of the most successful strategies for treating OCD is a form of cognitive behavioral therapy called Exposure and Response Prevention, or E.R.P.

E.R.P. is something I've been told to do since I was sixteen. Every therapist I've seen has recommended it, along with medication.

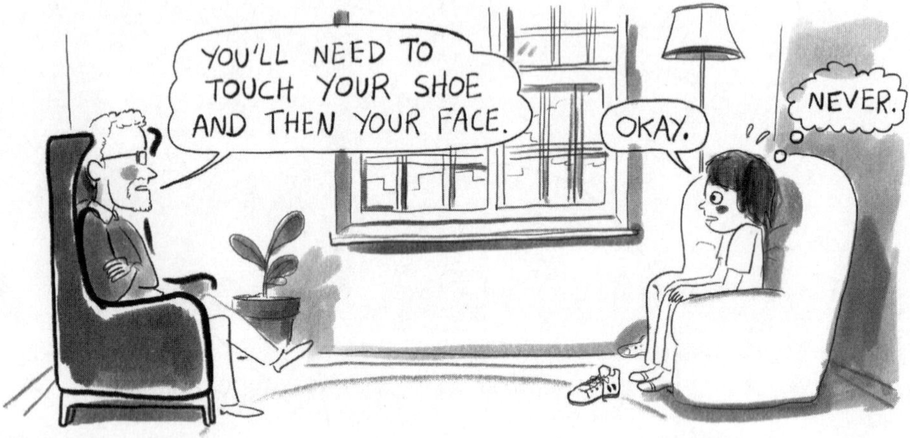
YOU'LL NEED TO TOUCH YOUR SHOE AND THEN YOUR FACE.
OKAY.
NEVER.

The problem, of course, is that E.R.P. sucks ass. I have to face all of my fears in increasing intensity seven to ten times a day.

I keep putting this off, but now I can't get out of bed without having a panic attack.

This feels like rock bottom.

And things look different when I've hit rock bottom.

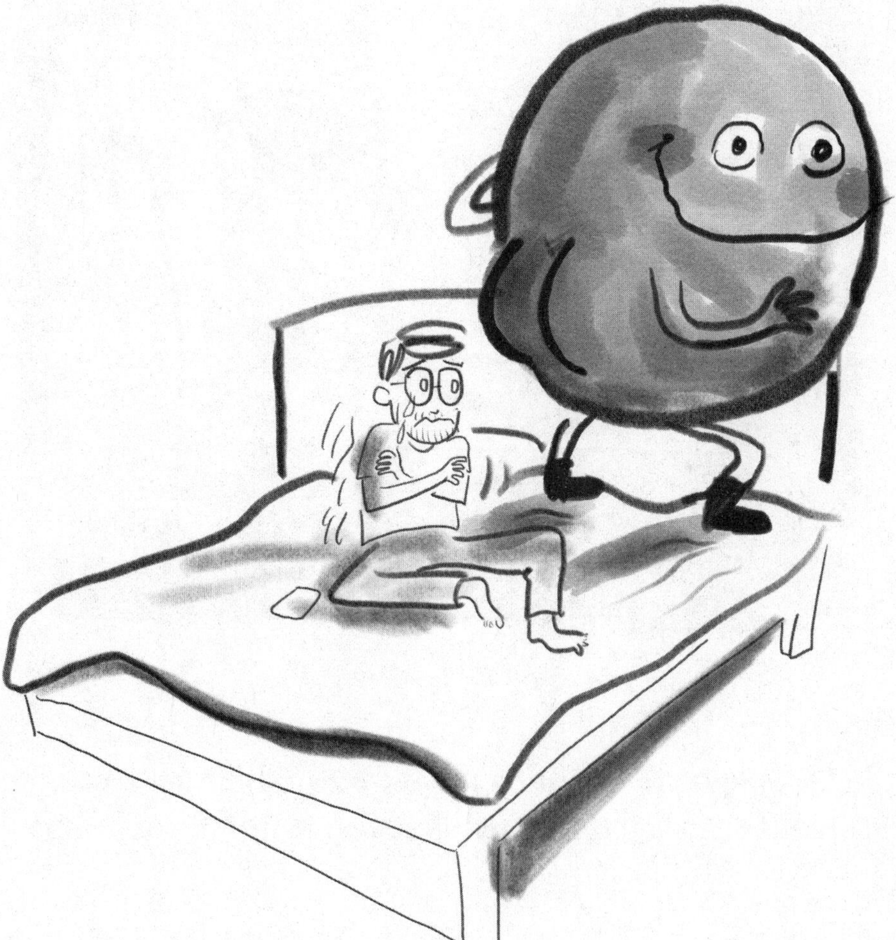

Behold, my "contaminated" shoe.

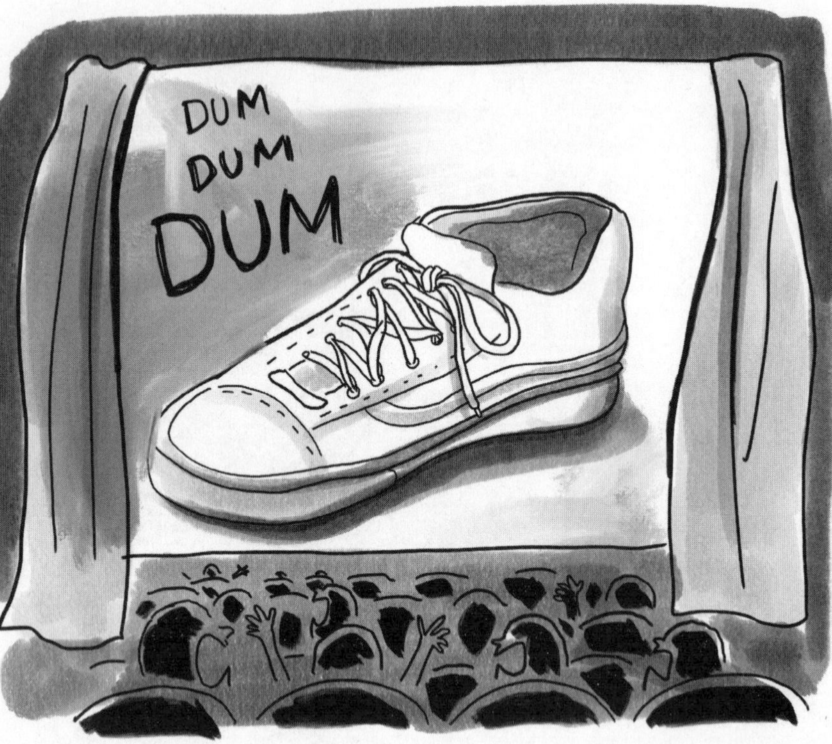
DUM
DUM
DUM

I'm supposed to touch my shoe and then my face, without washing afterward, seven to ten times a day.

It's supposed to feel terrible, to set off an alarm in my brain.

THINK ABOUT EVERYTHING YOUR SHOES HAVE STEPPED ON IN THIS CITY!

THAT'S WHAT YOU'RE TOUCHING!

As I keep touching my shoe and then my face, the sound of the alarm should grow fainter. I'm teaching my brain that what feels like an emergency isn't actually one.

I can't make the thoughts stop, but I can take away their legitimacy.

First, I summon the thought on purpose.

EXPOSURE

I want to perform my compulsion. It feels like I need to perform my compulsion to remain safe. I refuse to do it.

FEEL LIKE...
I SHOULD RUN...

RESPONSE PREVENTION

I do this over and over again, teaching my brain that what feels threatening doesn't hurt.

Until, eventually...

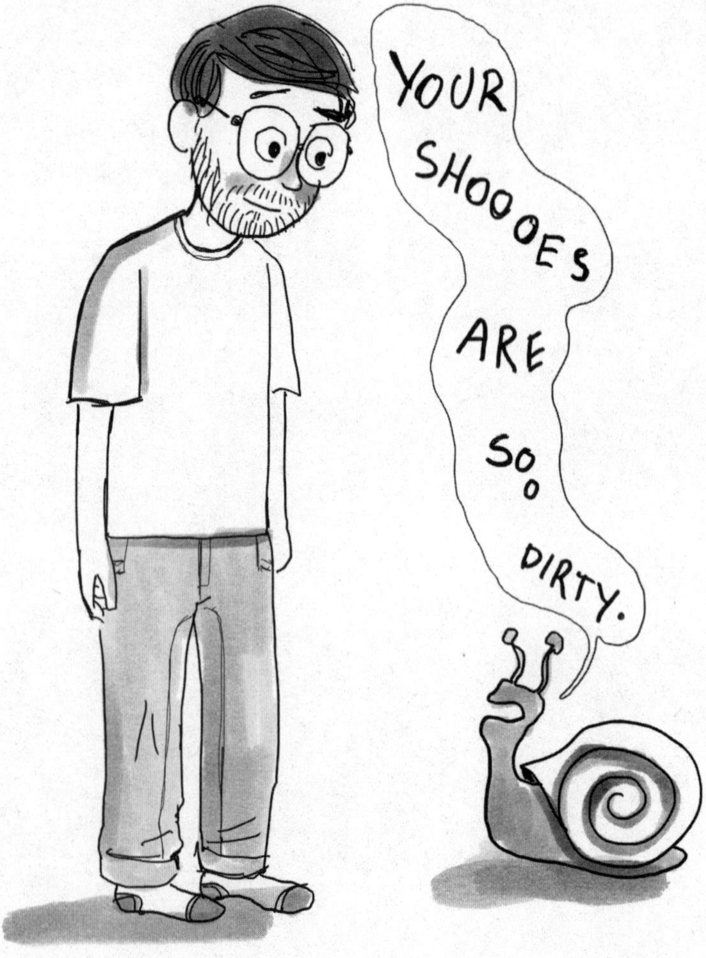
YOUR SHOOOOES ARE SOoo DIRTY.

OCD patients make a hierarchy of their
fears, from least to most intense.

1. NO MORE BALL
2. THUNDER SOUNDS
3. CAR SOUNDS
4. OTHER SOUNDS

When an E.R.P. exercise begins to feel more manageable,
I move on to the next item on my hierarchy.

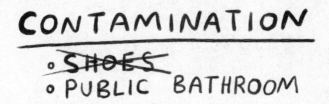

CONTAMINATION
- ~~SHOES~~
- PUBLIC BATHROOM

I'm encouraged to get creative with exposures.

My guilty obsessions are all ways I may have hurt or angered someone, or the potential dire consequences of something I've done.

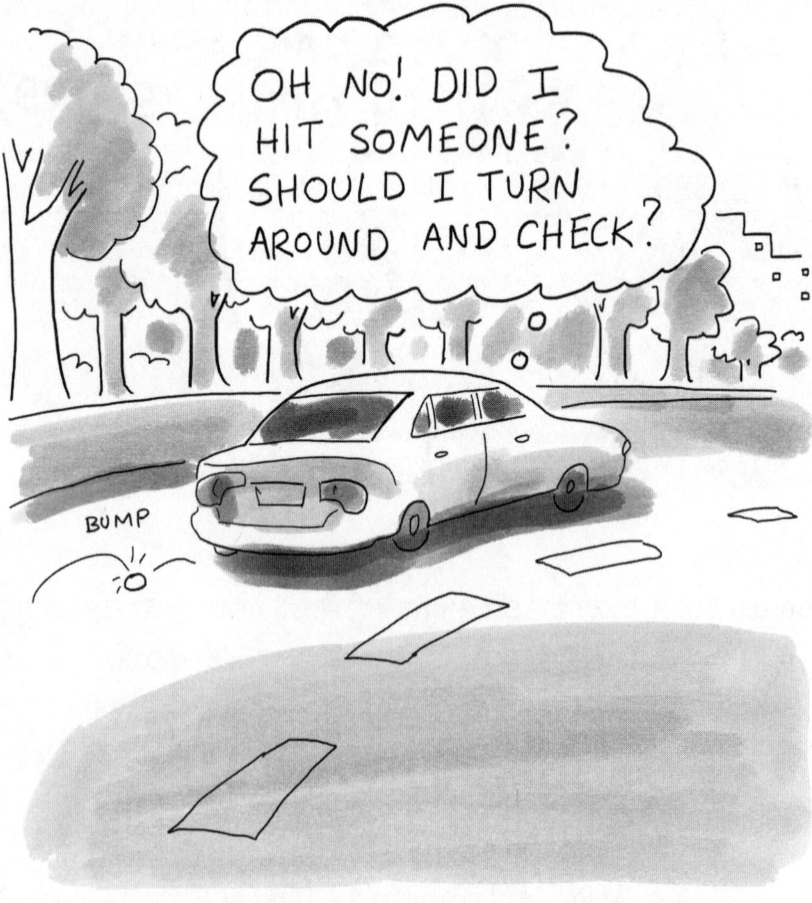
OH NO! DID I HIT SOMEONE? SHOULD I TURN AROUND AND CHECK?
BUMP

A small bump in the road becomes a corpse.

I'm supposed to rewrite the scene and amp up the drama. Sometimes, if I make it ridiculous enough, it stops haunting me.

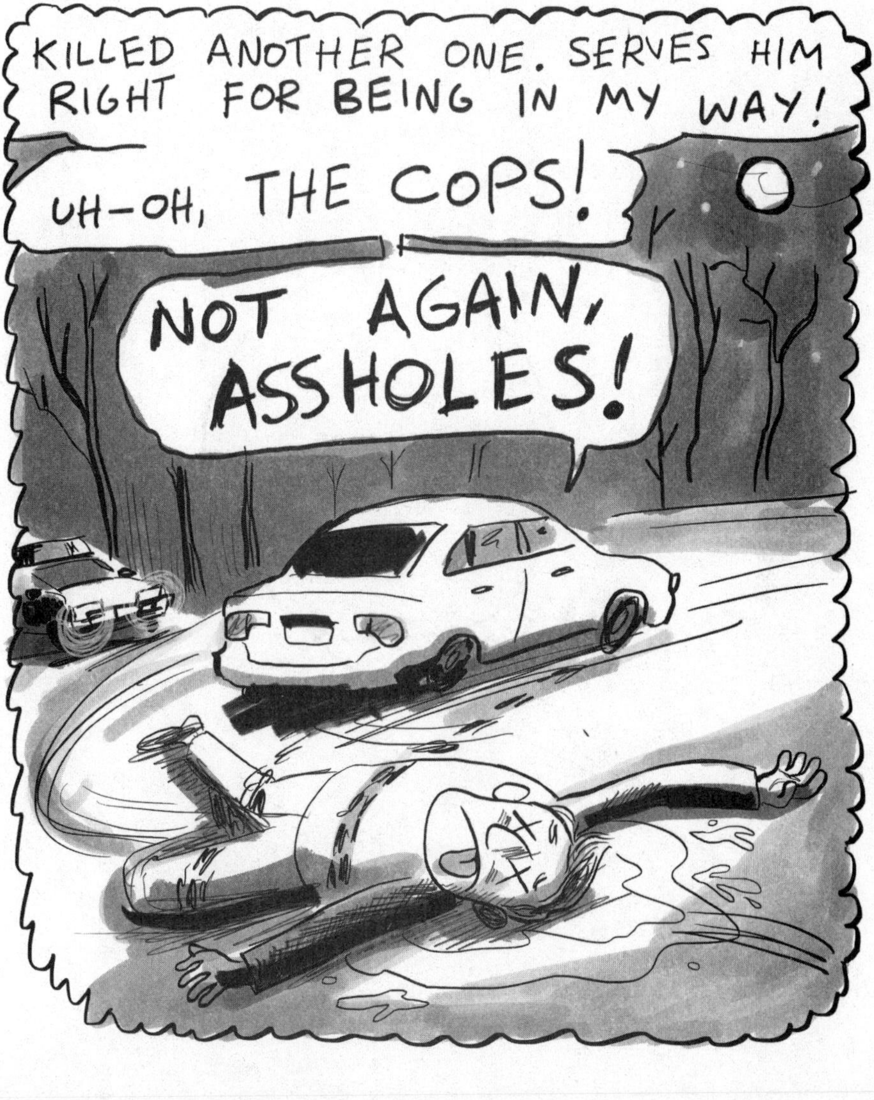
KILLED ANOTHER ONE. SERVES HIM RIGHT FOR BEING IN MY WAY!
UH-OH, THE COPS!
NOT AGAIN, ASSHOLES!

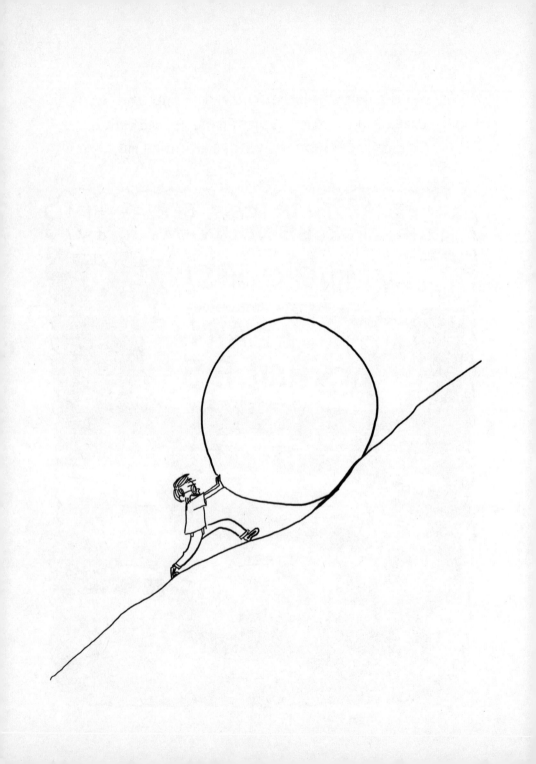

Another treatment strategy is meds. I see a psychiatrist.

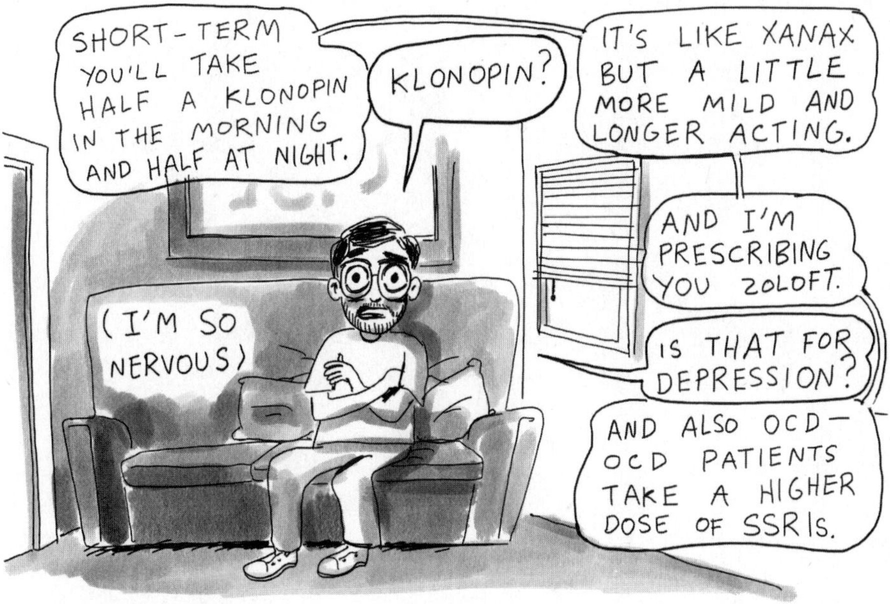
SHORT-TERM YOU'LL TAKE HALF A KLONOPIN IN THE MORNING AND HALF AT NIGHT.
KLONOPIN?
IT'S LIKE XANAX BUT A LITTLE MORE MILD AND LONGER ACTING.
AND I'M PRESCRIBING YOU ZOLOFT.
(I'M SO NERVOUS)
IS THAT FOR DEPRESSION?
AND ALSO OCD— OCD PATIENTS TAKE A HIGHER DOSE OF SSRIs.

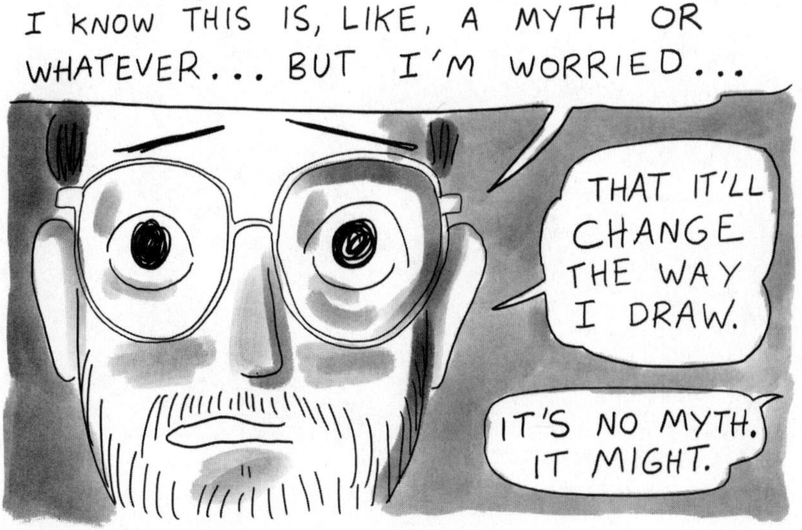
I KNOW THIS IS, LIKE, A MYTH OR WHATEVER... BUT I'M WORRIED...
THAT IT'LL CHANGE THE WAY I DRAW.
IT'S NO MYTH. IT MIGHT.

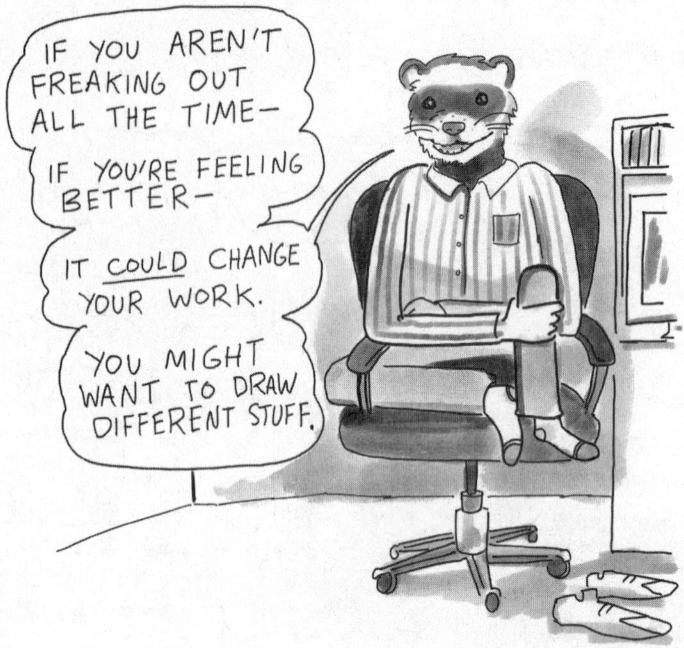
IF YOU AREN'T FREAKING OUT ALL THE TIME—
IF YOU'RE FEELING BETTER—
IT COULD CHANGE YOUR WORK.
YOU MIGHT WANT TO DRAW DIFFERENT STUFF.

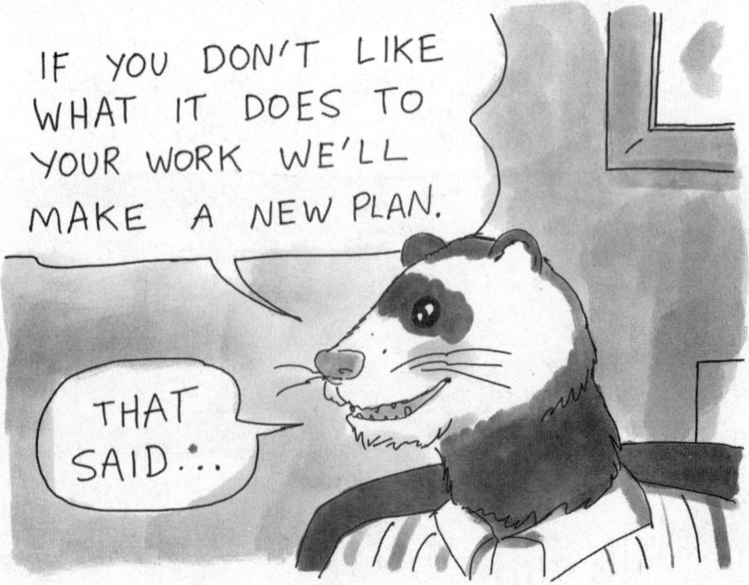
IF YOU DON'T LIKE WHAT IT DOES TO YOUR WORK WE'LL MAKE A NEW PLAN.
THAT SAID...

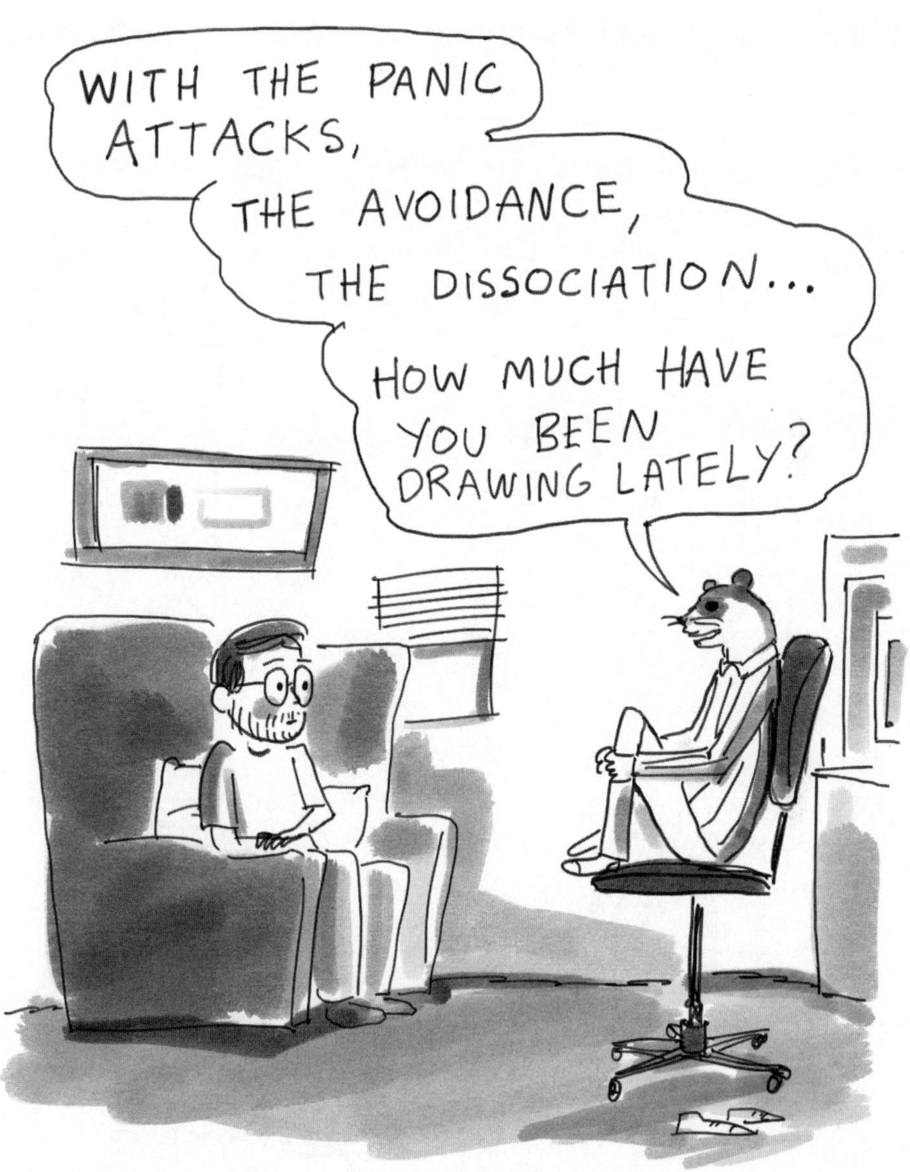
WITH THE PANIC ATTACKS,
THE AVOIDANCE,
THE DISSOCIATION...
HOW MUCH HAVE YOU BEEN DRAWING LATELY?

I worry that I'll stop feeling like myself. Whatever that means.

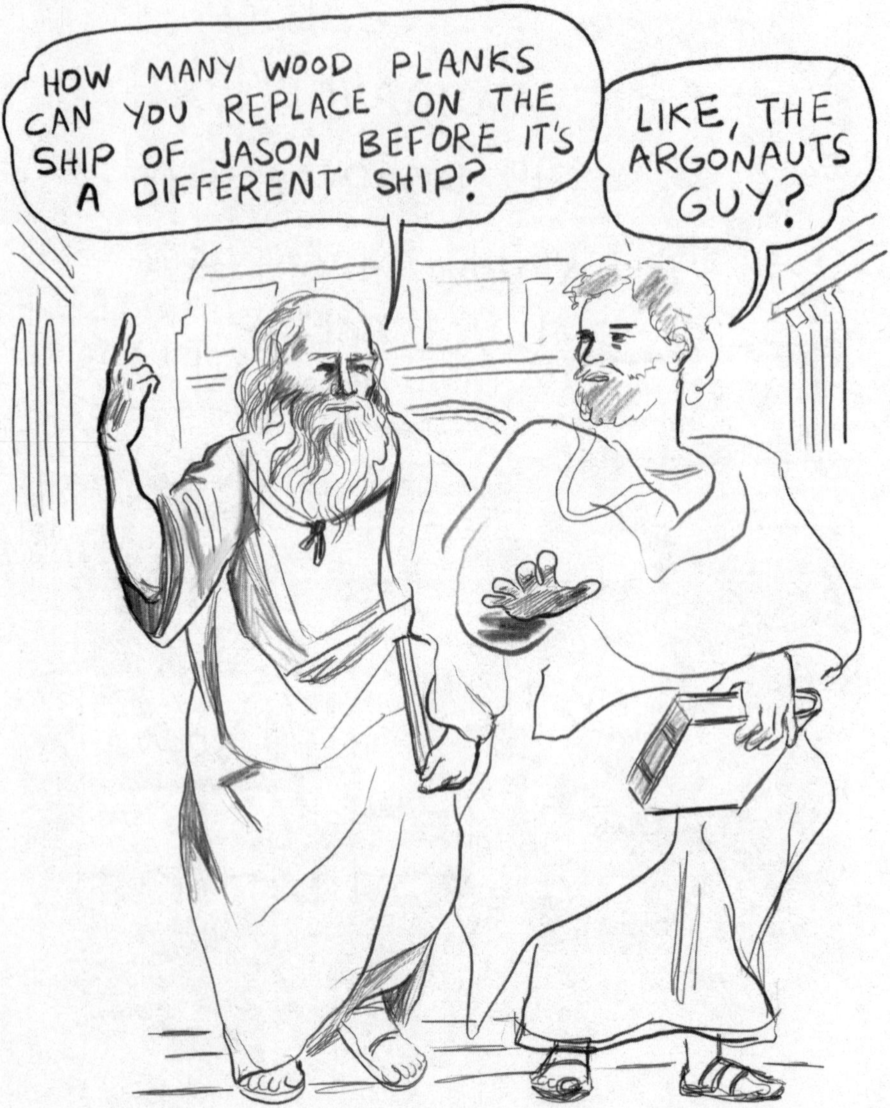
HOW MANY WOOD PLANKS CAN YOU REPLACE ON THE SHIP OF JASON BEFORE IT'S A DIFFERENT SHIP?
LIKE, THE ARGONAUTS GUY?

I have to admit that my anxiety and sadness often come with a feeling of superiority. If you're not as sad as me, you must not be paying attention.

This feeling has been reinforced by fifty percent of all movies ever made.

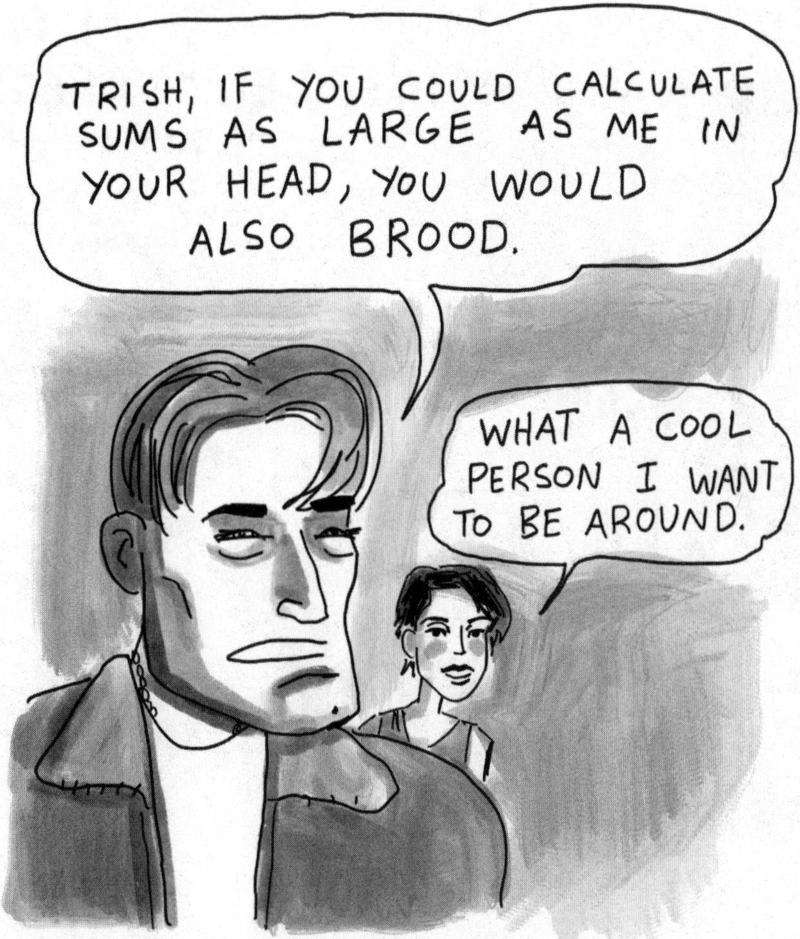
TRISH, IF YOU COULD CALCULATE SUMS AS LARGE AS ME IN YOUR HEAD, YOU WOULD ALSO BROOD.
WHAT A COOL PERSON I WANT TO BE AROUND.

And aren't my anxiety and sadness what make my work interesting? What make ME interesting? This is what the other fifty percent of movies has taught me.

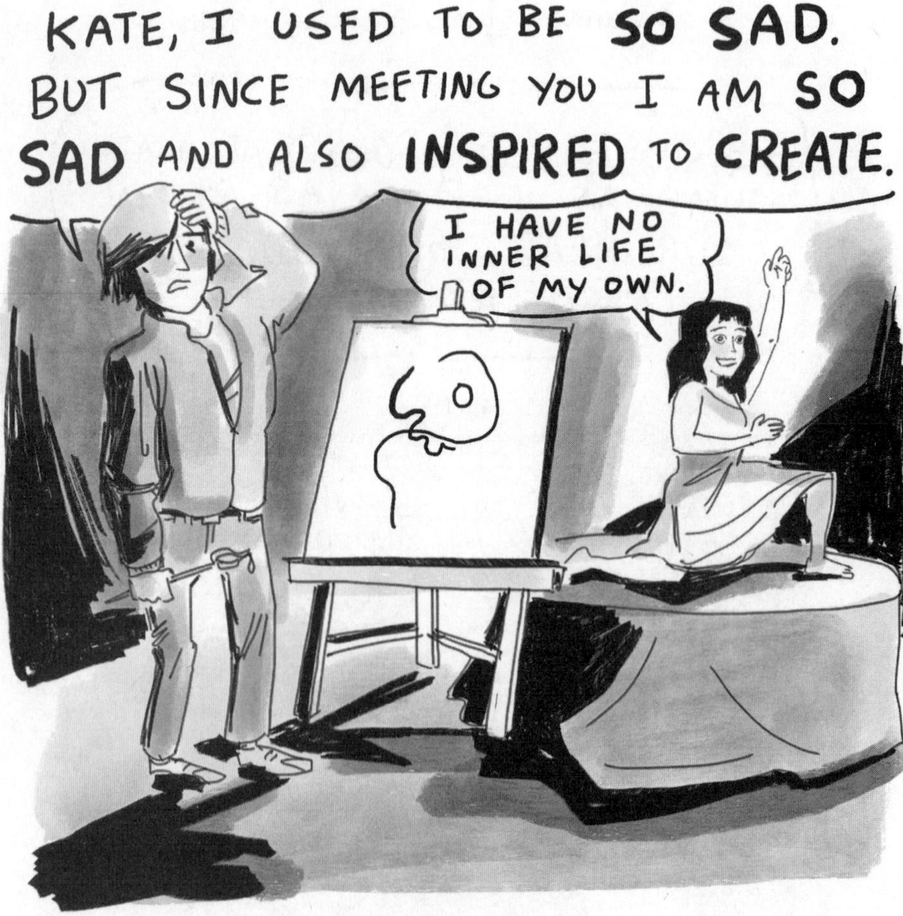
KATE, I USED TO BE **SO SAD.** BUT SINCE MEETING YOU I AM **SO SAD** AND ALSO **INSPIRED** TO **CREATE.**
I HAVE NO INNER LIFE OF MY OWN.

This pain is romantic. It's evidence of my heightened sensibility to the truth of things, and it's my job to show the world that truth.

These kinds of thoughts are insidious and persuasive, and the argument of all four versions of *A Star Is Born*. I know I shouldn't believe them, but part of me does.

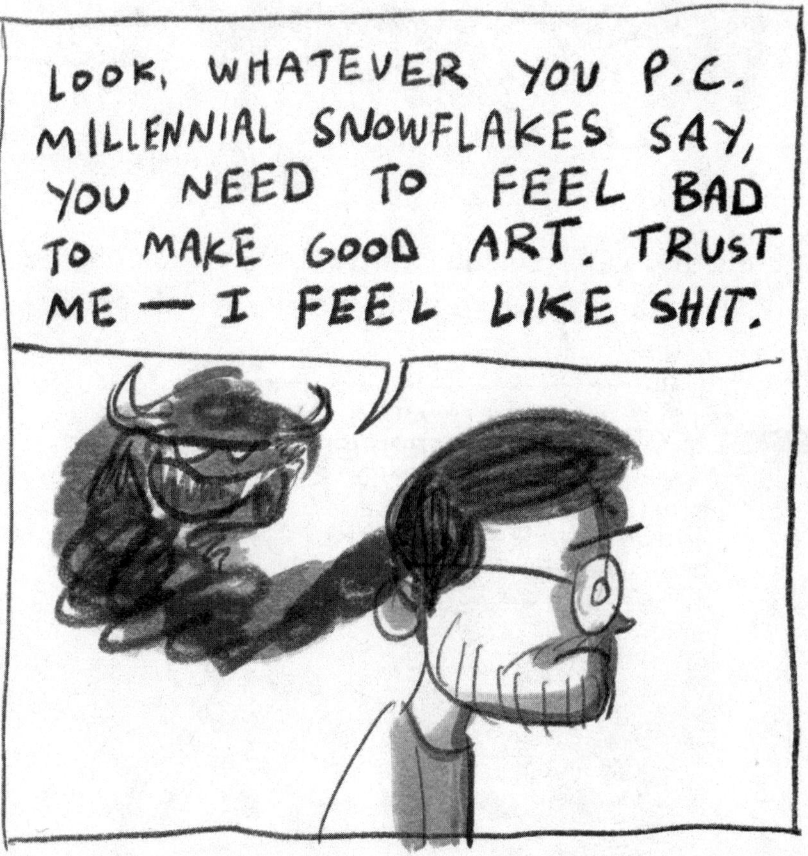
LOOK, WHATEVER YOU P.C. MILLENNIAL SNOWFLAKES SAY, YOU NEED TO FEEL BAD TO MAKE GOOD ART. TRUST ME — I FEEL LIKE SHIT.

A common refrain in OCD therapy is, "It's not me — it's my OCD." Another is, "I am not my brain."

It's a framework I've always had trouble accepting.

BUT... YOU'RE ALL JUST ME IN BAD DISGUISES.

I understand why I should isolate and unmask obsessive thoughts. It does take away some of their power.

JOKE YOU TOLD AT A PARTY THAT YOU'RE TERRIFIED WAS IN BAD TASTE AND KEEP RUMINATING ABOUT, LET'S SEE WHO YOU **REALLY** ARE.

But I've always identified so reflexively with my creativity. I am a cartoonist. It's an identity I have trouble extricating from my anxiety. I am an anxious cartoonist.

One tactic I've learned in therapy is to call my distressing thoughts a product of my "creative brain."

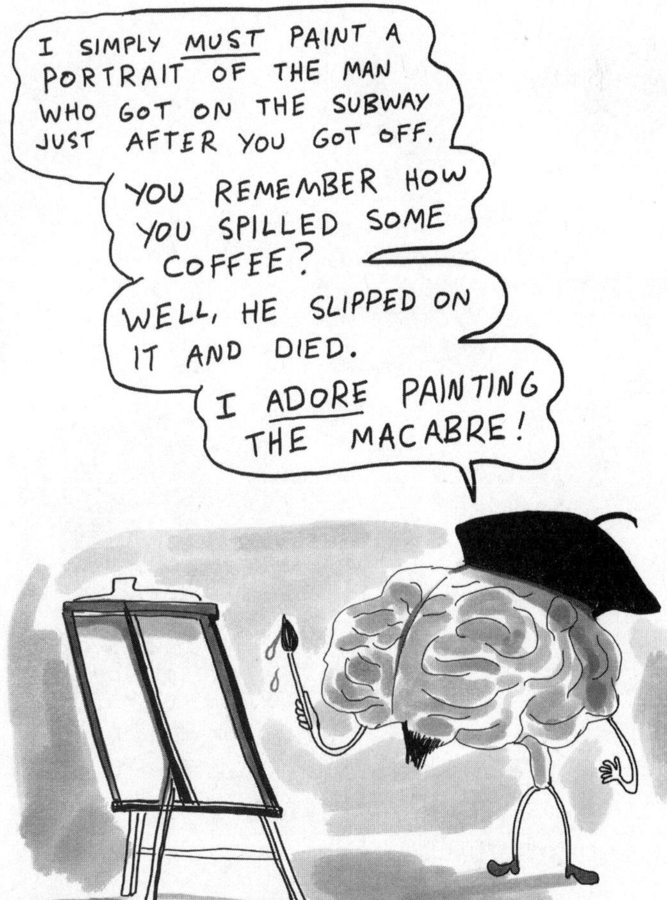
I SIMPLY MUST PAINT A PORTRAIT OF THE MAN WHO GOT ON THE SUBWAY JUST AFTER YOU GOT OFF.
YOU REMEMBER HOW YOU SPILLED SOME COFFEE?
WELL, HE SLIPPED ON IT AND DIED.
I ADORE PAINTING THE MACABRE!

My temptation is to see my anxiety as the catalyzing force for my creativity.

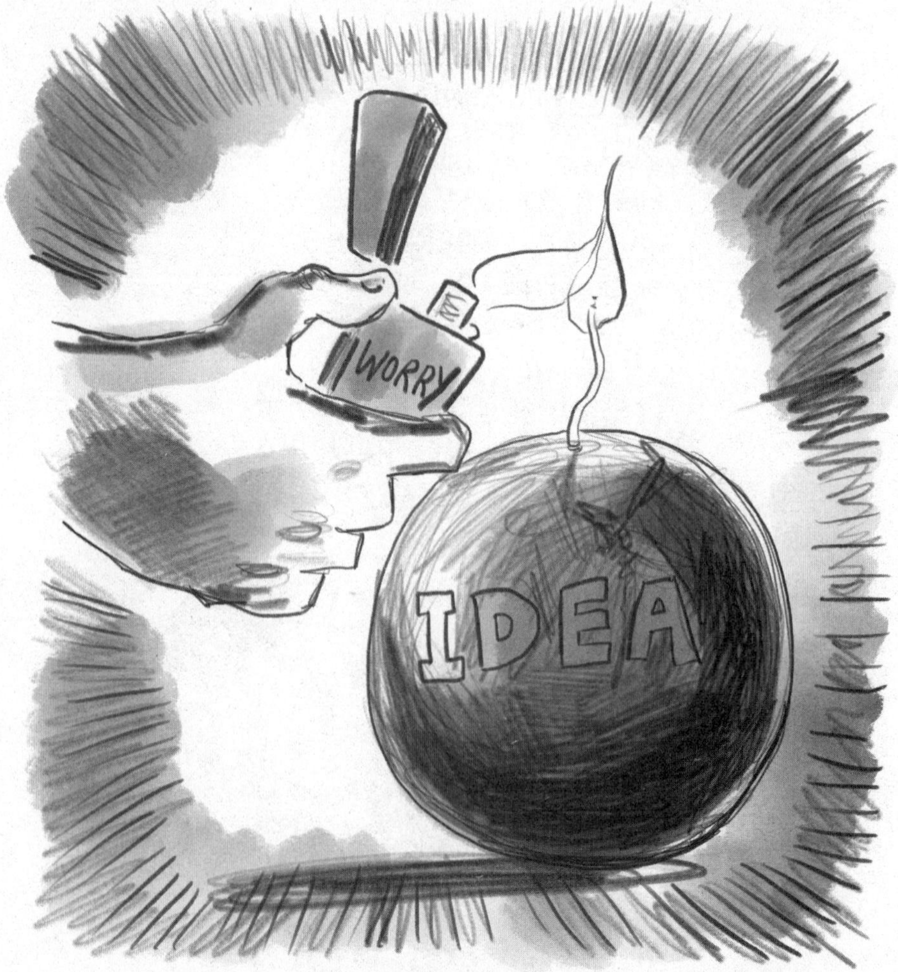
WORRY
IDEA

One throwaway thought sends me on a journey
through increasingly tenuous associations.
I discover new things to fear.

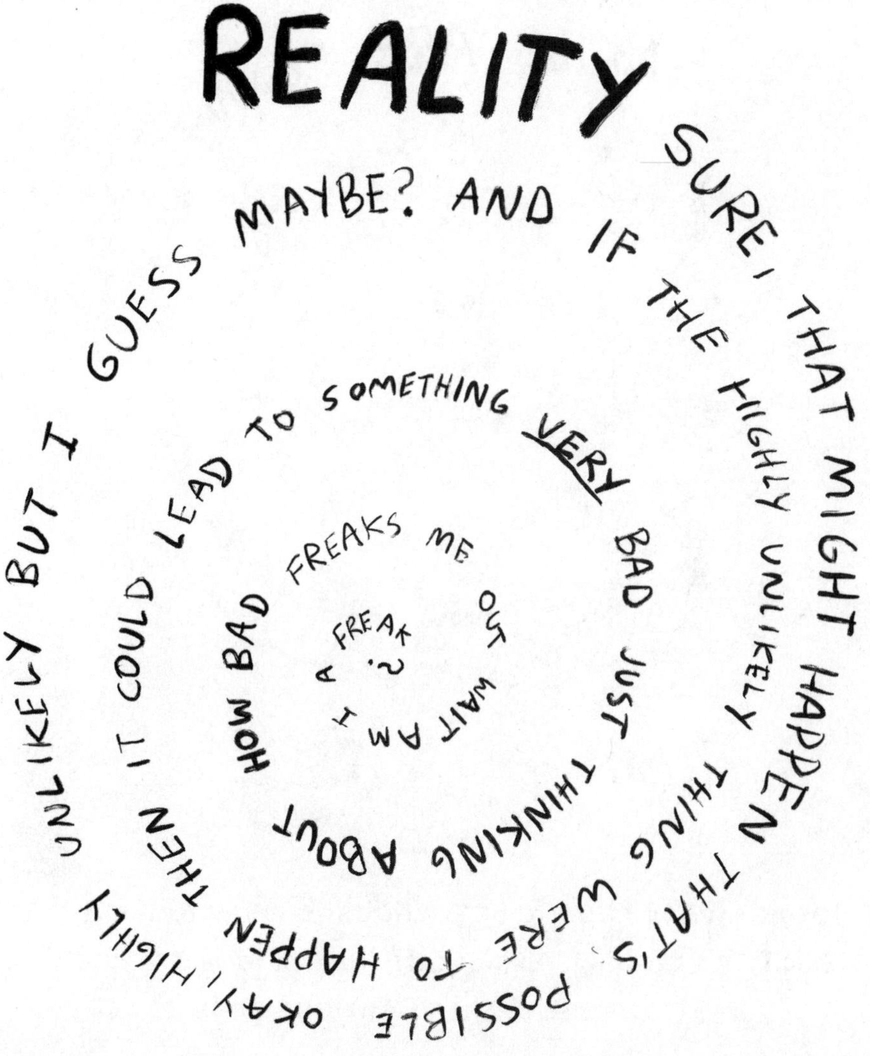
REALITY
SURE, THAT MIGHT HAPPEN THAT'S POSSIBLE OKAY, HIGHLY UNLIKELY BUT I GUESS MAYBE? AND IF THE HIGHLY UNLIKELY THING WERE TO HAPPEN THEN IT COULD LEAD TO SOMETHING VERY BAD JUST THINKING ABOUT HOW BAD FREAKS ME OUT WAIT AM I A FREAK?

This series of increasingly tenuous associations is also how I come up with cartoons.

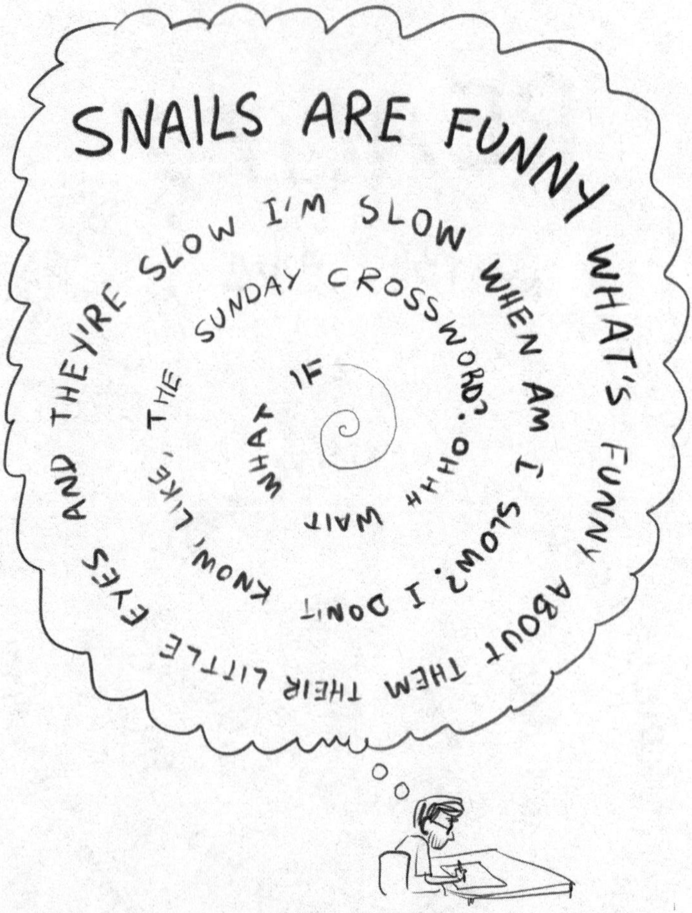
SNAILS ARE FUNNY WHAT'S FUNNY ABOUT THEM THEIR LITTLE EYES AND THEY'RE SLOW I'M SLOW WHEN AM I SLOW? I DON'T KNOW, LIKE, THE SUNDAY CROSSWORD? OHHH WAIT WHAT IF

It's not that I need to be anxious to make art, but that the way my thoughts spiral can lead me toward creative conclusions and anxious ones.

My tendency is to forget where reality ends and imagination takes over. This helps me live in a world of fictional characters. These characters refer back to my own experiences, but break the laws of my reality.

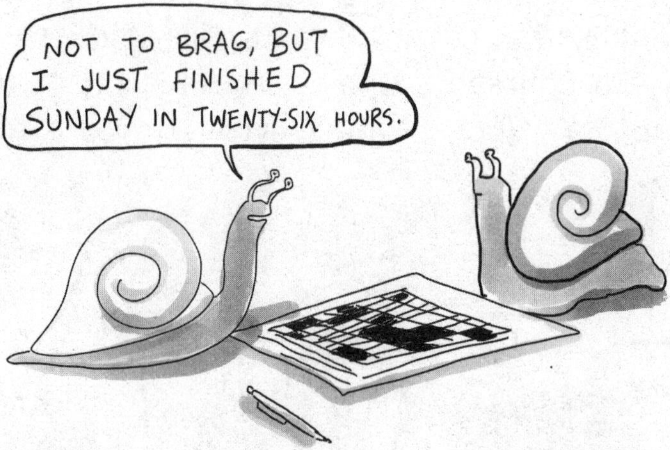
NOT TO BRAG, BUT I JUST FINISHED SUNDAY IN TWENTY-SIX HOURS.

An obsessive thought is an act of imagination that forgets it is imagination, a windmill I confuse for a dragon. I compulsively tilt.

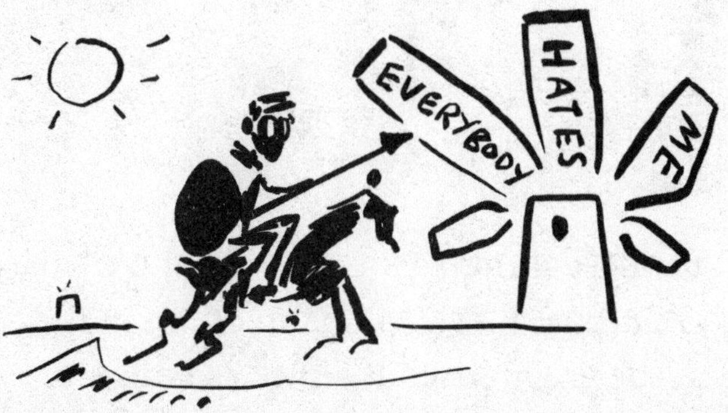
EVERYBODY
HATES
ME

Anxiety hasn't been a flashpoint for ideas, it's been keeping me from drawing anything at all.

I decide to try the pills.

It's not like I've never taken anything. I'm afraid of flying — of course I am. Once, on a flight to California next to Ana, I took a Xanax I'd bought from a friend.

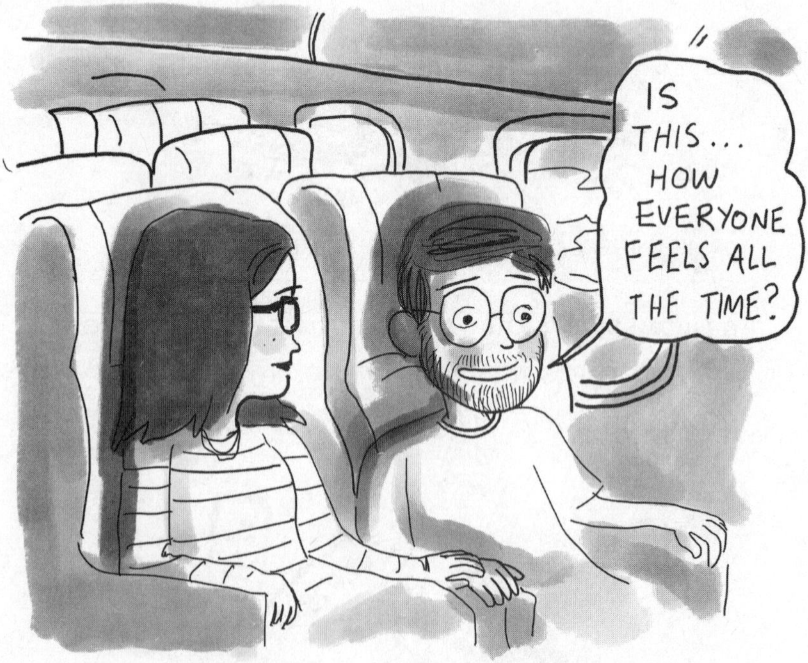
IS THIS... HOW EVERYONE FEELS ALL THE TIME?

On that plane I felt the absence of the physical manifestations of anxiety I took for granted would always be there.

I begin to take a small dose of Klonopin every morning and evening. It's a benzoamphetamine, which gives immediate relief from physical panic symptoms. It's very addictive, so I need to be careful with the dosage, and the plan is to wind down after a month.

I keep two in my pocket throughout the day in case of emergency.

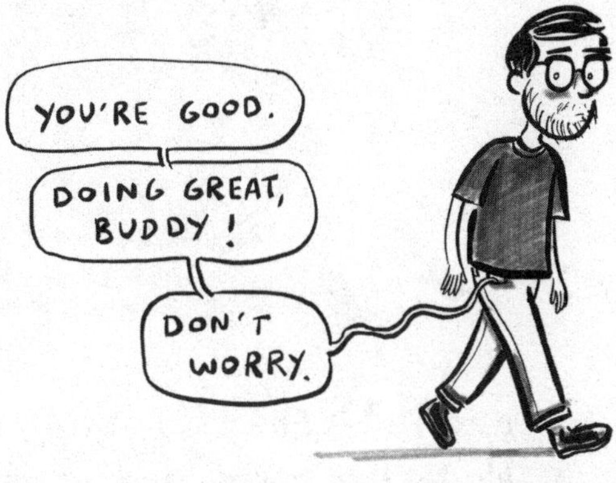
YOU'RE GOOD.
DOING GREAT, BUDDY!
DON'T WORRY.

When I feel near a panic attack, I clutch them.

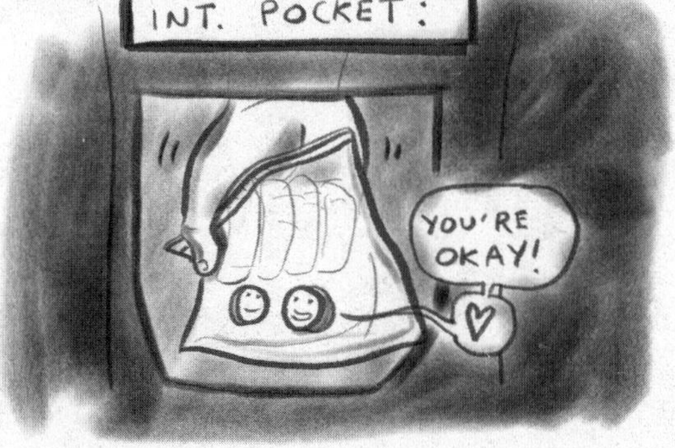
INT. POCKET:
YOU'RE OKAY!

My baseline reaction to most situations has usually tended toward one of two options:

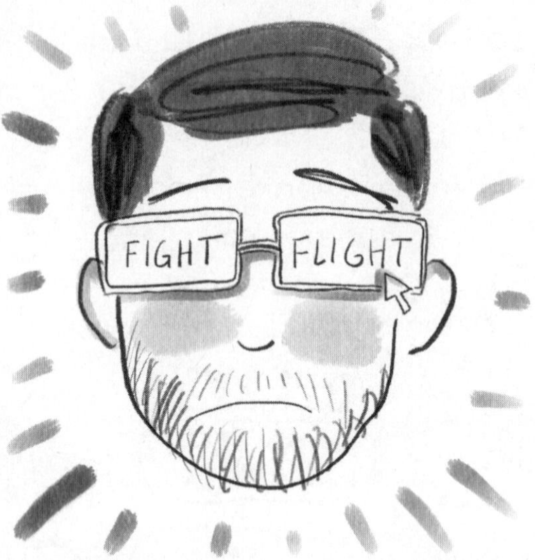
FIGHT
FLIGHT

Taking a benzo feels like I can stop and look around for a minute. Maybe this is how everyone feels all the time.

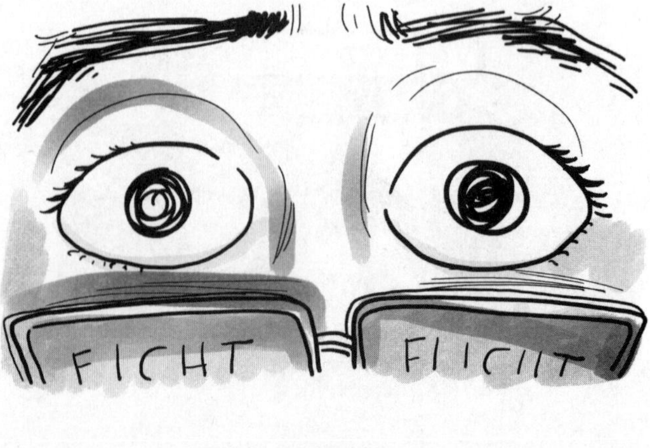

I begin taking Zoloft the same day.

Zoloft is a selective serotonin reuptake inhibitor, or SSRI. The OCD brain doesn't get enough serotonin, and a high dose of an SSRI can help.

It's supposed to take a few weeks to kick in, but I immediately worry about potential side effects.

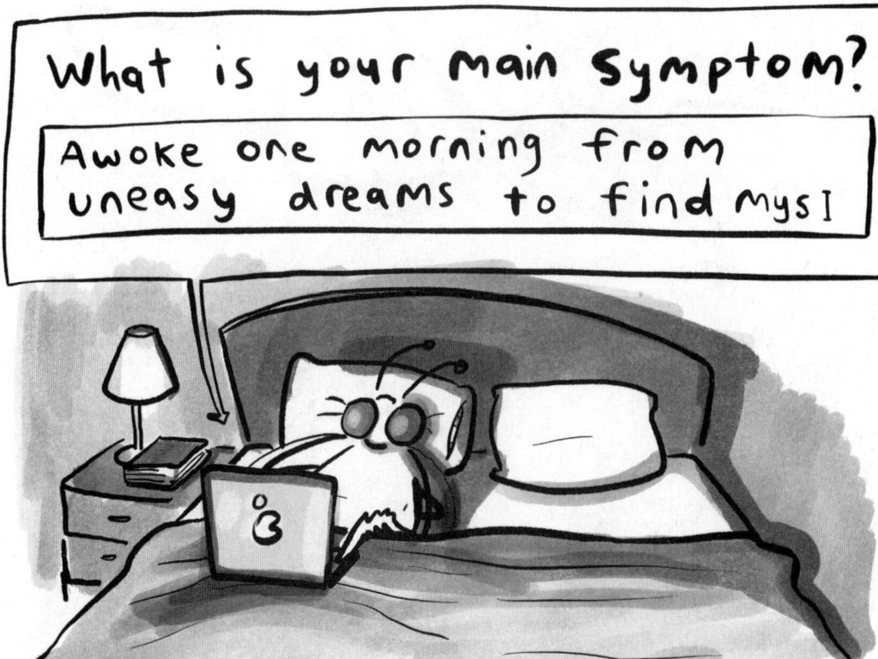
What is your main symptom?
Awoke one morning from uneasy dreams to find mysl

A few weeks in, I'm drawing a portrait of Shakespeare for a book.

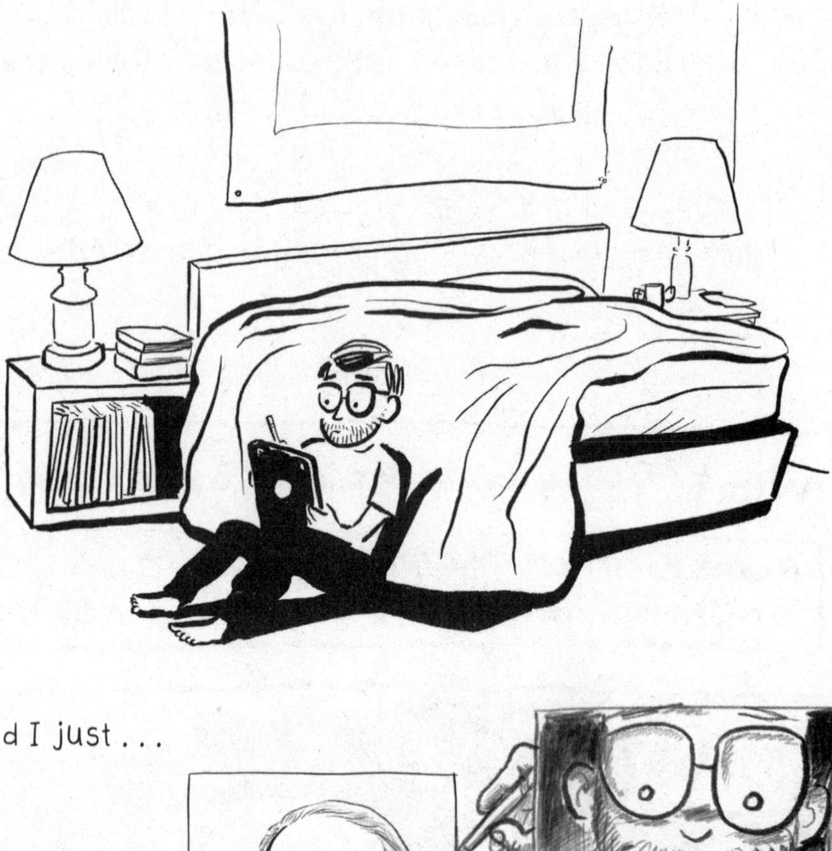

And I just . . .

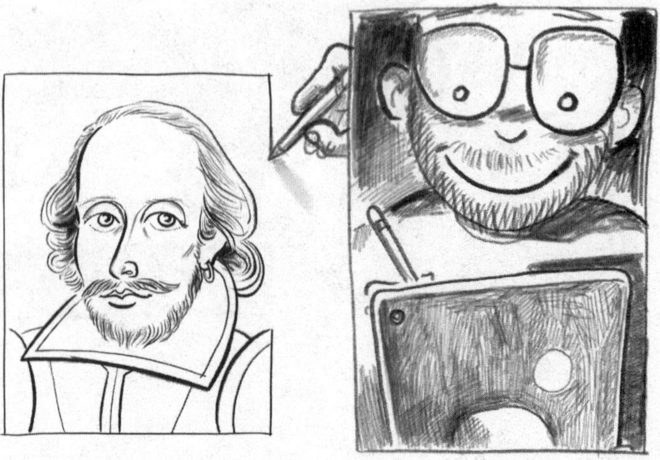

. . . remember how much I love to draw.

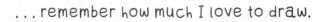

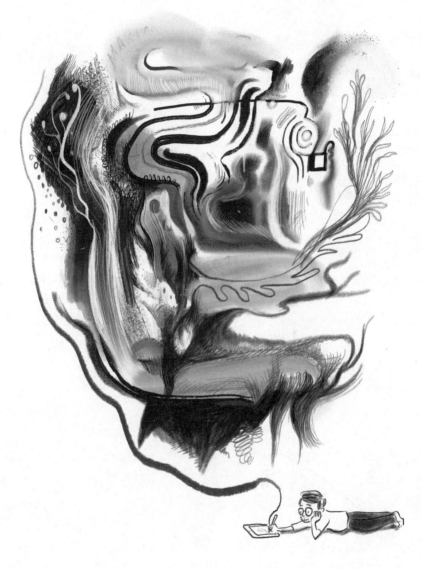

I hadn't even realized I'd forgotten.

I'm back on my feet. I've weaned off the klonopin.
I can leave my room. I can function.

I've run out of excuses to avoid E.R.P.

I begin at the bottom of the hierarchy:
touching my shoe and then my face.

Even the thought of doing this fills me with distress.

Why am I doing this to myself?

I've turned back
into a little kid,
sick with fear.

I want to stop the exposure, but I know where stopping leads.

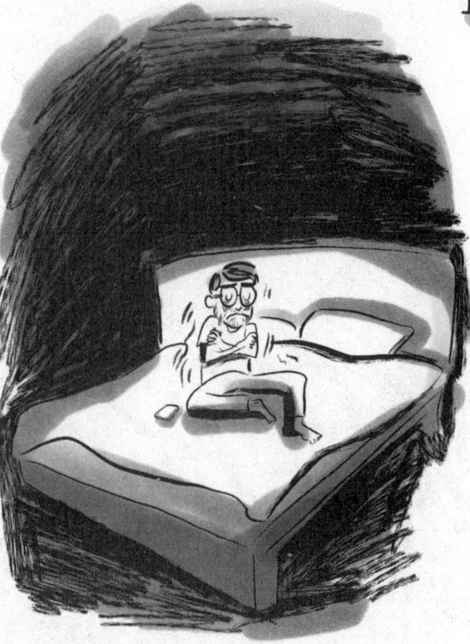

I don't want to do that to myself anymore.

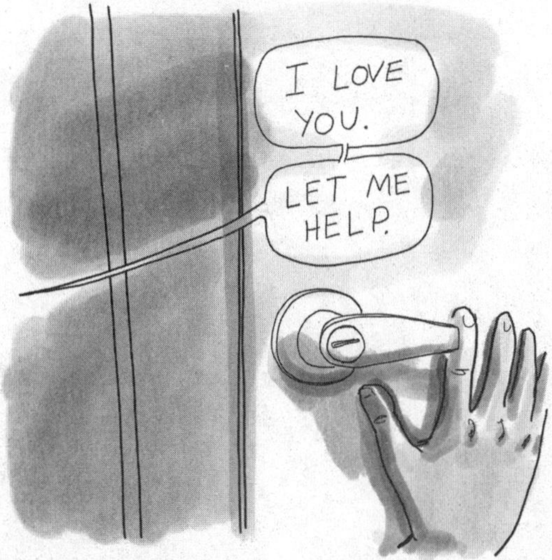
I LOVE YOU.
LET ME HELP.

I don't want to do that to my friends anymore.

Fuck it. I poke the bear.

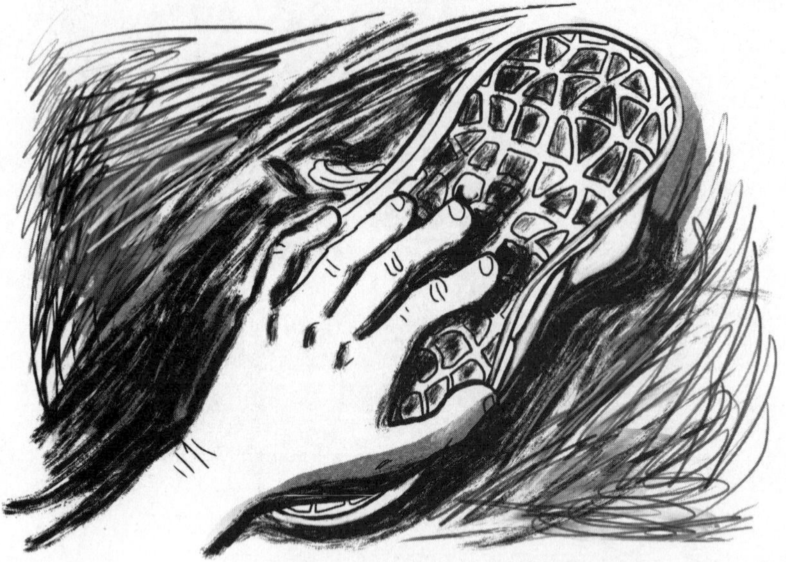

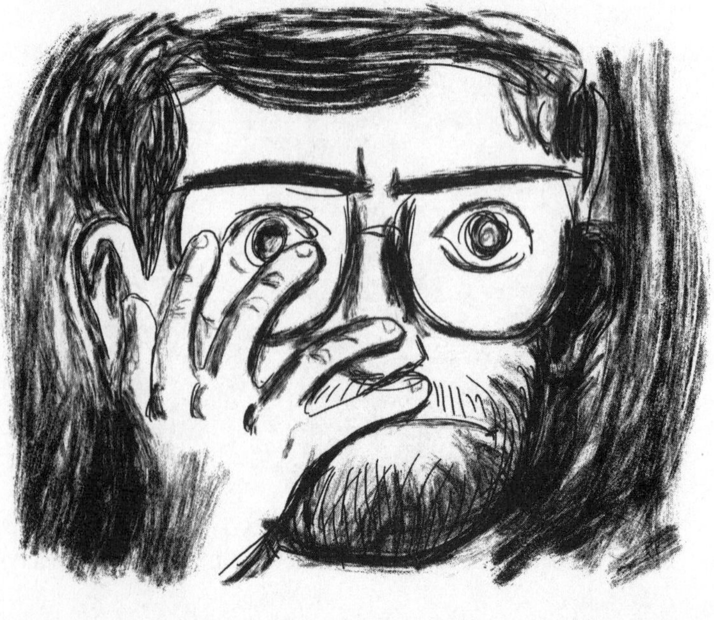

I touch my shoe and then my face over and over again.
I'm tired of complimenting the cat.

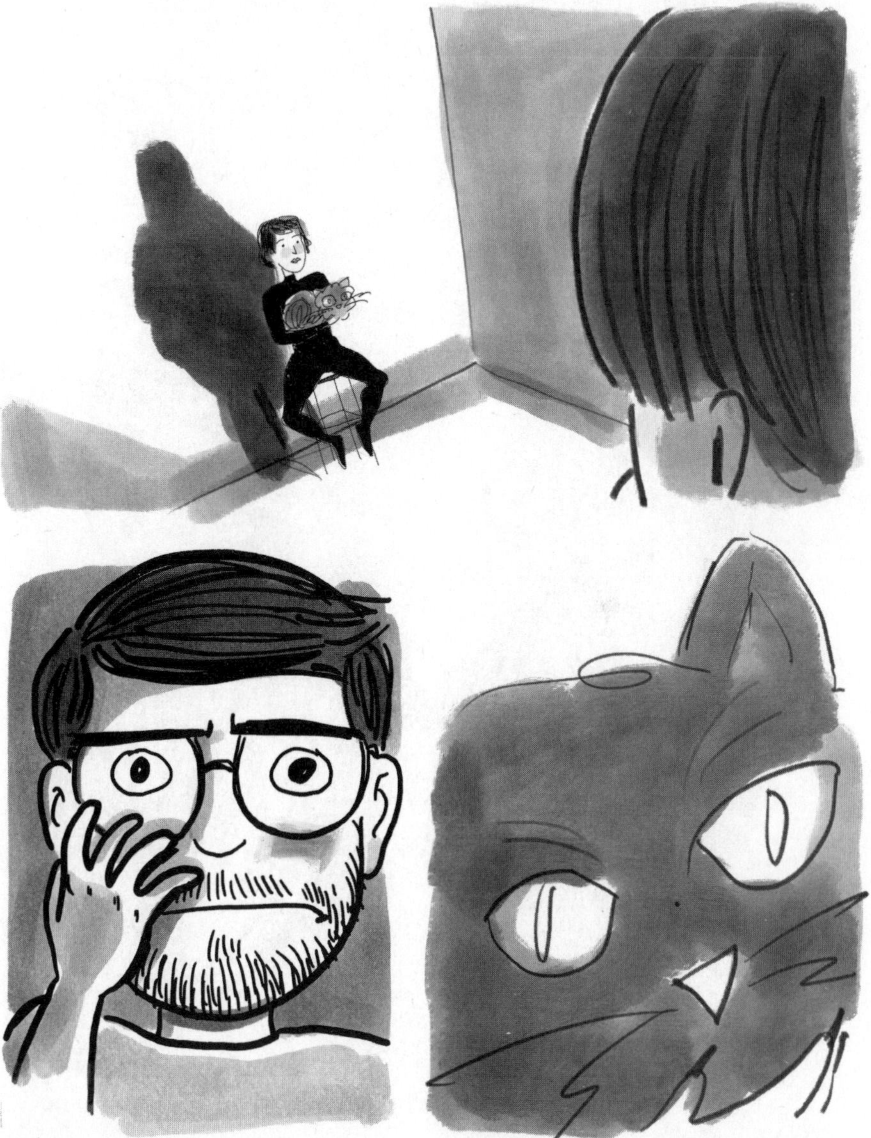

This won't work. Almost everything inside me screams that this won't work. Ten times a day I do this, and for days it feels like shit. This won't work.

One lone, little voice says, "Keep going on faith alone. Maybe there's an ending you can't yet see."

After a week of the exposure . . .

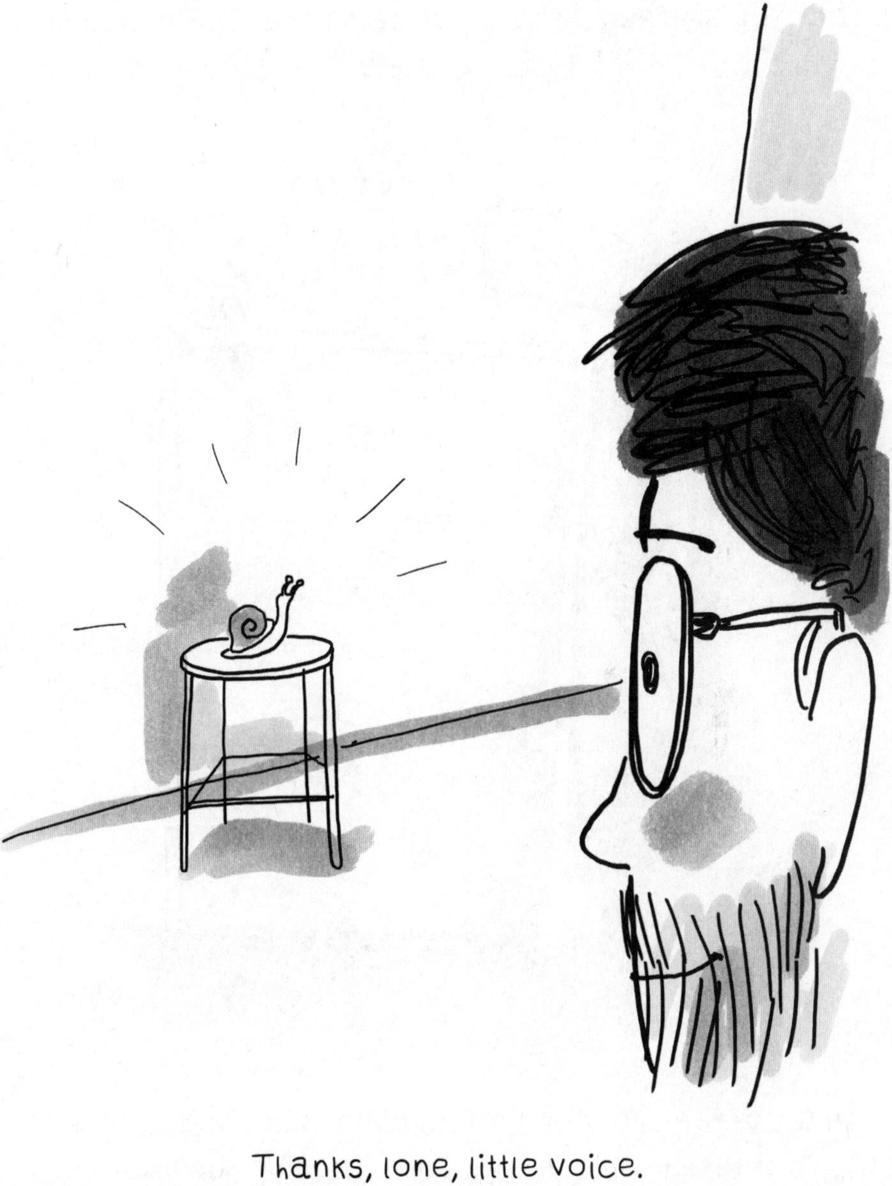

Thanks, lone, little voice.

Now I've set a precedent. Something that's always been an emergency can stop being one. I can change the way I feel. I. Can. Change. The. Way. I. Feel.

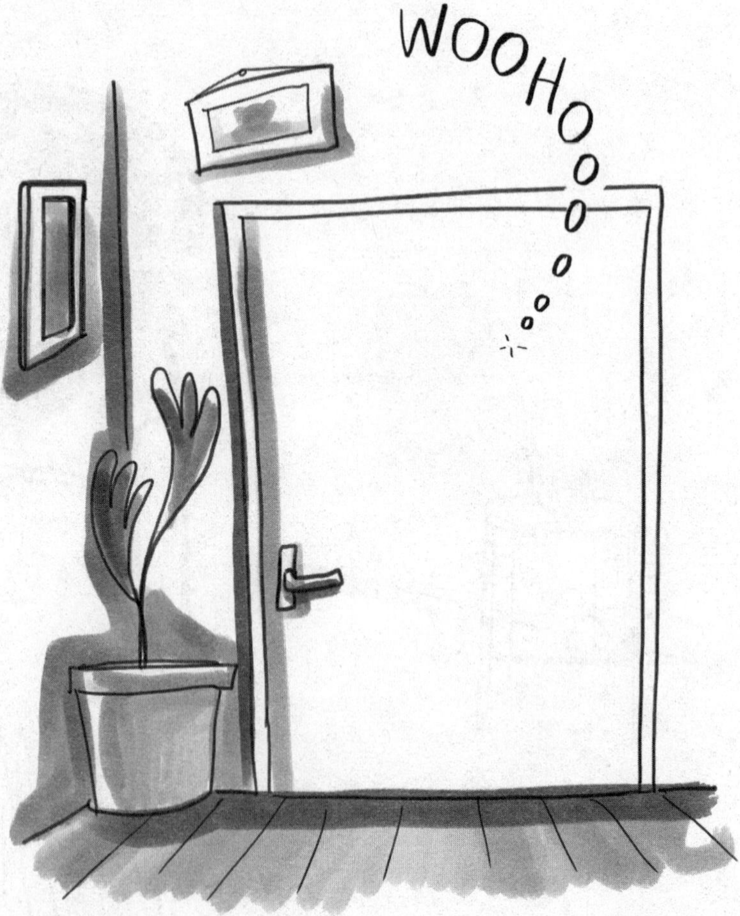
WOOHOOOOOOO

In a coffee shop, I sit on a public toilet seat for the first time in five years. I'm a fucking superhero.

Guilt doesn't run as smoothly as contamination.
Contamination exposures only put me "in danger,"
but in order to confront my irrational guilt I
need to put other people "in harm's way."

Whenever I pick up my laundry from the dryer, I move my
hand around the machine to see if it's still burning hot.
I'm afraid someone else will put their clothes in and burn
their hand. I stay in my laundromat until I can confirm the
machine has cooled down enough for someone else to use.

I walk around New York in constant fear that something small might fall out of my pocket. A baby or dog will see this, immediately put it in their mouth, and choke to death.

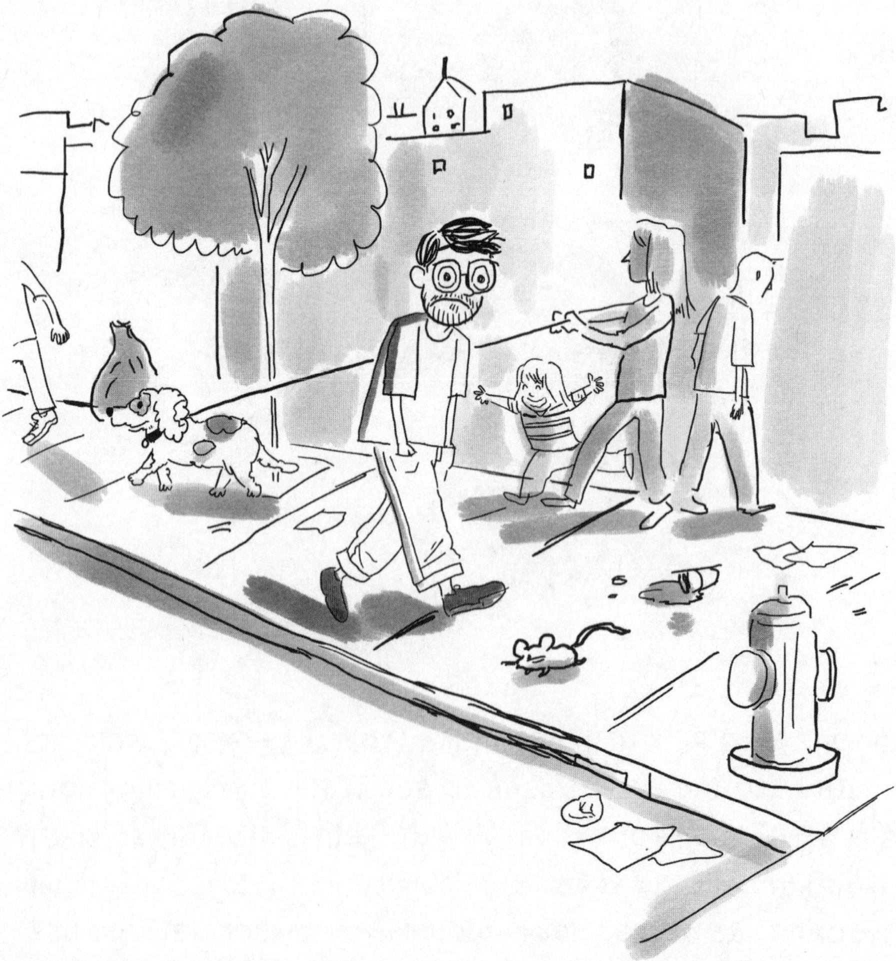

I'm supposed to throw a coin onto the ground on purpose . . .

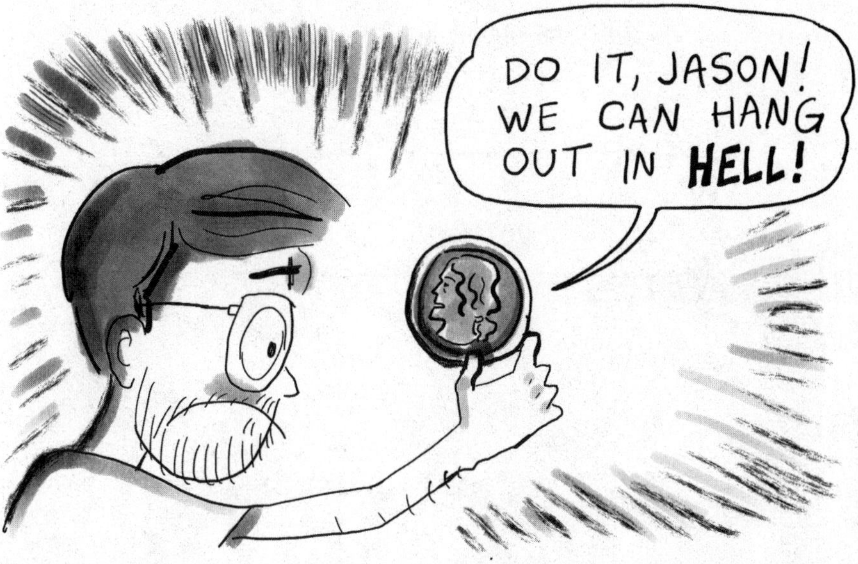
DO IT, JASON! WE CAN HANG OUT IN **HELL!**

. . . but I'm not there yet.

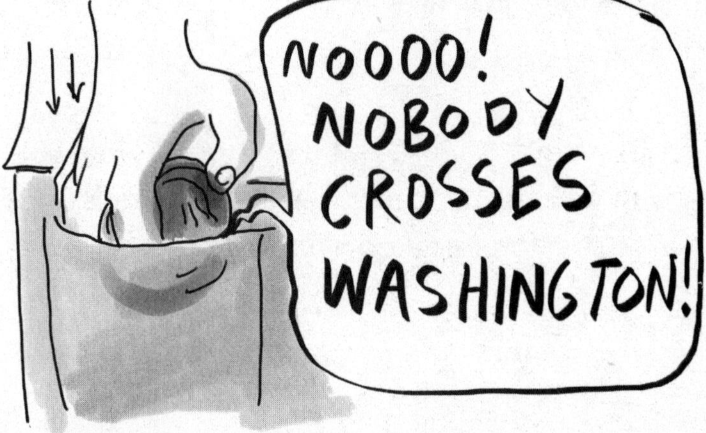
NOOOO! NOBODY CROSSES WASHINGTON!

I've begun meeting for group therapy sessions with other OCD patients. We all have different triggers, but our brains work the same way.

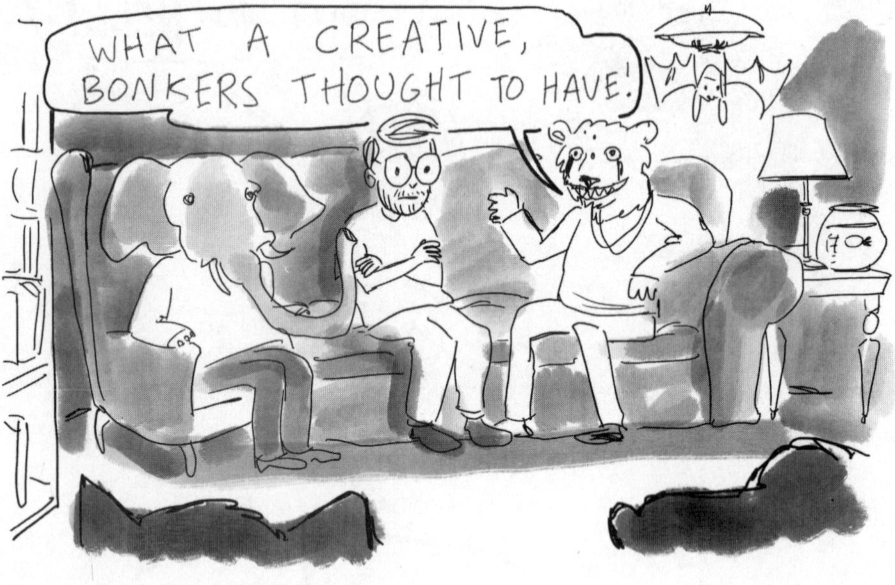
WHAT A CREATIVE, BONKERS THOUGHT TO HAVE!

It takes me a bit to get used to the way the group gives each other shit for their specific obsessions and compulsive behaviors.

I learn that this roasting is a technique to take power back from the distressing thoughts.

It's not me that's the butt of the joke, it's my OCD.

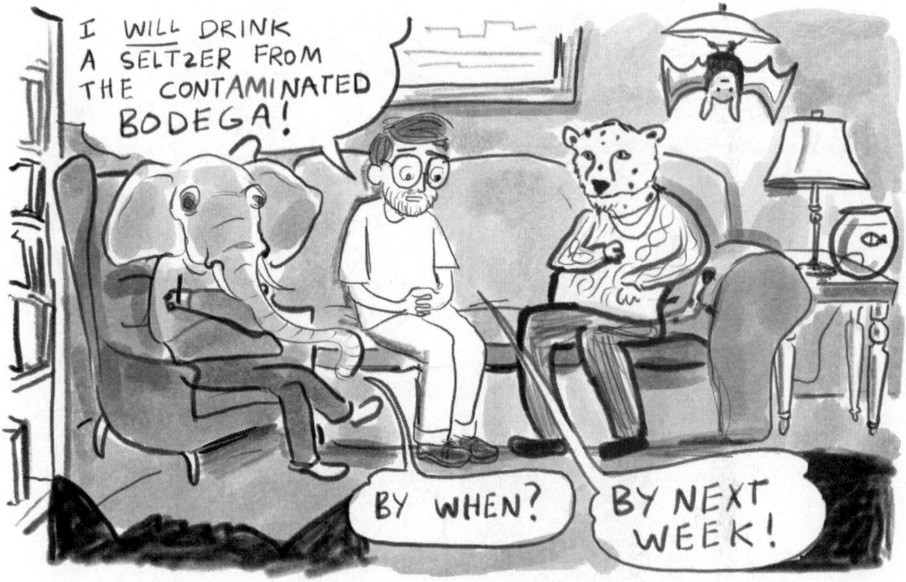
I WILL DRINK A SELTZER FROM THE CONTAMINATED BODEGA!
BY WHEN?
BY NEXT WEEK!

The group holds me accountable to my E.R.P. work.

I begin talking about my nightmare thoughts in group, and the thoughts begin to lose their hold on me.

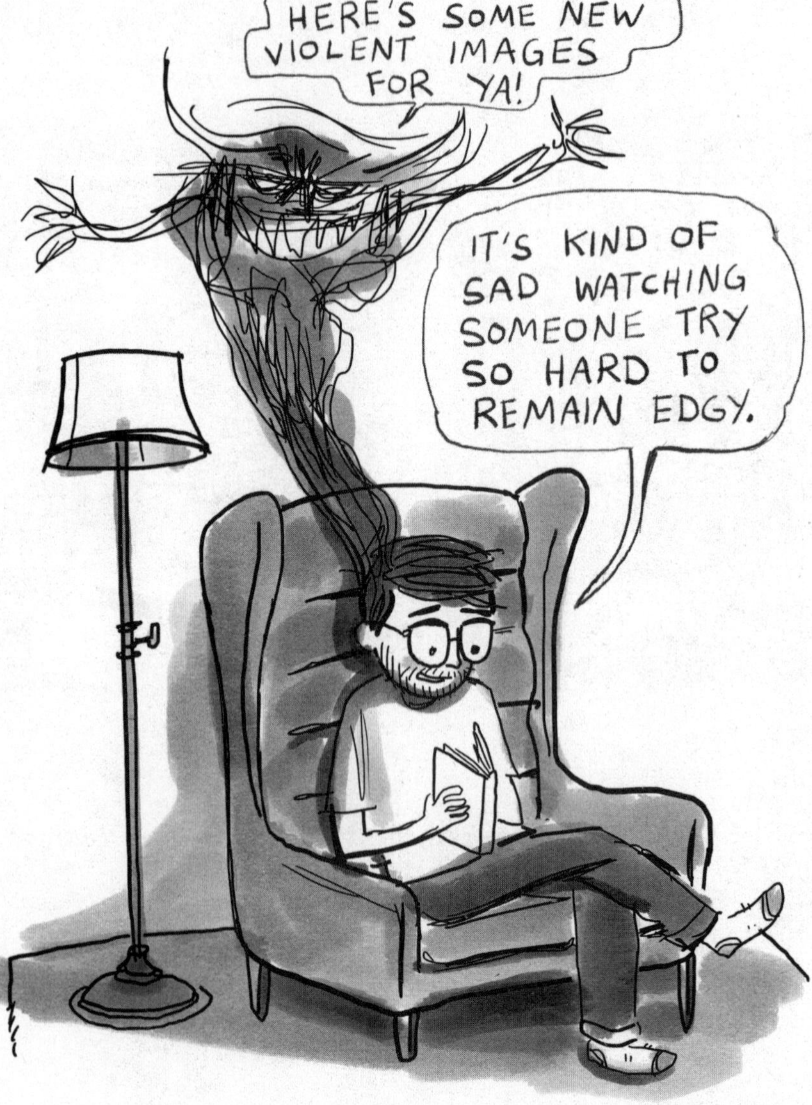
HERE'S SOME NEW VIOLENT IMAGES FOR YA!
IT'S KIND OF SAD WATCHING SOMEONE TRY SO HARD TO REMAIN EDGY.

One day:

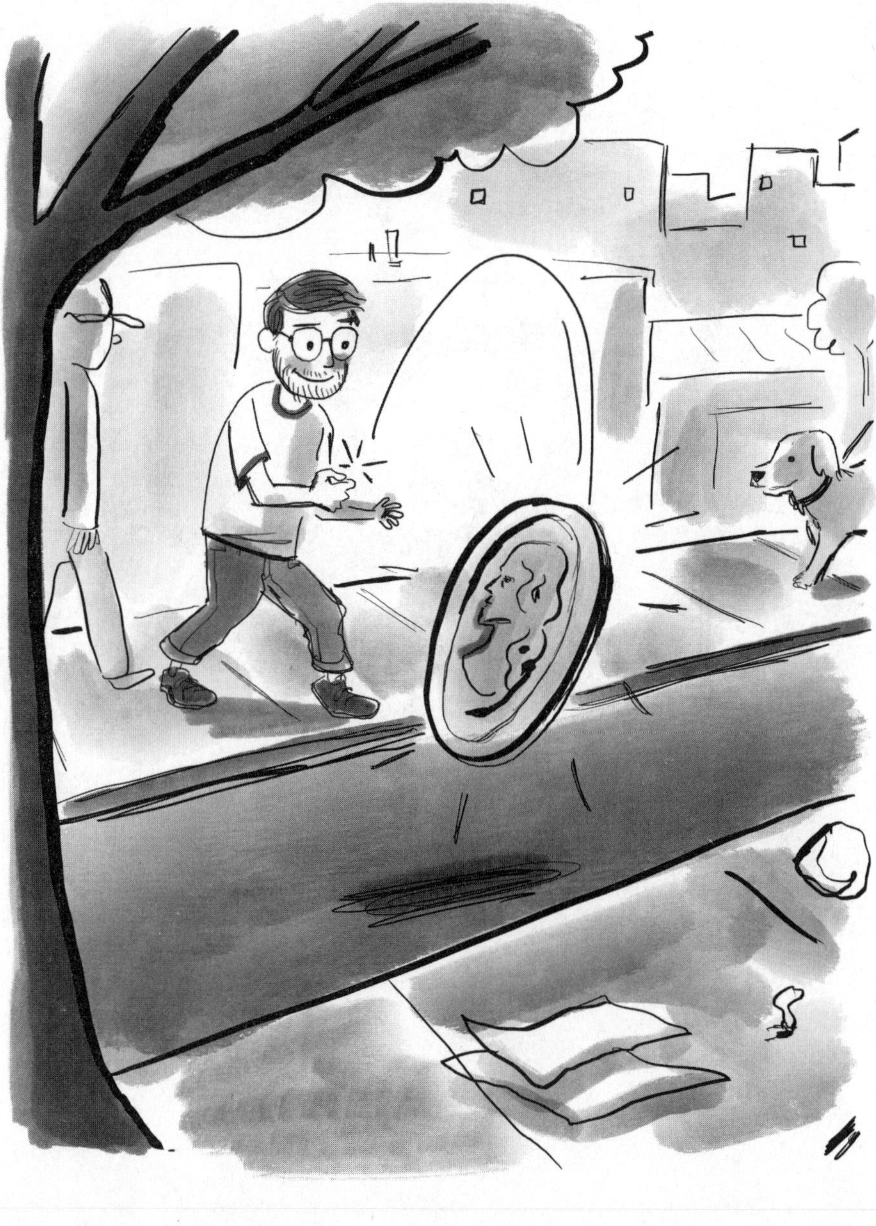

And that week in group . . .

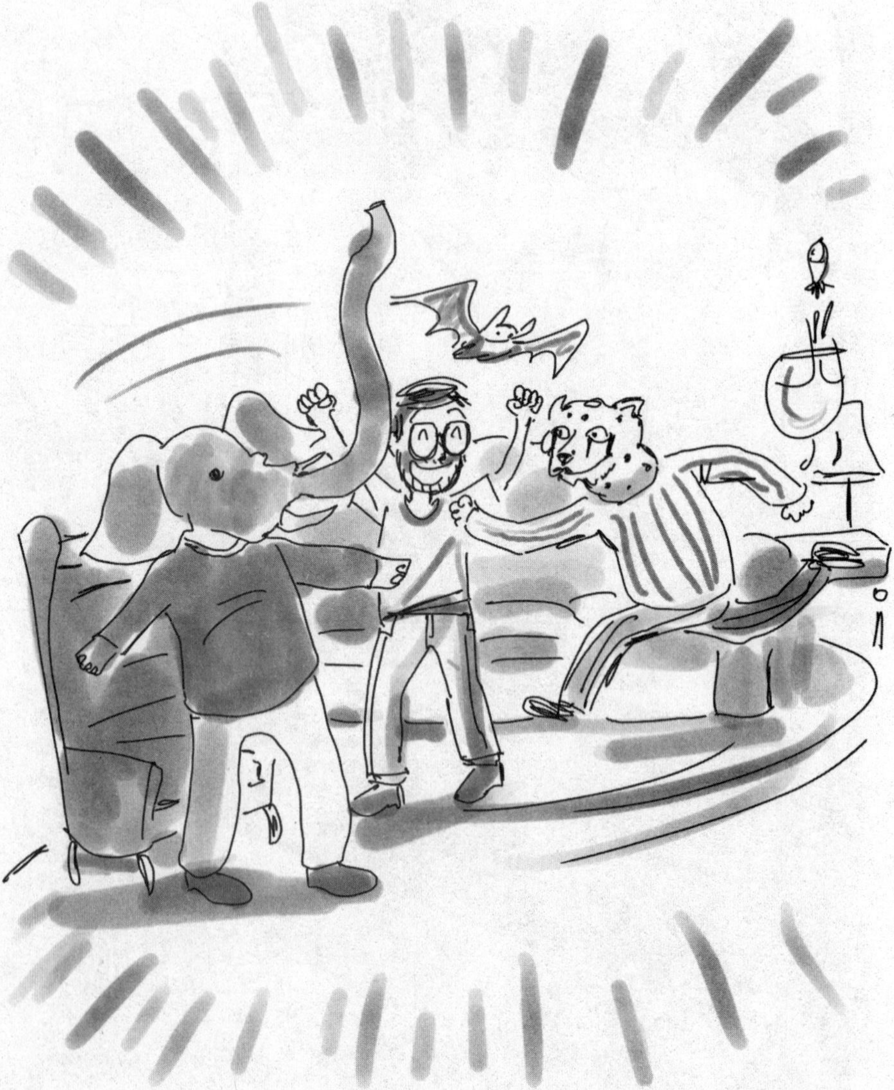

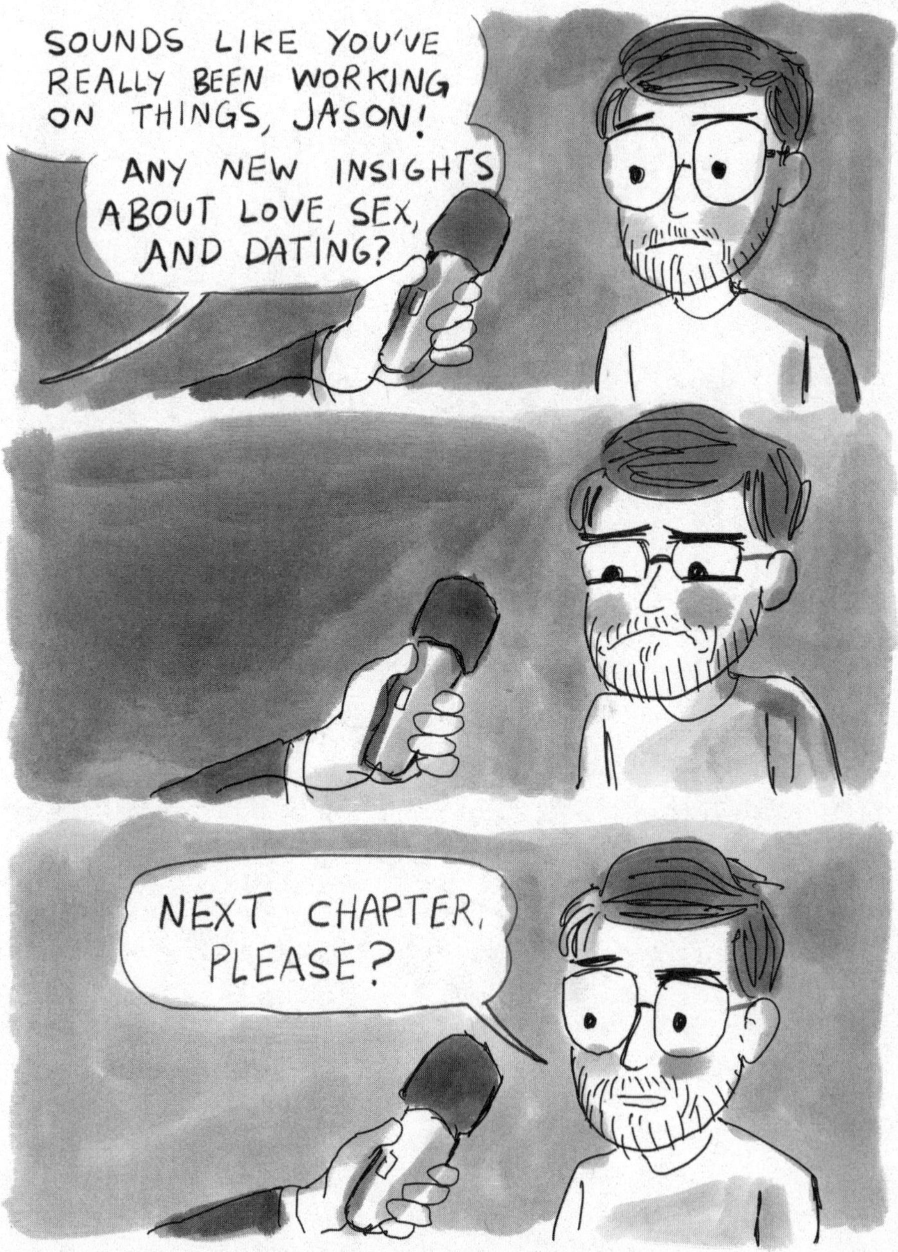
SOUNDS LIKE YOU'VE REALLY BEEN WORKING ON THINGS, JASON!
ANY NEW INSIGHTS ABOUT LOVE, SEX, AND DATING?
NEXT CHAPTER, PLEASE?

Lately, the volume of my symptoms is down to a dull hum.

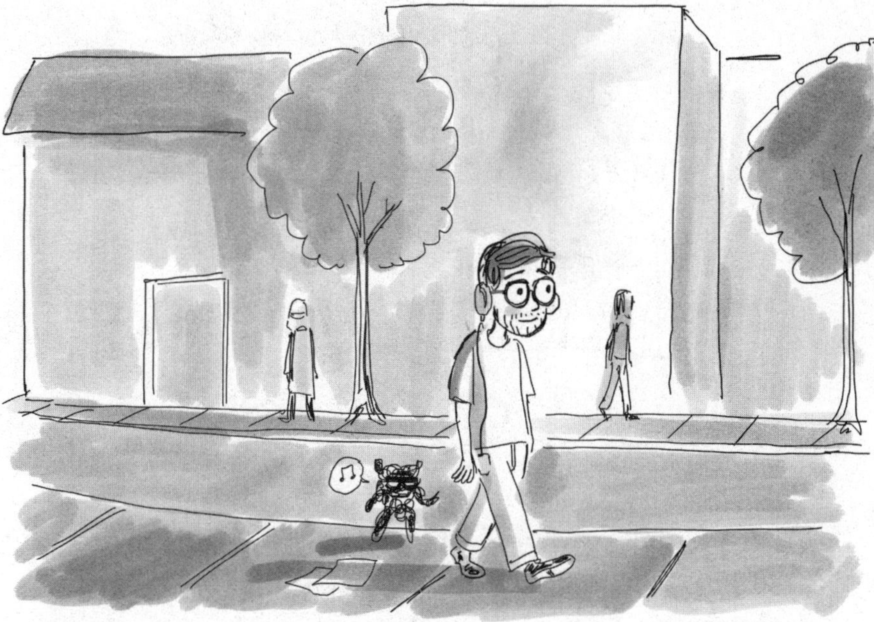

And still, my anxieties stare calmly back at me just out of frame.

That's okay.

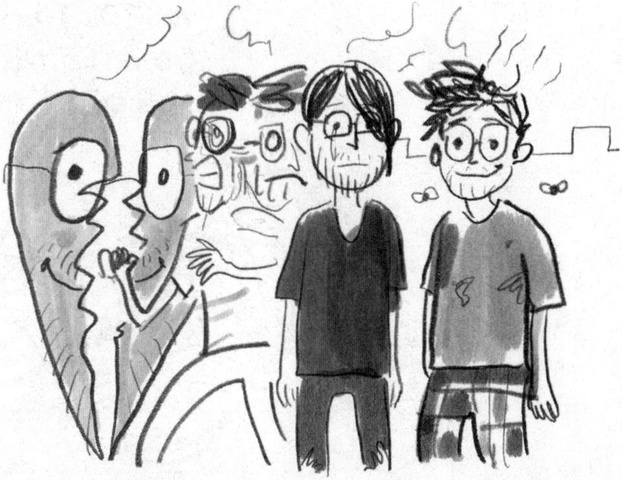

Sometimes I have small epiphanies:

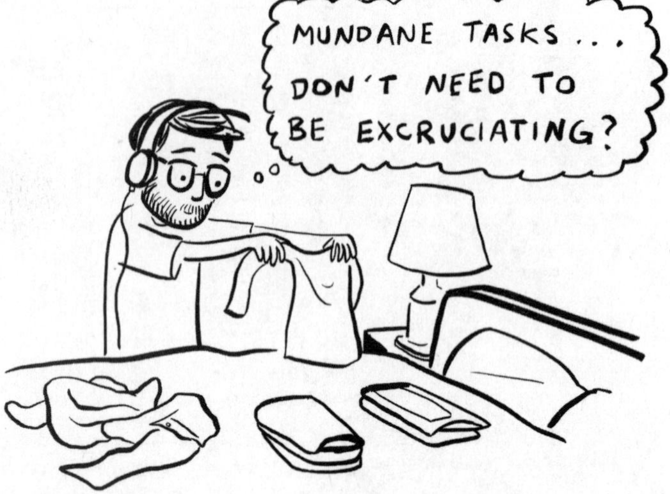
MUNDANE TASKS . . .
DON'T NEED TO
BE EXCRUCIATING?

The exposure therapy, the meds, the whole trying to be healthy thing? It's changing me.

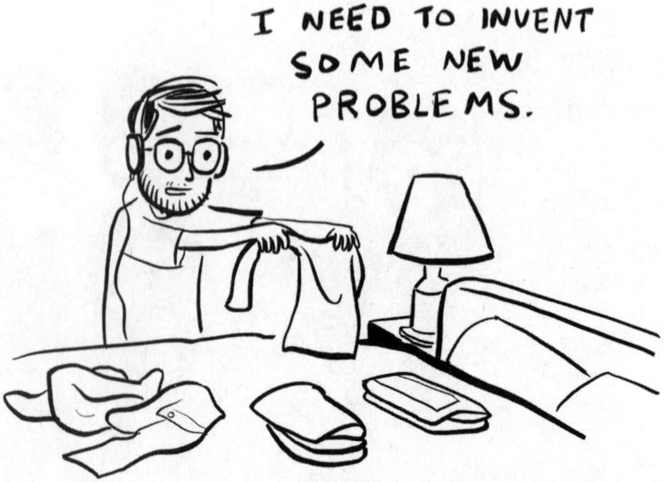
I NEED TO INVENT
SOME NEW
PROBLEMS.

I do low-level exposures every day, to remind myself that my obsessions aren't threats. I'm like a pianist practicing scales.

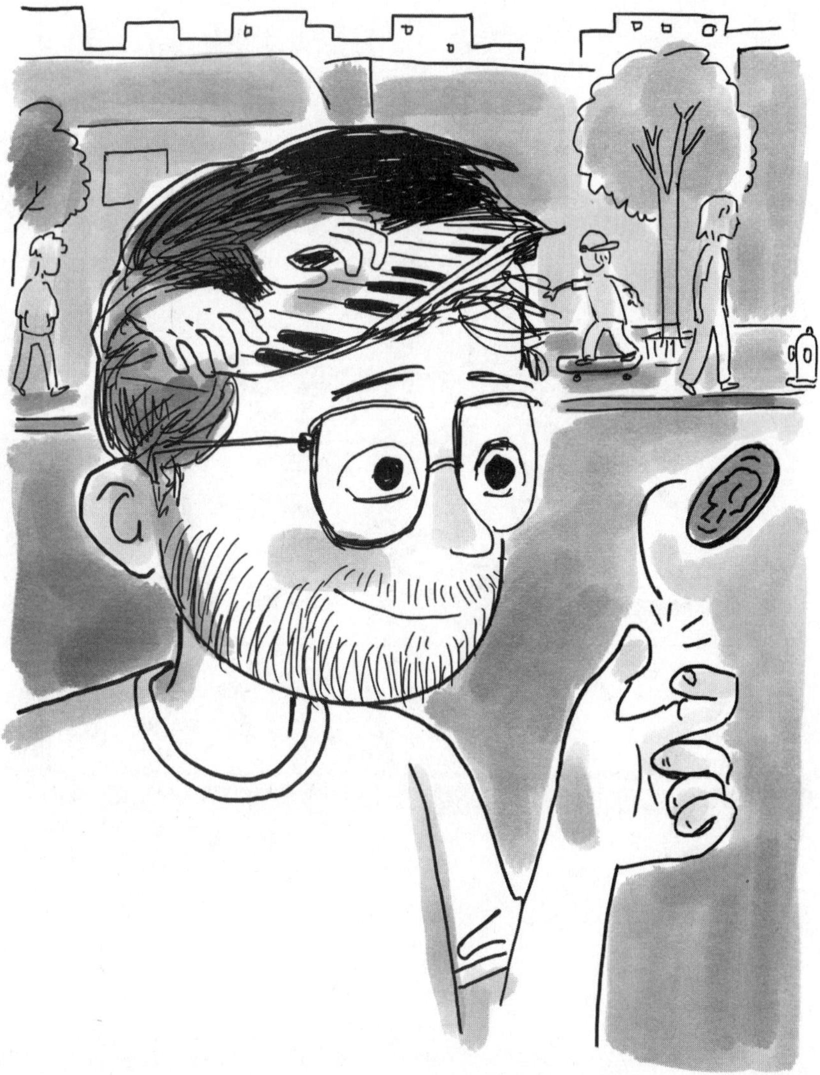

When I obeyed my anxieties, my days could be very circumscribed. There was some comfort in this. The rules were always clear.

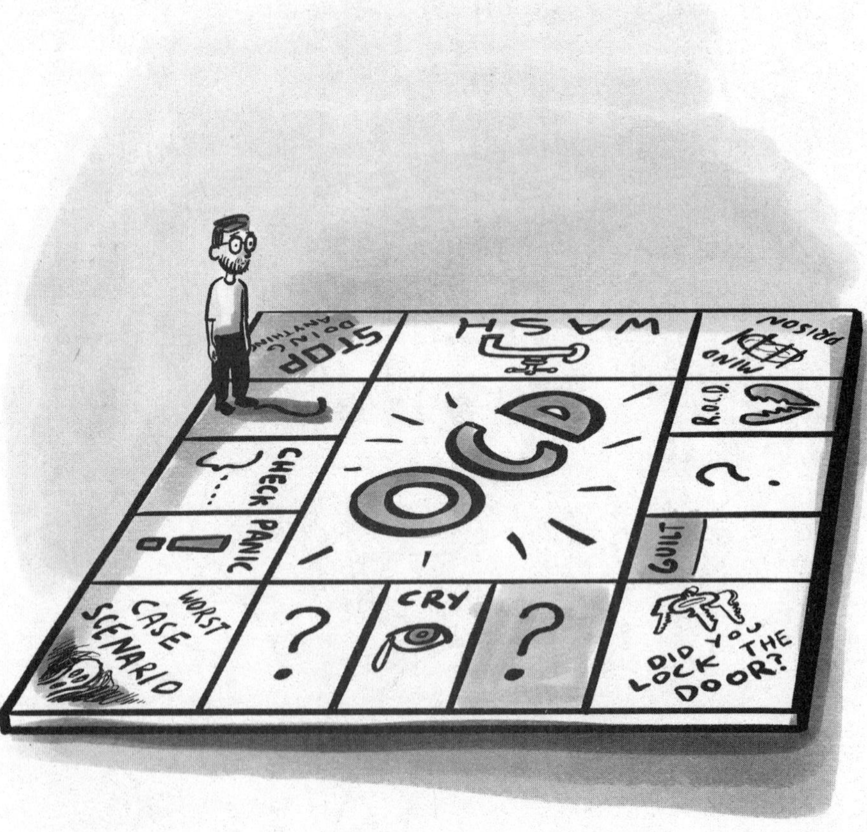
STOP DOING ANYTHING
WASH
MIND PRISON
R.O.C.D.
?
OCD
CHECK
PANIC
GUILT
WORST CASE SCENARIO
?
CRY
?
DID YOU LOCK THE DOOR?

All of the self-imposed restrictions on what I could touch, how I could behave, where I could go, what I could do . . . they hurt me all the time, sure. They also ordered my universe.

I go looking for new kinds of order.

I decide to get in to cooking.

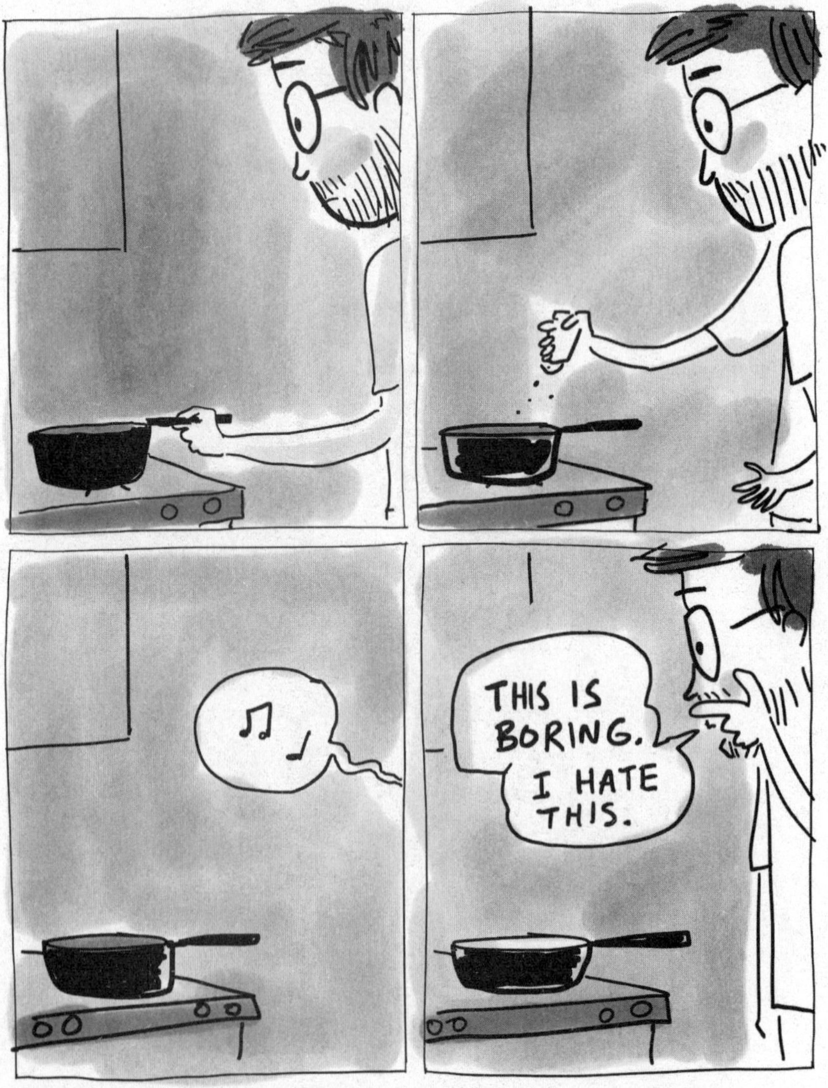
♫ ♩
THIS IS BORING.
I HATE THIS.

I try jogging.

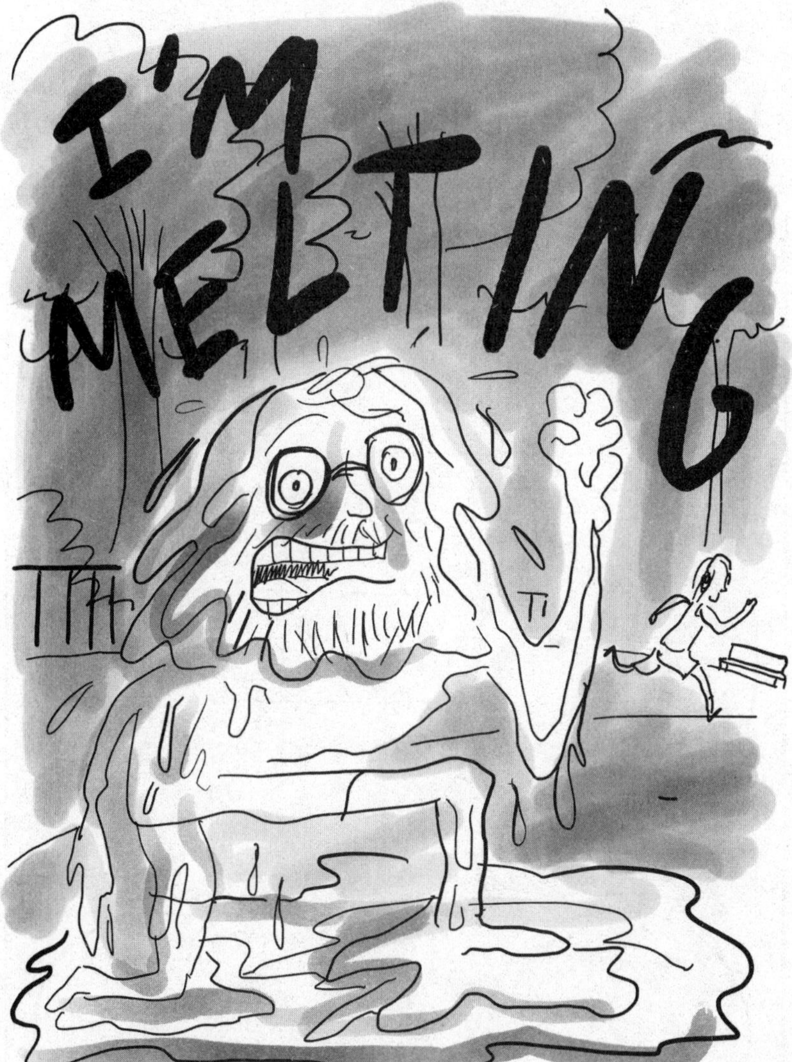
I'M MELTING

It's not for me.

In therapy, I get a cheesy worksheet.

What are my values?

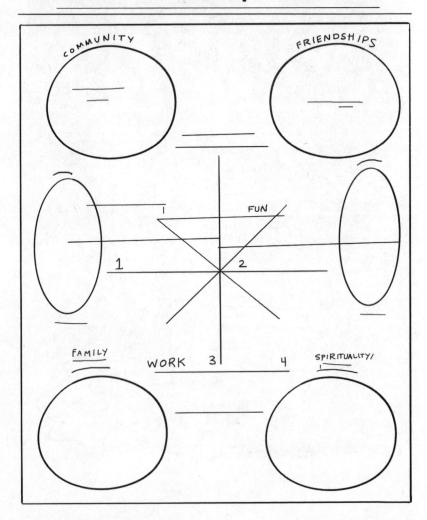

COMMUNITY

FRIENDSHIPS

FUN

1

2

FAMILY

WORK   3

4

SPIRITUALITY/

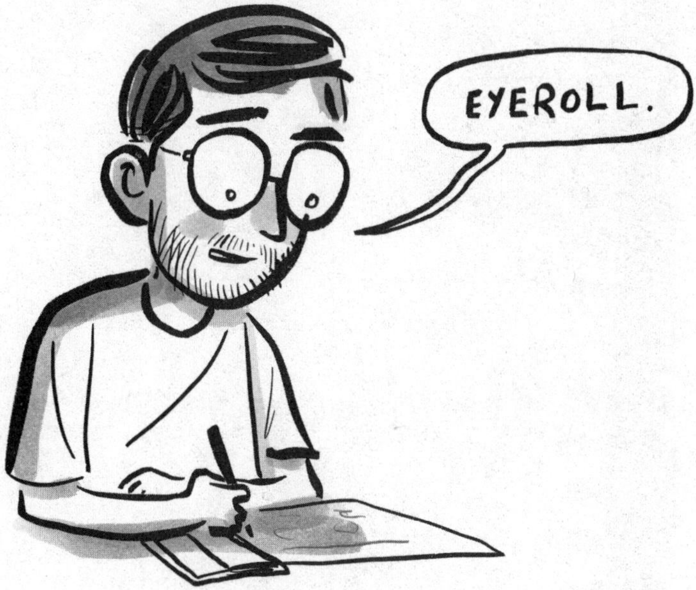
EYEROLL.

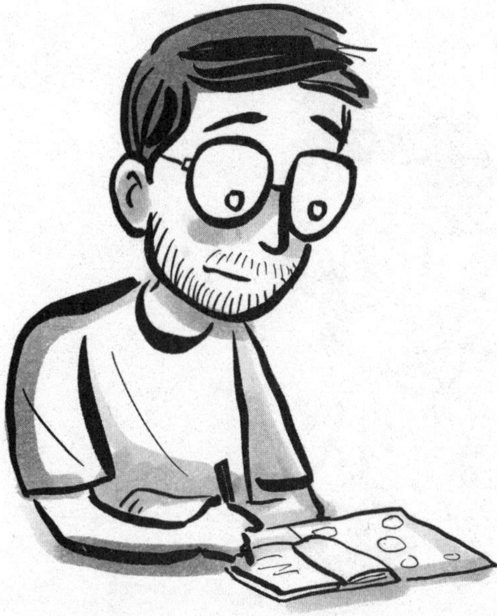

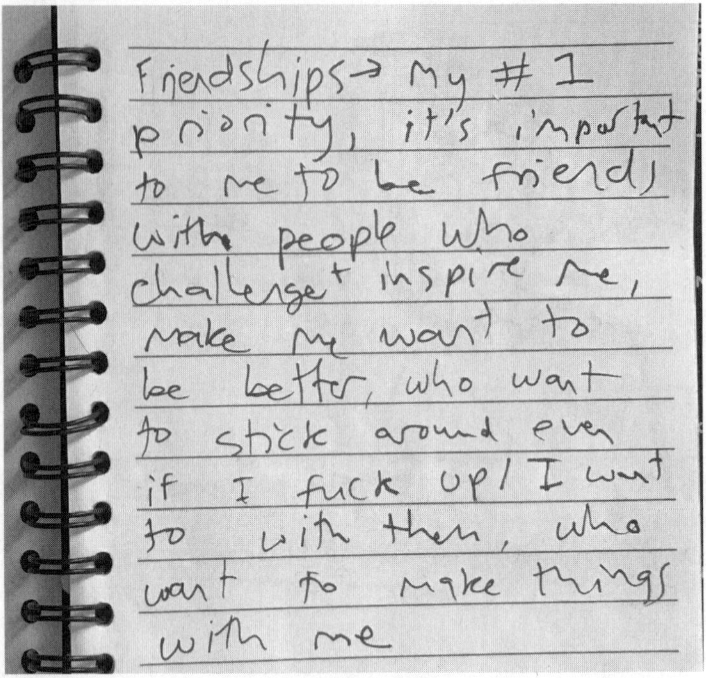
Friendships → my #1
priority, it's important
to me to be friends
with people who
challenge + inspire me,
make me want to
be better, who want
to stick around even
if I fuck up / I want
to with them, who
want to make things
with me

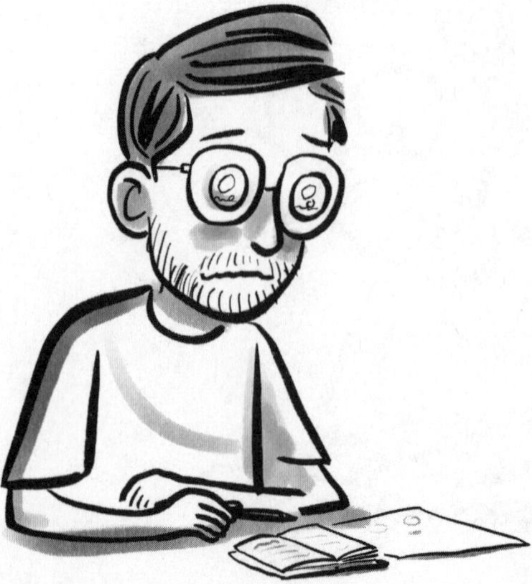

Every morning I wake up early and go to my coffee shop, so I can begin my day interacting with other people. Or, trying to interact.

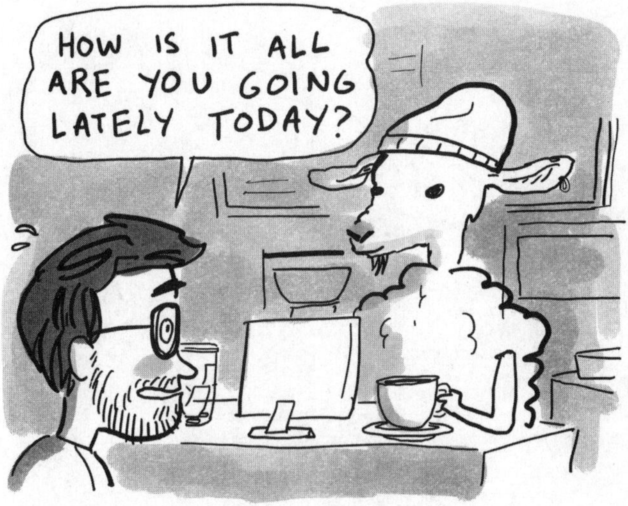
HOW IS IT ALL
ARE YOU GOING
LATELY TODAY?

I leave my phone at home. I sit outside and read Jenny Odell.

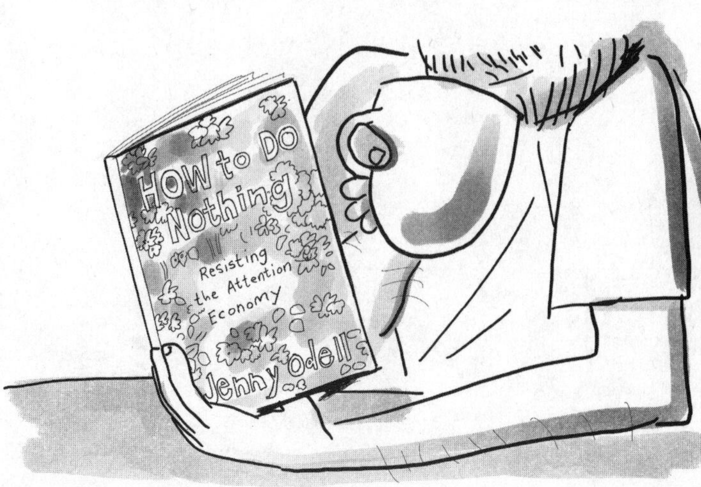
HOW to DO Nothing
Resisting the Attention Economy
Jenny Odell

I take the long way home through the park. I try to notice my body. I try to notice the world. If I pay close enough attention, I can hear the birds sing.

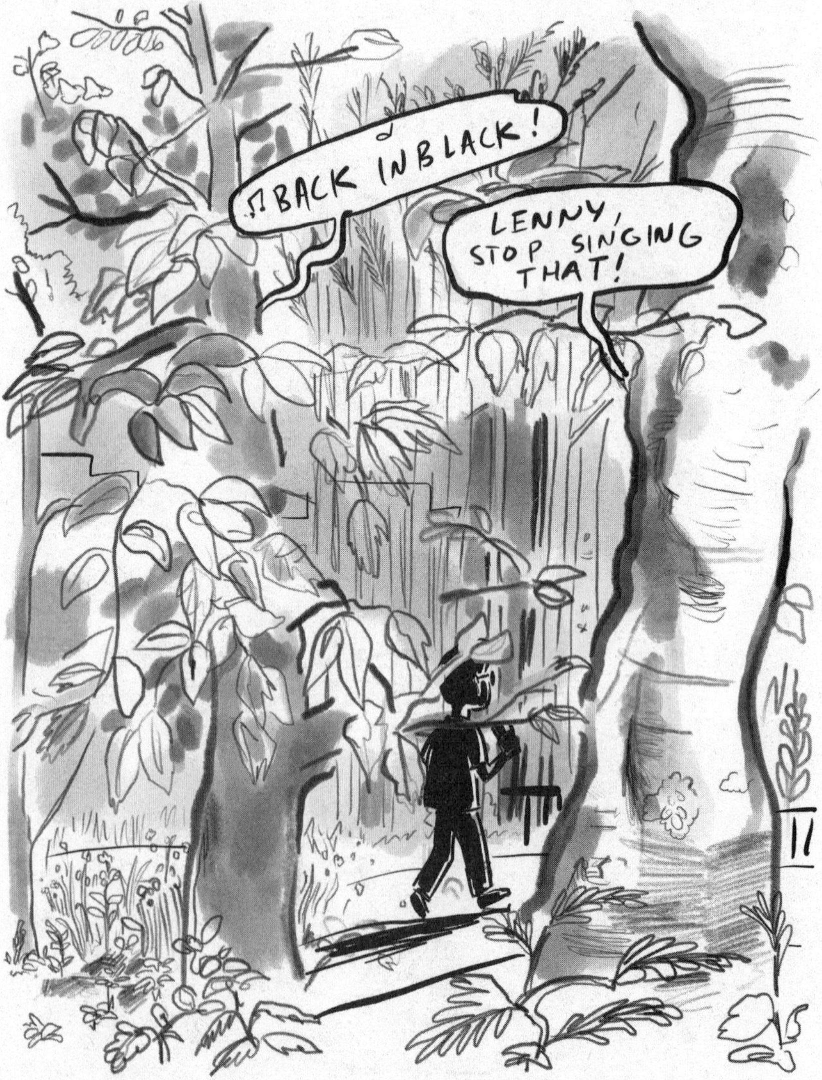
♫ BACK IN BLACK!
LENNY, STOP SINGING THAT!

When I get back to my apartment . . .

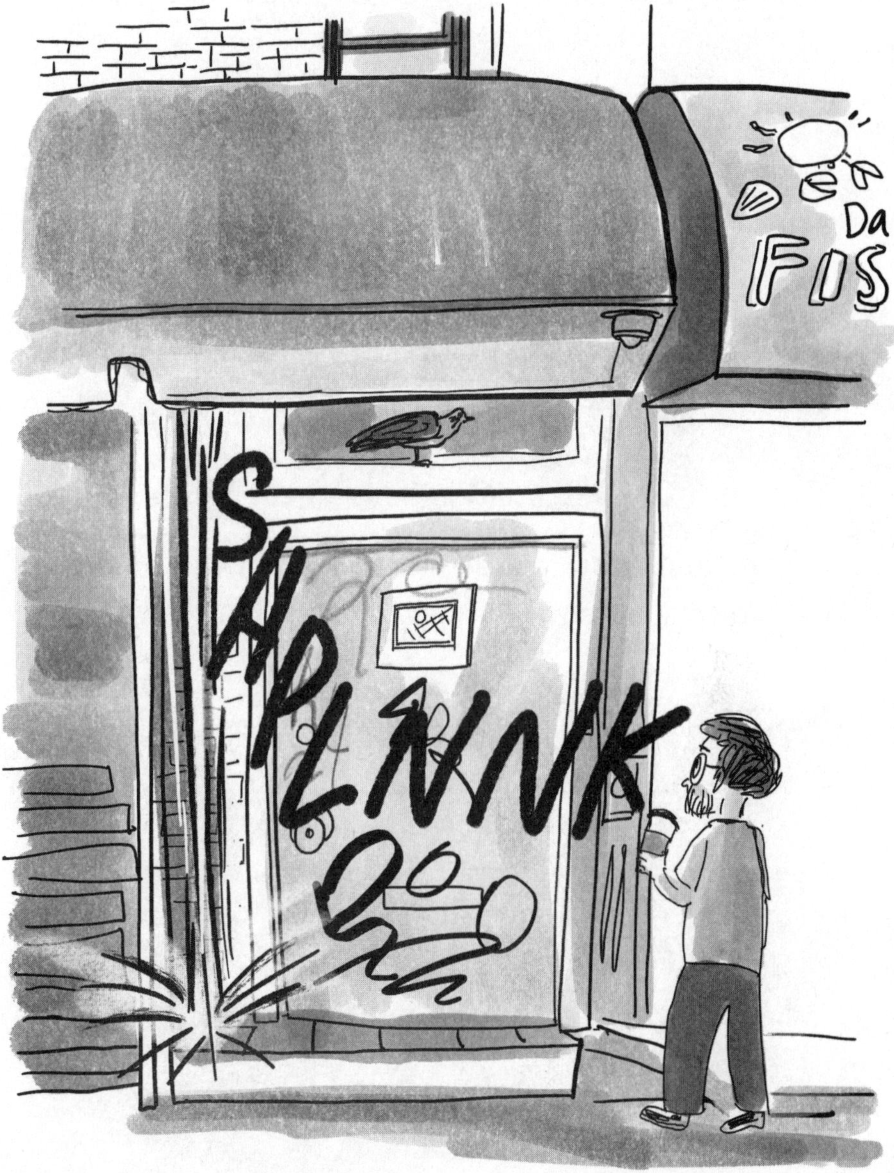
Da
FIS
SHPLNNK

In the little gap between our neighbor's awning and our front door, a bunch of pigeons have made their home.

I've just seen one of these pigeons fall to earth. He can't, or he won't, fly away.

I really try to let nature work this one out on its own,
but when I open the door . . .

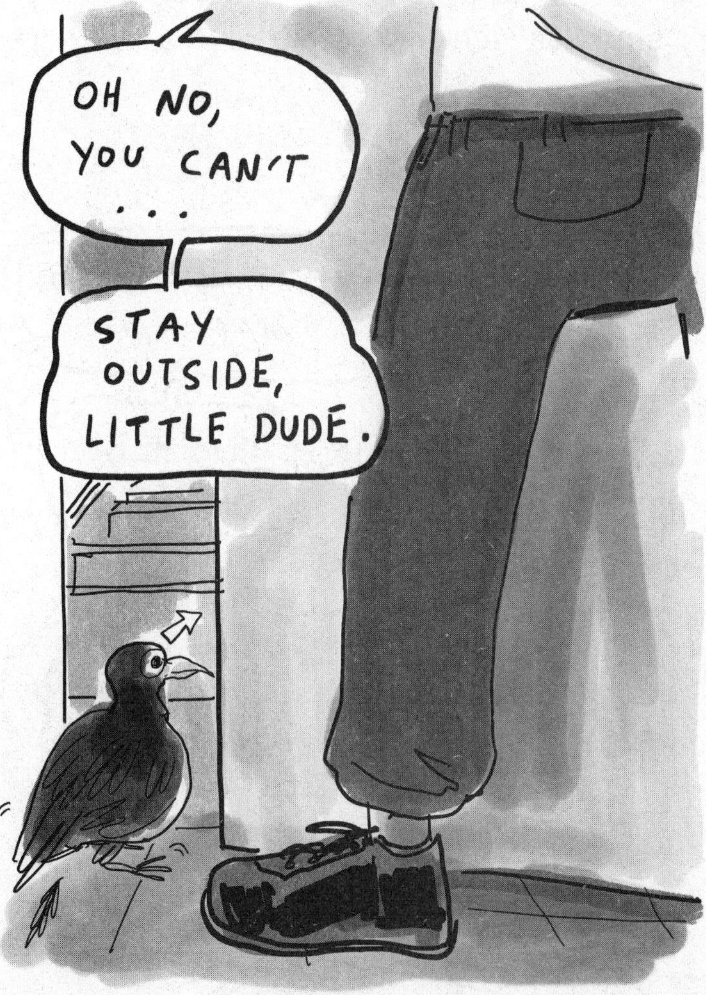
OH NO, YOU CAN'T . . .
STAY OUTSIDE, LITTLE DUDE.

I name him Birdston Moore, and any hope I had of not being responsible for his well-being goes out the window.

The internet says to put him in a cardboard box, which I do. Wildlife Bird Fund says to leave him water, so I do. I wonder why small, vulnerable animals keep wandering into my stairwell, seeking protection from me personally.

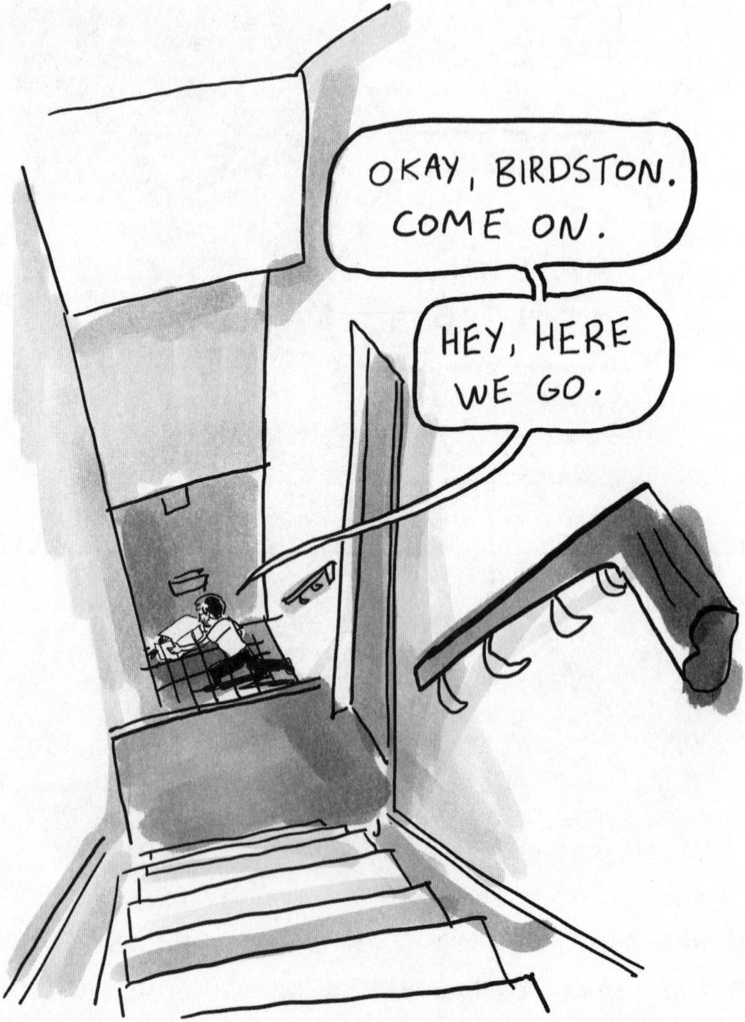
OKAY, BIRDSTON. COME ON.
HEY, HERE WE GO.

I wonder if I'll lose a week to caring for this sick bird, if the panic attacks will start back up, if the delicate Jenga game that is my newfound mental stability will crumble.

When I check on Birdston, somebody has left him food.

I love New York.

I briefly consider that a little kid may walk by my front door, see the bird in the box and pick him up. This will lead to either an *Of Mice and Men* situation, or result in the kid getting sick. Either way it will be my fault.

I suspect this may be an irrational thought and that to act on it would be a compulsion. I text my group thread to confirm that it's irrational, and when they all say, YES OF COURSE YES, I let that be the final word. I go back to living my very exciting life.

MEANWHILE, SOMEWHERE UPTOWN, SAMANTHA WAS AT A DIFFERENT KIND OF BALL...

Later, I decide to let Birdston out of his box.
Maybe he'll fly away. Please, I hope he'll fly away.

He hobbles like he's drunk. He flaps his wings and gets a little air, then grounds again. Come on, Birdston.

I look away briefly. And when I look back . . .

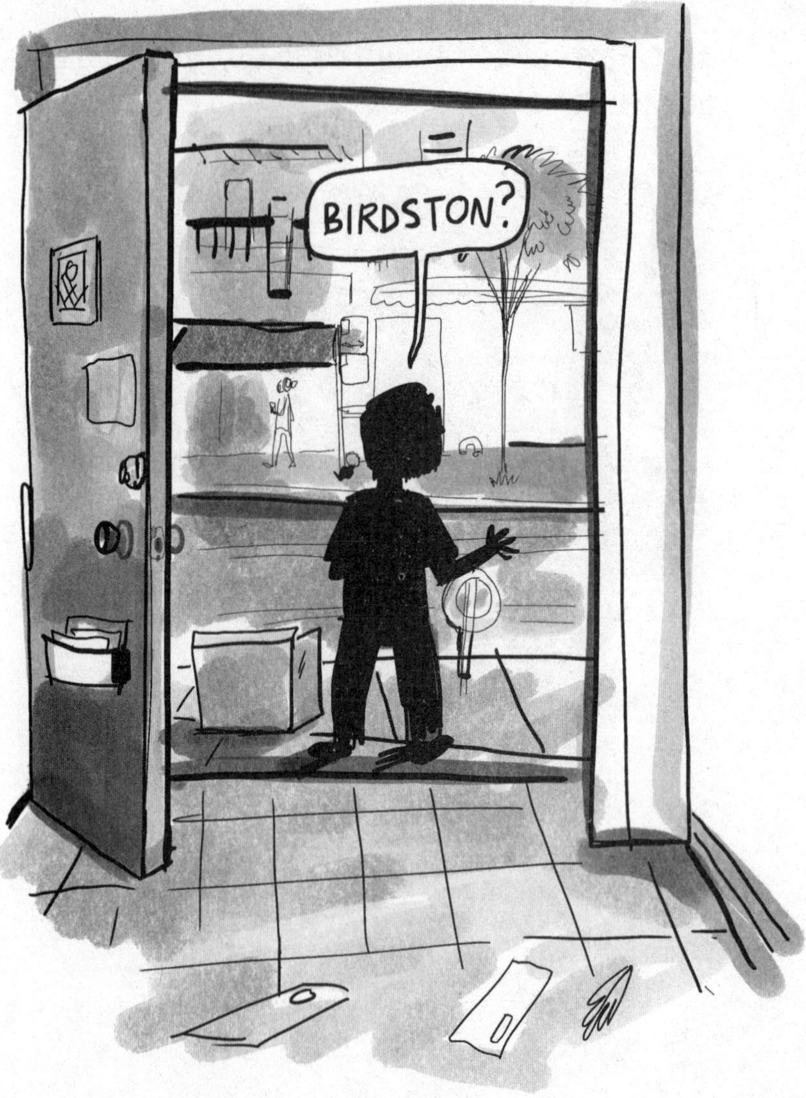
BIRDSTON?

I'll never know if he ran and hid under something, or managed to fly away, or was quickly eaten by a street cat. I tried to help, did my best, and didn't fall to pieces.

I go on with my day.

It's early autumn in New York. We have a merciful pocket of perfect weather.

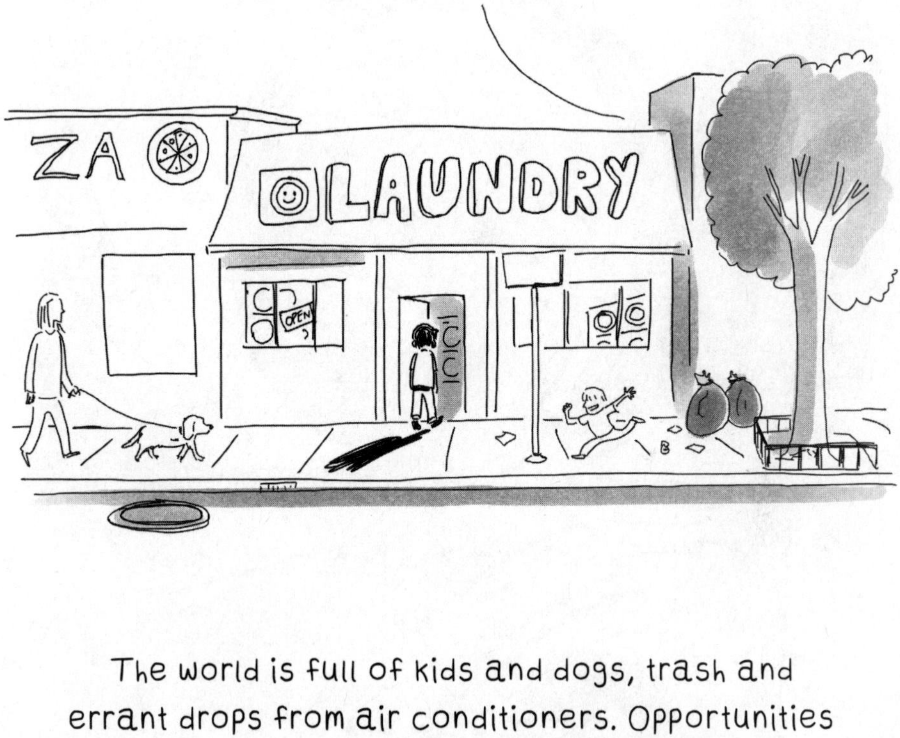
ZA
LAUNDRY
OPEN

The world is full of kids and dogs, trash and errant drops from air conditioners. Opportunities abound for social interactions gone wrong. Rats run from piles of trash to other piles of trash, right in front of my feet. Somewhere, friends of mine are angry with me. I may have left the oven on and the door unlocked.

These thoughts come and go, but none stick.

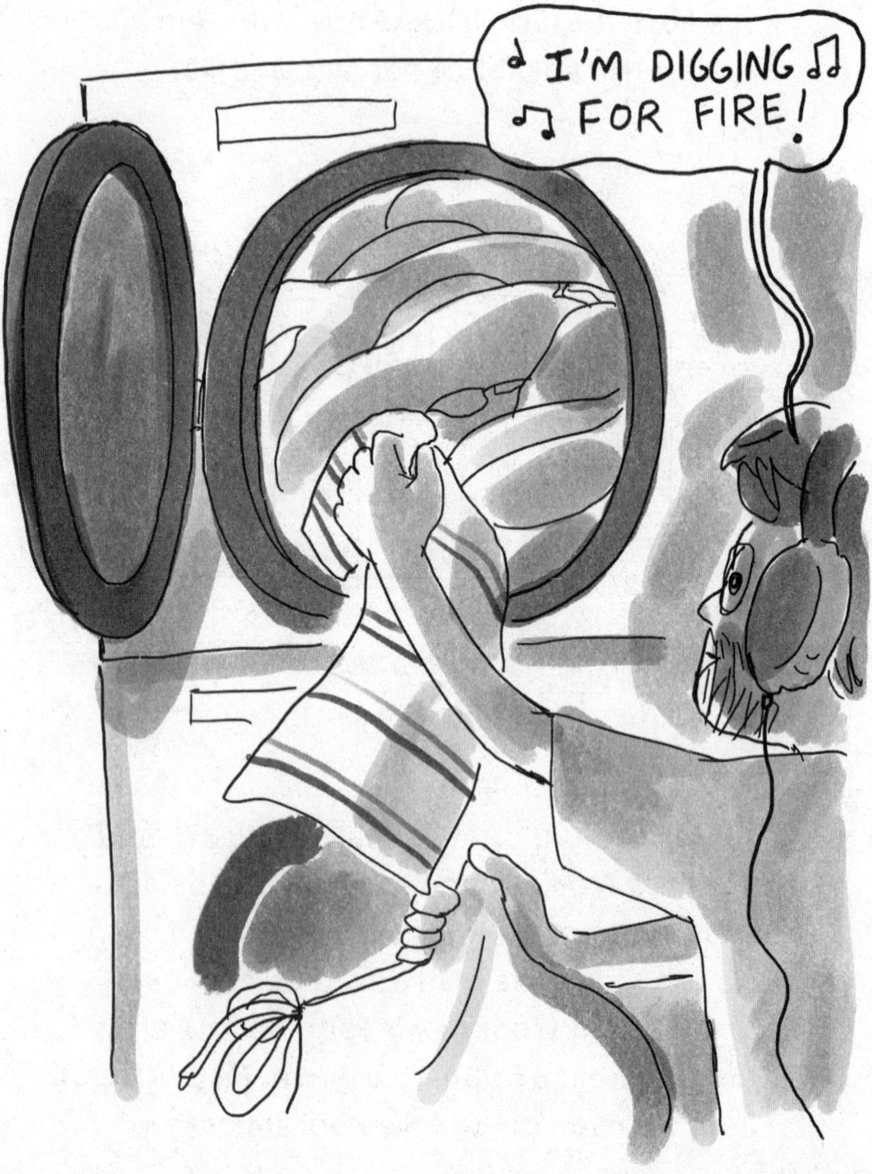
♩ I'M DIGGING ♫
♫ FOR FIRE!

The real problem in front of me is, will I have enough time to fold my laundry before meeting a friend for dinner, or will I need to leave it in a heap? Later, I'll be tired, maybe a little drunk, and the last thing I want to do is put laundry away.

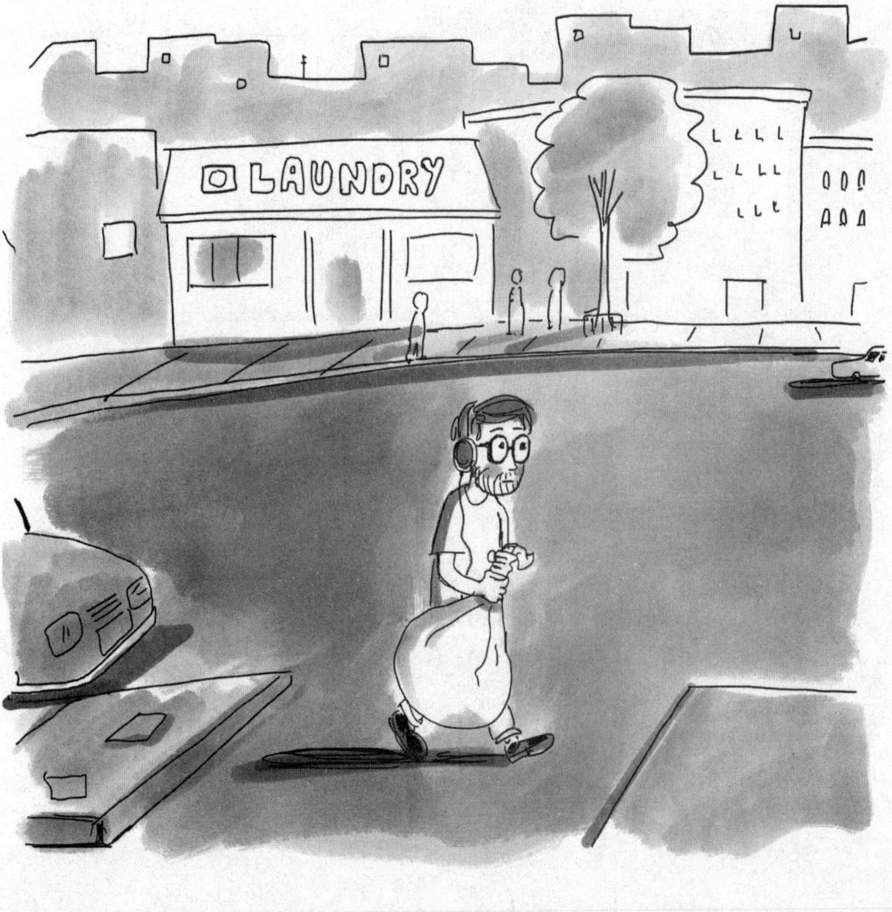
LAUNDRY

Later, at dinner, my mind drifts for a second:
I never ran my hand across the dryer.

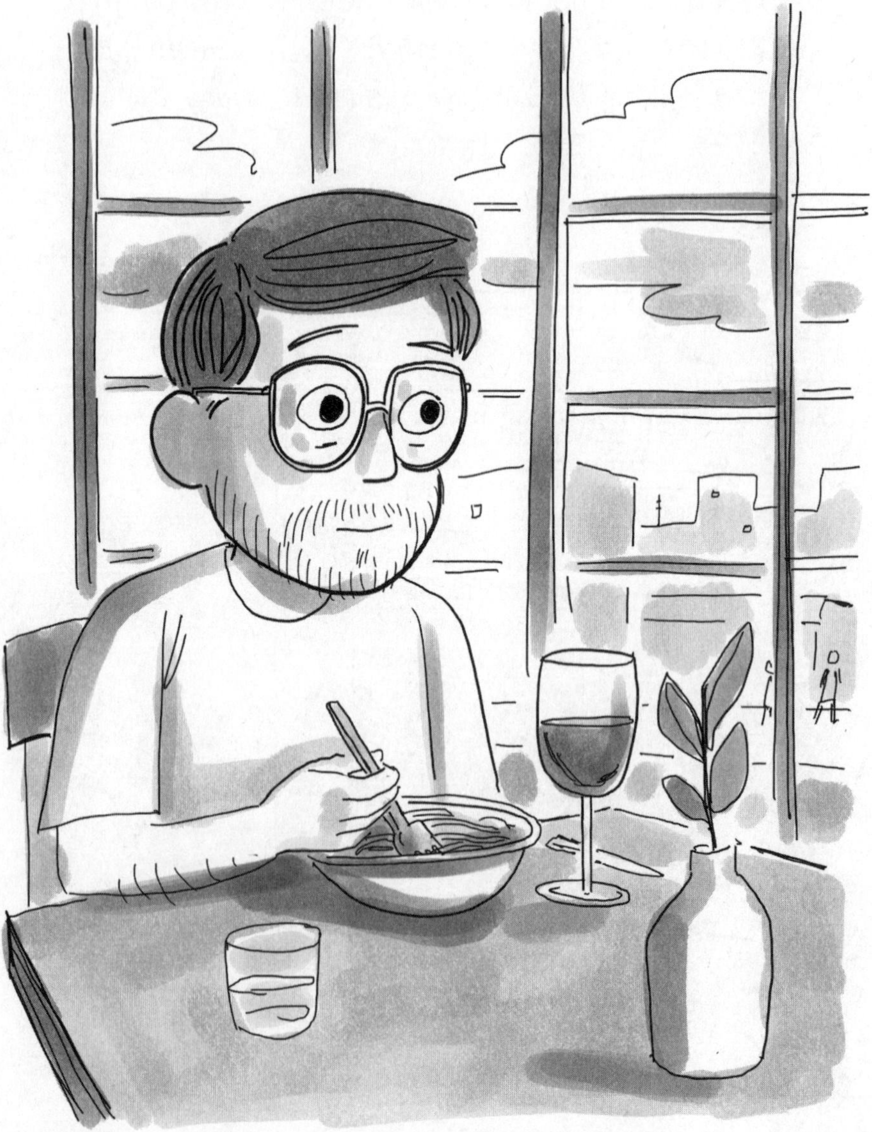

Then I rejoin the coversation.

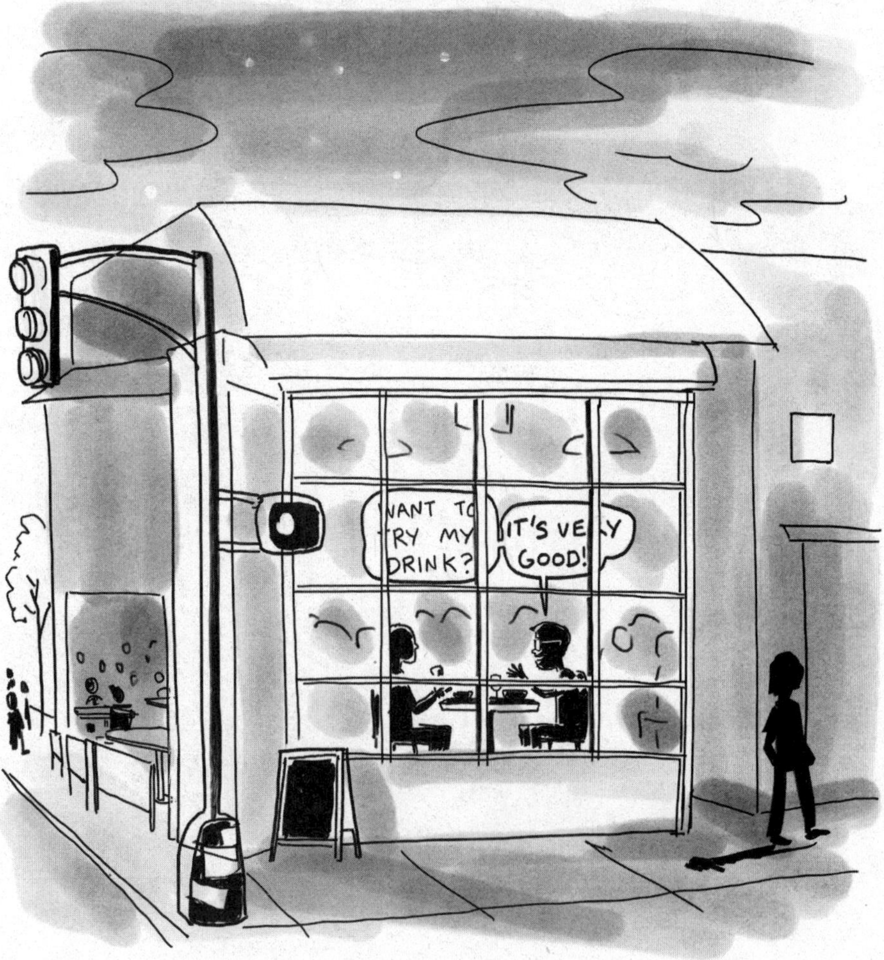

WANT TO TRY MY DRINK?
IT'S VERY GOOD!

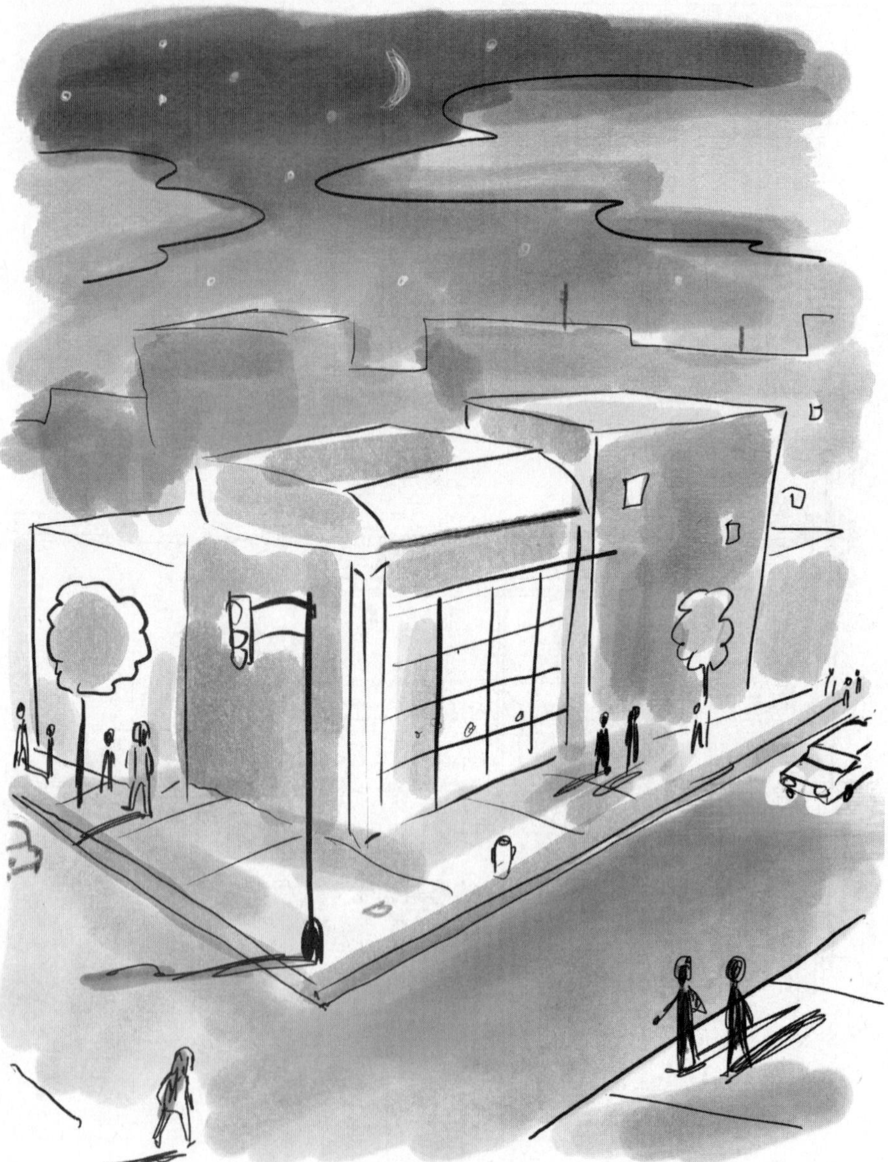

Acknowledgments

Thank you to Sarah Haugen, whose last word on this book I trust enough to even let it see the light of day. You took my whirlwind and helped me tell a story. You are amazing.

Dan Mandel, you believed in this project when it was just a few scattered cartoons, and I'll always be grateful that you saw something here. We did the thing!

Everyone at HarperCollins, I feel so impressed and taken care of. Thank you Megan, Falon, Jen, and the whole design team.

To a group of people I love, I owe my ability to even leave my room. There wouldn't be a book without you, of course.

A lot of you I have not drawn into this comic nor have you been turned into animals. This isn't because you don't matter, but rather because this story unfolds mostly in my broken brain. You matter more than anything I could draw.

Dema, Ethan, Sofia, Dana, Hanna, Dylan, Jordan, Matt, Emily, Sarah, Garren, Amy, Ellis, Hilary, Ema, Adrien, Zain, David, Will, Sky, Elias, Barry, Frank, Stephen, Paul, Anna, Adam, Hannah, Lila, Ally, Sabina, Celine, Erin, Julia, Shelby, Colin, Emma, Lauren, Aditi, Jason, Sammy, Blythe, Ginny, Neima, Ivy, Sara, Andie, Kate, Maya, Natalia. <3.

Emma Allen and Colin Stokes, thank you for your friendship and for believing in my work enough to put it in *The New Yorker.* I wouldn't be here without you.

Dr. Scott, you taught me to draw comics and showed me Kirby and Ditko. This starts with you. Steven T. Seagle, you believed in me when I had no credits to my name, and I tried to rise to the occasion. For my career, I have you to thank. Sam Viviano, you took my work seriously when I wasn't yet serious, and your advice will always hover over me like a superego. Let's never stop getting lunch.

The Usual Gang of Idiots at MAD: Ryan, Dave, Charlie, John, Joe, Doug, Sam, Dick, you were my heroes before we met—I get to be friends with my heroes.

My MacDowell comrades, you inspire me and play a great game of "Mafia," and it was a privilege to work all day on this book and eat with you every night. You're incredible artists, and you made me want to rise to your level.

To my family, Mom, Dad, Gaetano, Robin, Heather, Grandma, Grandpa, Jeremy, Becky, Kiara, Lorenzo,

Hannah, Jade, Nonna, Luci, Lara, Phillipe, Bruno, Chris: everything I've ever gotten to do I owe to you. Thank you for your love, support, generosity, encouragement, art classes, pun contests, for reading things I wrote, showing me my new favorite artists, taking me seriously, and never once discouraging me from thinking I could make comic books for my whole life. You encouraged me to make "Comics" my Bar Mitzvah theme. Look what you've done.

Thank you to Dweebs coffee shop, Wesleyan University, *Current Affairs*, *The New Yorker*, Dr. Lohitsa, Michelle, Zoloft, Klonopin, sweatpants, Georg's custom brushes, BK Jani, *Man of Action*, The Center for Cognitive Behavioral Therapy, Steven Phillipson, and Foster Sundry.

Amy Bloom, Joan Larkin, Sofia Warren, Natalia Winkelman, Dema Paxton Fofang: you all read drafts of this and told me what you thought. Listening to you has made this a better book. Thank you. Thank you. Thank you.

About the Author

Jason Adam Katzenstein is a cartoonist and writer for print and television. His work has appeared in *The New Yorker*, the *New York Times*, and *MAD Magazine*, and on Cartoon Network. He is the illustrator of *The White Man's Guide to White Male Writers of the Western Canon* and the graphic novel *Camp Midnight*. He is also a visiting professor at Wesleyan University.

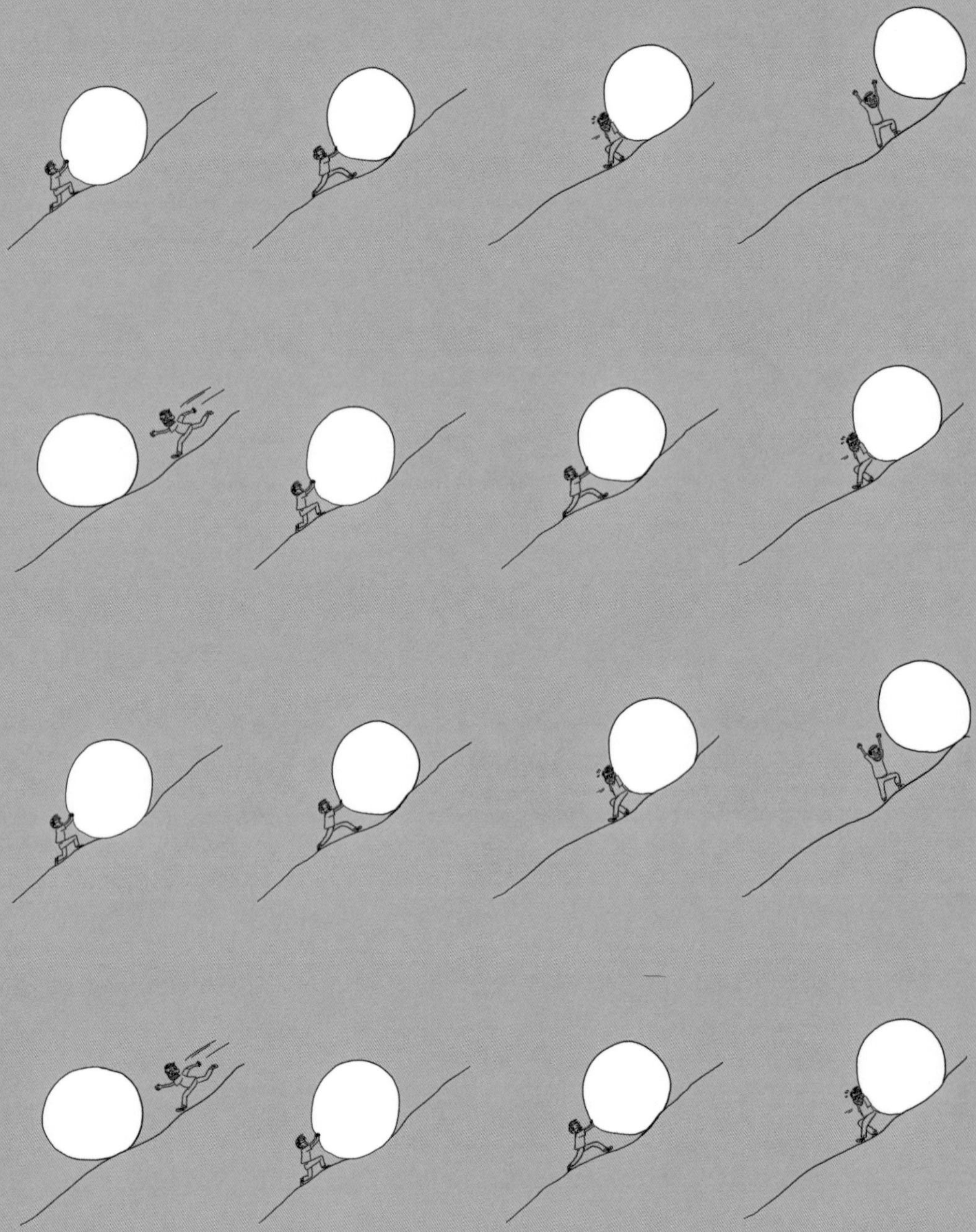